second edition

Writing Arguments

A Rhetoric with Readings
Concise Edition

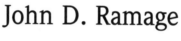

John D. Ramage
Arizona State University

John C. Bean
Seattle University

June Johnson
Seattle University

Allyn and Bacon

Boston ▪ *London* ▪ *Toronto* ▪ *Sydney* ▪ *Tokyo* ▪ *Singapore*

Vice President: Eben W. Ludlow
Editorial Assistant: Grace Trudow
Executive Marketing Manager: Lisa Kimball
Editorial Production Administrator: Susan Brown
Editorial-Production Service: Matrix Productions, Inc.

Text Designer: Denise Hoffman
Composition Buyer: Linda Cox
Manufacturing Buyer: Suzanne Lareau
Compositor: Omegatype Typography, Inc.
Cover Administrator: Linda Knowles

Credits: Page 14. Gordon F. Adams, "Petition to Waive the University Math Requirement." Reprinted with the permission of the author. Page 23. George F. Will, "Lies, Damned Lies, and . . ." from *Newsweek* (March 29, 1999). Copyright © 1999 by the Washington Post Writers Group. Reprinted with permission. Page 31. Ellen Goodman, "A New Campaign for Pay Equity" from the *Boston Globe* (1985). Copyright © 1985 by the Boston Globe Company. Reprinted with permission of the Washington Post Writers Group. Page 98. David Langley, " 'Half-Criminals' or Urban Athletes? A Plea for Fair Treatment of Skateboarders." Reprinted with the permission of the author. Page 126. Ellen Goodman, "Minneapolis Pornography Ordinance" from the *Boston Globe* (1985). Copyright © 1985 by the Boston Globe Company. Reprinted with the permission of the Washington Post Writers Group. Page 163. John Leo, "The Stereotypes No Phantom in New 'Star Wars' Movie" from the *Seattle Times* (July 6, 1999). Copyright © 1999 by John Leo. Reprinted with the permission of the author. Page 165. Kathy Sullivan, "Oncore, Obscenity, and the Liquor Control Board." Reprinted with the permission of the author. Page 184. Daeha Ko, "The Monster That Is High School" from the *University of Washington Daily* (May 9, 1999). Copyright © 1999 by the *University of Washington Daily*. Reprinted with the permission of the publisher. Page 197. T. D. Hylton, "Don't Fake Sirens!" Reprinted with the permission of the author. Page 198. Michael D. Lubrecht, "Creeping Loopholism Threatens Our Rights" from the *Seattle Times* (June 23, 1999). Reprinted with the permission of the author and the *Seattle Times*. Page 211. Pat Inglenook, "The Spice Girls: Good at Marketing but Not Good for the Market." Reprinted with the permission of the author. Page 228. Stephen Bean, "What Should Be Done about the Mentally Ill Homeless?" Reprinted with the permission of the author. Page 248. Michael Levin, "The Case for Torture" from *Newsweek* (June 7, 1982). Copyright © 1982 by Michael Levin. Reprinted with the permission of the author. Page 272. Lynnea Clark, "Women Police Officers: Should Size and Strength Be Criteria for Patrol Duty?" Reprinted with the permission of the author.

Library of Congress Cataloging-in-Publication Data
Ramage, John D.
   Writing arguments : a rhetoric with readings / John D. Ramage,
John C. Bean, June Johnson. — Concise ed., 2nd ed.
     p.   cm.
   Includes index.
   ISBN 0-205-31747-2 (alk. paper)
   1. English language—Rhetoric. 2. Persuasion (Rhetoric)
3. College readers. 4. Report writing. I. Bean, John C.
II. Johnson, June. III. Title.
PE1431.R33 2000b
808'.042—dc21   00–038621

Printed in the United States of America

10 9 8 7 6 5 4 3 2 1   RRDV   04 03 02 01 00

brief contents

contents

PART TWO
PRINCIPLES OF ARGUMENT   59

CHAPTER 4   The Core of an Argument:
A Claim with Reasons   61

PART THREE
ARGUMENTS IN DEPTH:
SIX TYPES OF CLAIMS   135

CHAPTER 9   An Introduction to Types of Claims   137

CHAPTER 10   Categorical and Definitional Arguments: X Is (Is Not) a Y   146

CHAPTER 15   Ethical Arguments   238

APPENDIXES   250

APPENDIX TWO   A Concise Guide to Evaluating and Documenting Sources   257

preface

Overview

Through five editions, *Writing Arguments* has earned its place as the leading college textbook in argumentation. In this second Concise Edition of *Writing Arguments*, we have tried to create the most up-to-date, accessible, and teachable short rhetoric of argument on the market. Based on the fifth edition of *Writing Arguments*, this Concise Edition covers the essentials of argument without sacrificing clarity or flexibility. It can be used successfully as a stand-alone rhetoric text or as a compact companion to an anthology of readings.

As in the Regular and Brief Editions of *Writing Arguments*, our aim in the Concise Edition is to integrate a comprehensive study of argument with a process approach to writing and critical thinking. Our class-tested discussion questions and short writing assignments, combined with clear and effectively sequenced explanations, teach the critical thinking that helps students *write* arguments. By treating argument as a means of discovery as well as persuasion and by emphasizing audience and rhetorical context at every stage of the construction of an argument, we show students how arguing involves productive dialogue in search of the best solutions to problems rather than pro-con debate with winners and losers. Adopters of *Writing Arguments* testify that students using this text produce better arguments of their own—arguments that are more critically thoughtful, more fully developed and elaborated, and more attuned to the demands of audience.

Judicious changes in the second Concise Edition reflect our evolving understanding of the theory and practice of argumentation and our awareness of what concepts and skills students need to write thoughtful and effective arguments. We have increased the book's interest level for students by using examples and readings that connect more directly to their lives. In both its treatment of argumentation and its approach to teaching writing, our text is rooted in current research and theory. Our emphasis throughout is on creating a concise teaching tool that really works in the classroom.

This new edition is particularly strengthened by the presence of a new coauthor, June Johnson, a colleague of John Bean's at Seattle University. Her background in contemporary literary and rhetorical theory and her research interests in popular culture and civic argument—along with extensive classroom experience and training in pedagogy—make June an invaluable writing partner.

What's New in the Second Edition?

The new edition contains the following improvements:

- Substantial revision of Chapter 2, "Reading Arguments," aimed at increasing student interest and showing how experienced readers cope with ambiguity and seek synthesis. We replaced the lengthy Charles Murray article on welfare reform with short opposing arguments by George Will and Ellen Goodman on gender pay equity, and we added a model student essay that analyzes sources of disagreement between Will and Goodman. Besides teaching summary writing and critical analysis, Chapter 2 shows students how to seek alternative views and use disagreement productively to prompt further investigation. Throughout, we treat the process of reading arguments as a step toward writing arguments.

- Reconceptualization of Chapter 9, "An Introduction to the Types of Claims," to reflect our evolving understanding of stasis theory. Using lasik eye surgery as an extended example, we show how knowledge of claim types—combined with an analysis of audience—can help writers focus an argument and generate ideas. Also, we added a sixth claim type, called "simple categorical arguments."

- A revision of Chapter 10, now titled "Categorical and Definitional Arguments." The revised chapter explains both simple categorical arguments and definitional arguments. The chapter makes it easy for students to appreciate the universality of these two claim types, to understand the argumentative moves they entail, and to produce their own categorical or definitional arguments.

- An expanded Appendix 2, "A Concise Guide to Evaluating and Documenting Sources," to include instruction on the logic of Internet searching and the evaluation of Web sites. Throughout the text, we treat the Web as a resource and exemplify how to use Web materials in a critically responsible way.

- More attention to visual arguments (we include photographs on Kosovo and on Makah whaling) with a special section devoted to visual arguments in Chapter 7, "Moving Your Audience: Audience-Based Reasons, *Ethos*, and *Pathos*." We also added screen captures from Web sites on gender pay equity (Chapter 2) and on sweatshops (Appendix 2).

- Five new student essays selected for the quality of their arguments and the appeal of their subject matter. Drawn from popular culture issues and other contemporary concerns, these readings connect effectively to the interests of today's students. For example, one student essay persuades readers to change their misconception of skateboarders ("'Half-Criminals' or Urban Athletes? A Plea for Fair Treatment of Skateboarders," pp. 98–100); another evaluates the marketing wizardry of the Spice Girls ("The Spice

Girls: Good at Marketing but Not Good for Their Market," pp. 211–13); still another identifies high school cliques as a possible cause for the Columbine massacre ("The Monster That Is High School," pp. 184–85). We also added to Chapter 1 student writer Gordon Adams's "Petition to Waive the University Mathematics Requirement," a popular teaching tool from the Brief and Regular Editions of *Writing Arguments*.

- Three new professional essays, also chosen for their appeal to student interests. In addition to the Will and Goodman arguments on gender pay equity, we include John Leo's analysis of racial stereotypes in the film *The Phantom Menace* ("Stereotypes No Phantom in New *Star Wars* Movie," pp. 163–64).

What Hasn't Changed? The Distinguishing Features of *Writing Arguments, Concise Edition*

Building on earlier success, the second edition retains successful features from the first edition:

- Focus throughout on writing arguments. Grounded in composition theory, this text combines explanations of argument with class-tested discussion tasks, exploratory writing tasks, and sequenced writing assignments aimed at developing skills of writing and critical thinking.

- Four different, complementary approaches to argument—the enthymeme (a claim with *because* clause); the Toulmin system; the classical appeals of *logos, ethos,* and *pathos;* and the stasis system (six categories of claims). These approaches allow flexibility for instructors and provide students with a range of argumentative strategies. Teachers can emphasize one, two, three, or all four of these approaches.

- Focus on the reading and writing of arguments, with emphasis on argument as inquiry and discovery as well as persuasion.

- Focus on the critical thinking that underlies effective arguments, particularly the skills of critical reading, of believing and doubting, of empathic listening, of active questioning, and of negotiating ambiguity and seeking synthesis.

- Focus on strategies for analyzing rhetorical context, for rooting arguments in the values and beliefs of the intended audience, and for basing decisions about content, structure, and style on analysis of audience and context.

- Concise treatment of documentation, including two student examples of researched arguments—one using the MLA system and one using the APA system.

- Numerous "For Class Discussion" exercises and sequenced writing assignments designed to teach critical thinking and build argumentative skills. All "For Class Discussion" exercises can be used for whole-class discussions or for collaborative group tasks.

- Effective student and professional arguments used to illustrate argumentative strategies and stimulate discussion, analysis, and debate. The text includes eight student arguments and five professional arguments.

Structure of the Text

The text has three main parts and two appendixes. Part One gives an overview of argumentation. Its three chapters present our philosophy of argument, showing how argument helps writers clarify their own thinking and connect with the values and beliefs of a questioning audience. Throughout we link the process of arguing—articulating issue questions, formulating propositions, examining alternative points of view, and creating structures of supporting reasons and evidence—with the processes of reading and writing.

Part Two examines the principles of argument. Chapters 4 through 6 show that the core of an argument is a claim with reasons. These reasons are often stated as enthymemes, the unstated premise of which must sometimes be brought to the surface and supported. Discussion of Toulmin logic shows students how to discover the stated and unstated premises of their arguments and to provide structures of reasons and evidence to support them. Chapters 7 and 8 focus on the rhetorical context of arguments. These chapters discuss the writer's relationship with an audience, particularly with finding audience-based reasons, with using *pathos* and *ethos* effectively and responsibly, and with accommodating arguments to audiences ranging from sympathetic to neutral to resistant.

Part Three discusses six different types of argument: simple categorical arguments, definitional arguments, causal arguments, resemblance arguments, evaluation arguments, and proposal arguments. These chapters introduce students to two recurring strategies of argument that cut across the different category types: criteria-match arguing, in which the writer establishes criteria for making a judgment and argues whether a specific case does or does not meet those criteria, and causal arguing, in which the writer shows that one event or phenomenon can be linked to others in a causal chain. The last chapter of Part Three deals with the special complexities of moral arguments.

The text concludes with two appendixes. Appendix 1 gives an overview of informal fallacies. Appendix 2 shows students how to evaluate research sources, particularly Web sites, and provides an overview of the MLA and APA systems for citing and documenting sources.

Writing Assignments

We provide a variety of sequenced writing assignments, including exploratory tasks for discovering and generating arguments, "microthemes" for practicing basic argumentative moves (for example, supporting a reason with evidence), cases, and numerous other assignments calling for complete arguments. Thus, the text provides instructors with a wealth of options for writing assignments on which to build a coherent course.

An Expanded and Improved Instructor's Manual

The Instructor's Manual has been revised and expanded to make it more useful for teachers and writing program administrators. Written by co-author June Johnson, the new Instructor's Manual has the following features:

- Discussion of planning decisions an instructor must make in designing an argument course: for example, how to use readings; how much to emphasize or deemphasize Toulmin or claim-type theory; how much time to build into the course for invention, peer review of drafts, and other writing instruction; and how to select and sequence assignments.

- Three detailed sample syllabi showing how *Writing Arguments*, Concise Edition can support a variety of course structures and emphases:

  Syllabus #1: This course emphasizes argumentative skills and strategies, uses readings for rhetorical analysis, and asks students to write on issues drawn from their own experience.

  Syllabus #2: This more rigorous course works intensely with the logical structure of argument, the classical appeals, the Toulmin schema, and claim-type theory. It uses readings for rhetorical analysis and for an introduction to the argumentative controversies that students will address in their papers.

  Syllabus #3: This course asks students to experiment with genres of argument (for example, op-ed pieces, white papers, visual arguments, and researched freelance or scholarly arguments) and focuses on students' choice of topics and claim types.

- For instructors who include Toulmin, an independent, highly teachable introductory lesson on the Toulmin schema.

- For new teachers, a helpful discussion of how to sequence writing assignments and how to use a variety of collaborative tasks in the classroom to promote active learning and critical thinking.

- Chapter-by-chapter responses to the "For Class Discussion" exercises.

- Numerous teaching tips and suggestions placed strategically throughout the chapter material.

- Helpful suggestions for discussing and critiquing readings in Part Three, "Arguments in Depth: Six Types of Claims." By focusing on rhetorical context as well as the strengths and weaknesses of these arguments, our suggestions will help students connect their reading of arguments to their writing of arguments.

Companion Web Site

The *Writing Arguments* Companion Web Site, http://www.abacon.com/ramage, enables instructors to access online writing activities and Web links keyed to specific chapters, post and make changes to their syllabi, hold chat sessions with individual students or groups of students, and receive e-mail and essay assignments directly from students.

Acknowledgments

We are happy for this opportunity to give public thanks to the scholars, teachers, and students who have influenced our approach to composition and argument. We would especially like to thank Darlene Panvini of Vanderbilt University for her advice on our treatment of the wetlands controversy in Chapter 10. Additional thanks go to Seattle University librarian Sandra Brandt for her help with our explanations of library and Internet databases and retrieval. Thanks also to Susan Meyer, Stephen Bean, and Sarah Bean for their research assistance.

Particular thanks go to the following reviewers, who gave us helpful and cogent advice at various stages of the revision process: Jonathan Ayres, the University of Texas at Austin; Linda Bensel-Meyers, University of Tennessee–Knoxville; Deborah Core, Eastern Kentucky University; Richard Fulkerson, Texas A&M University–Commerce; Carol A. Lowe, McLennan Community College; David Mair, University of Oklahoma; Tim McGee, the College of New Jersey; Thomas A. Wallis, North Carolina State University; and Irene Ward, Kansas State University, for their reviews of *Writing Arguments,* Fourth Edition, and draft chapters of this fifth edition.

We also would like to thank our editor of more than fifteen years, Eben Ludlow, who well deserves his reputation as a premier editor in college publishing. In fact, it has been a joy for us to work with the whole Allyn & Bacon English team: Lisa Kimball, English marketing manager; Susan Brown, editorial production administrator; and Doug Day, English sales specialist. Additional thanks go to Merrill Peterson of Matrix Productions, who professionally managed many key aspects of production.

Finally, we would like to thank our families. John Bean: Thanks to my wife, Kit, whose own work as an ESL instructor has produced wonderful discussions of argument and pedagogy in a multicultural setting, and to my children Matthew, Andrew, Stephen, and Sarah for their love and support. June Johnson: Thanks to my husband, Kenneth Bube, and my daughter, Jane Ellen, for their keen insights, loving encouragement, and inspirational humor.

part one

Overview
of Argument

1 Argument
An Introduction

One ought to begin a book on argument by telling the reader straight out what argument is. But we can't. Philosophers and rhetoricians have disagreed for centuries about the meaning of the term and about the goals that arguers should set for themselves. So in place of a simple definition, we'll show you several different ways of thinking about argument as a way of helping you become a more powerful arguer yourself.

After explaining how arguments make claims and provide justifications for those claims, we will consider argument from two different perspectives—as product and process. We'll also explain how arguments combine two distinct and sometimes conflicting purposes—truth seeking and persuasion. Because of the importance of this last distinction, we'll explore extensively the debate over truth versus victory as the goal of argument.

WHAT DO WE MEAN BY ARGUMENT?

Let's begin by rejecting two popular synonyms for "argument": *fight* and *debate*.

Argument Is Not a Fight or a Quarrel

The word *argument* often connotes anger, as when we say, "I just got in a huge argument with my roommate!" We may picture heated disagreements, rising pulse rates, and slamming doors. We may conjure up images of shouting talk-show guests or fist-banging speakers.

But to our way of thinking, argument doesn't necessarily imply anger. In fact, arguing can be pleasurable. It can be a creative and productive activity that engages our minds and our hearts in conversations with people we respect about ideas that we cherish. For your primary image of argument, we invite you to think not of a fist-banging speaker but of a small group of reasonable persons seeking the best solution to a problem. We will return to this image throughout the chapter.

Argument Is Not Pro-Con Debate

Another popular conception of argument is debate—a presidential debate, perhaps, or a high school or college debate tournament, in which, according to one popular dictionary, "opposing speakers defend and attack a given proposition." While formal debates can develop our critical thinking powers, they stress winning and losing, often to the detriment of cooperative inquiry.

To illustrate the limitations of debate, consider one of our former students, a champion high school debater, who spent his senior year debating prison reform. Throughout the year he argued for and against such propositions as "The United States should build more prisons" and "We must find innovative alternatives to prison." One day we asked him, "What do you personally think is the best way to reform prisons?" "I don't know," he replied. "I've never thought about it that way."

Nothing in the atmosphere of pro-con debate had engaged this bright, articulate student in the important process of clarifying his own values and taking a personal stand. As we explain throughout this text, argument entails a desire for truth seeking, not necessarily Truth with a capital T but truth as a desire to find the best solutions to complex problems. Of course, arguers often passionately support their own points of view and expose weaknesses in other views. However, arguers' passionate defenses and relentless probings are not moves in a win-lose game but rather moves toward discovering and promoting the best belief or best course of action.

Arguments Can Be Explicit or Implicit

Before proceeding to some defining features of argument, we should note also that arguments can be either explicit or implicit. An *explicit* argument states directly a controversial claim and supports it with reasons and evidence. An *implicit* argument, in contrast, doesn't look like an argument. It may be a poem or short story, a photograph or cartoon, a personal essay, or an autobiographical narrative. But like an explicit argument, it persuades an audience toward a certain point of view. For example, a famous World War I poem (Wilfred Owen's *"Dulce et Decorum Est"*) challenges the patriotic notion that it is "sweet and fitting" to die for one's country. Instead of using the ordered thesis, reasons, and evidence found in explicit arguments, this poem employs a horrible image—a soldier drowning in his own fluids from a mustard gas attack—to impel readers to see the gruesome senselessness of war.

Visual images can also make implicit arguments, often by evoking powerful emotions in audiences. The perspective that photos take, the stories they tell, or the vivid details of place and time they display compel viewers literally to see the issue from a particular angle. Take, for instance, Figure 1.1, a photo of homeless Albanian refugees during the Kosovo War. By foregrounding the old woman, probably a grandmother, perched precariously atop a heavily loaded wheelbarrow, her canes or crutches sticking out from the pile, and the six persons in the scene hastening down a stark road against an ominous gray background, the photographer conveys the nightmare of this war. Here *showing* the urgency of the Albanians' flight for their lives and the helplessness of the two who can't walk is an effective strategy to arouse sympathy for the Albanians. Photographs of this kind regularly appeared in American newspapers during the war, serving to heighten U.S. support of NATO's bombing. Meanwhile, Serbs complained that no American newspapers showed photographs of KLA (Kosovo Liberation Army) atrocities against Serbs.

FIGURE 1.1   Albanian refugees during the Kosovo War
Newsweek 12 Apr. 1999: 33.

FOR CLASS DISCUSSION

Working individually or in small groups, describe a photograph that would create an implicit argument persuading (1) teenagers to avoid smoking, (2) teenagers to avoid becoming sexually active, (3) the general public to ban handguns, or (4) the general public to save endangered species.

> EXAMPLE: To create an implicit argument against legalizing hard drugs, you might photograph a blank-eyed, cadaverous teenager plunging a needle into her arm.

We'll return to implicit arguments later, especially in Chapter 7, where we describe the persuasive power of stories, narratives, and visual images. For now, however, and in most of this text, our predominant focus is on explicit argument.

ARGUMENT REQUIRES JUSTIFICATION OF ITS CLAIMS

To begin defining argument, let's turn to a humble but universal site of disagreement: the conflict between a parent and a teenager over rules. In what way and in what circumstances do these conflicts constitute arguments?

Consider the following dialogue:

> YOUNG PERSON (*racing for the front door while putting coat on*):   Bye. See you later.
>
> PARENT: Whoa! What time are you planning on coming home?
>
> YOUNG PERSON (*coolly, hand still on doorknob*):   I'm sure we discussed this earlier. I'll be home around two A.M. (*The second sentence, spoken very rapidly, is barely audible.*)
>
> PARENT (*mouth tightening*):   We did *not* discuss this earlier, and you're *not* staying out till two in the morning. You'll be home at twelve.

At this point in the exchange, we have a quarrel, not an argument. Quarrelers exchange antagonistic assertions without any attempt to support them rationally. If the dialogue never gets past the "Yes-you-will/No-I-won't" stage, it either remains a quarrel or degenerates into a fight.

Let us say, however, that the dialogue takes the following turn:

> YOUNG PERSON (*tragically*):   But I'm *sixteen years old!*

Now we're moving toward argument. Not, to be sure, a particularly well-developed or cogent one, but an argument all the same. It's now an argument because one of the quarrelers has offered a reason for her assertion. Her choice of curfew is satisfactory, she says, *because* she is sixteen years old.

The parent can now respond in one of several ways that will either advance the argument or turn it back into a quarrel. The parent can simply invoke parental authority ("I don't care—you're still coming home at twelve"), in which case argument ceases. Or the parent can provide a reason for his or her view ("You will be home at twelve because your dad and I pay the bills around here!"), in which case the argument takes a new turn.

So far we've established two necessary conditions that must be met before we're willing to call something an argument: (1) a set of two or more conflicting assertions and (2) the attempt to resolve the conflict through an appeal to reason. But good argument demands more than meeting these two formal requirements. For an argument to be effective, the arguer must clarify and support the reasons presented.

For example, "But I'm sixteen years old!" is not yet a clear support for the assertion "I should be allowed to set my own curfew." On the surface, Young Person's argument seems absurd. Her parent, of all people, knows precisely how old she is. What makes it an argument is that behind her claim lies an unstated assumption—all sixteen-year-olds are old enough to set their own curfews. What Young Person needs to do now is to support that assumption.* In doing so, she must anticipate the sorts of questions the assumption will raise in the minds of her parent: What is the legal status of sixteen-year-olds? How psychologically mature, as opposed to chronologically mature, is Young Person? What is the actual track record of Young Person in being responsible? Each of these questions will force Young Person to reexamine and clarify her assumptions about the proper degree of autonomy for sixteen-year-olds. And her response to those questions should in turn force the parents to reexamine their assumptions about the dependence of sixteen-year-olds on parental guidance and wisdom. (Likewise, the parents will need to show why "paying the bills around here" automatically gives them the right to set Young Person's curfew.)

As the argument continues, Young Person and Parent may shift to a different line of reasoning. For example, Young Person might say: "I should be allowed to stay out until two A.M. because all my friends get to stay out that late." (Here the unstated assumption is that the rules in this family ought to be based on the rules in other families.) The parent might in turn respond, "But I certainly never stayed out that late when I was your age"—an argument assuming that the rules in this family should follow the rules of an earlier generation.

As Young Person and Parent listen to each other's points of view (trying to figure out why their initial arguments are unpersuasive), both parties find themselves in the uncomfortable position of having to examine their own beliefs and to justify assumptions that they have taken for granted. Here we encounter one of the earliest senses of the term *to argue*, which is "to clarify." In response to her audience's failure to understand or assent to her view, the arguer must reshape her

---

*In Chapter 5 we will call the assumption underlying a line of reasoning its *warrant*.

argument to help her audience "see" her position. In the process she may, perhaps for the first time, come to understand that position herself. Thus Young Person might recast her argument so that it relates more directly to her parent's values:

> I should be allowed to stay out until two A.M. on a trial basis because I need enough space to demonstrate my maturity and show you I won't get into trouble.

The assumption underlying this argument is that it is good to give teenagers freedom to demonstrate their maturity. Because this reason is likely to appeal to her parent's values (the parent wants the daughter to mature) and because it is tempered by the qualifier "on a trial basis" (which reduces some of the threat of Young Person's initial demands), it may prompt productive discussion.

Whether or not Young Person and Parent can work out the best solution, the preceding scenario illustrates how argument leads persons to clarify their reasons and provide justifications that can be examined rationally. The scenario also illustrates two specific aspects of argument that we will explore in detail in the next sections: (1) Argument is both a process and a product. (2) Argument combines truth seeking and persuasion.

ARGUMENT IS BOTH A PROCESS AND A PRODUCT

In the preceding scenario, argument functioned as a *process* whereby two or more parties sought the best solution to a question or problem. But if we stopped the process at a given moment and looked at each person's contribution to the conversation, these contributions would be *products*. In an informal discussion, these products are usually brief, comprising a few sentences. In a more formal setting, such as an open-mike discussion of a campus issue or a presentation to a legislative subcommittee, the oral argument might be considerably longer.

Written versions of informal conversations occur online among members of chat groups or listservs. These e-mail messages are usually short and informal, albeit more carefully crafted than real-time oral rejoinders. And as these discussions (or *threads*) play out over several days, you may well see participants' ideas shift and evolve as they negotiate some sort of collectively agreeable view, or perhaps a simple truce.

Written versions of formal speeches, drafted over the course of days or weeks, may take the form of an academic argument for a college course; a grant proposal; a guest column for the op-ed* section of a newspaper; a legal brief; a letter to a member of Congress; or an article for an organizational newsletter, popular mag-

---

*Op-ed stands for "opposite-editorial." It is the generic name in journalism for signed arguments that voice the writer's opinion on an issue, as opposed to news stories, which are supposed to report events objectively.

azine, or professional journal. In such instances, the written argument (a product) enters a conversation (a process)—in this case, a conversation of readers, many of whom will carry on the conversation by writing their own responses or by discussing the writer's views with others.

ARGUMENT COMBINES TRUTH SEEKING AND PERSUASION

In producing her argument, the writer will find herself continually moving back and forth between truth seeking and persuasion—that is, between questions about the subject matter (What is the best solution to this problem?) and about audience (What reasons and evidence best speak to my audience's values?). Back and forth she'll weave, alternately absorbed in the subject matter of her argument and in the persuasiveness of her argument to her audience.

Rarely is either focus ever completely ignored, but their relative importance shifts during different phases of the argument's development. We could thus place "concern for truthfulness" at one end of a continuum and "concern for persuasiveness" at the other, and fit any argument somewhere along that continuum. At the far truth-seeking end might be an exploratory piece that lays out several alternative approaches to a problem and weighs the strengths and weaknesses of each. At the other end of the continuum would be outright propaganda, such as a political campaign advertisement that reduces a complex issue to sound bites. (At its most blatant, propaganda obliterates truth seeking; it will do anything, including distorting or inventing evidence, to win over an audience.) In the middle ranges of the continuum, writers shift their focuses back and forth between truth seeking and persuasion but with varying degrees of emphasis.

To illustrate the need for a shifting focus, consider the case of Kathleen, who in her college argument course addressed the definitional question "Should American Sign Language meet the university's foreign language requirement?" Kathleen had taken two years of ASL at a community college. When she transferred to a four-year college, her ASL proficiency was dismissed by the foreign language department chair. "ASL isn't a 'language,' " he said summarily. "It's not equivalent to learning French, German, or Japanese."

Kathleen disagreed and immersed herself in her argument. In her initial research she focused almost entirely on subject matter, searching for what linguists, brain neurologists, cognitive psychologists, and sociologists had said about ASL. She was only tacitly concerned with her audience, whom she mostly envisioned as her classmates and those sympathetic to her view. She wrote a well-documented paper, citing several scholarly articles, that made a good case to her classmates (and her professor) that ASL was indeed a distinct language.

Proud of the big red A the professor had placed on her paper and more secure in her position, Kathleen resubmitted her request (this time buttressed with a copy of her paper) to count ASL for her language requirement. The chair of the foreign language department read her paper, congratulated her on her good writing, but said her argument was not persuasive. He disagreed with the definition of *language* she used in the paper, and he took issue with several of the linguists she cited. He again turned down her request.

Stung by what she considered a facile rejection of her argument, Kathleen embarked on a second ASL paper for her argument class—this time aimed directly at the foreign language chair. She researched the history of her college's foreign language requirement and discovered that after being dropped in the 1970s, the requirement was revived in the 1990s, partly (her math professor confided) to revive flagging enrollments in foreign languages. She also interviewed foreign language teachers to uncover their assumptions about ASL. She discovered that many of them thought ASL was "easy to learn" and that given the option, many students would take ASL to avoid the rigors of "real" language classes. Additionally, she learned that foreign language teachers valued immersing students in a foreign culture; in fact, the foreign language requirement was seen as a key component in the college's attempt to improve multicultural education.

With her newly acquired understanding of her target audience, Kathleen reconceptualized her argument. She emphasized how difficult ASL was to learn (to counter her audience's belief that learning ASL was easy), how the deaf community formed a distinct culture with its own customs and literature (to show how ASL met the goals of multiculturalism), and how few students would transfer in with ASL credits (to allay fears that accepting ASL would threaten language enrollments). She concluded by citing her college's mission statement, which called for eradicating social injustice and for reaching out to the oppressed. Surely, she argued, encouraging hearing people to learn ASL would help integrate the deaf community more fully into the larger campus community. In sum, all her revisions—the reasons selected, the evidence used, the arrangement and tone—were guided by her desire to persuade.

Our point, then, is that all along the continuum writers are concerned both to seek truth and to persuade, but not necessarily with equal balance. Kathleen could not have written her second paper, aimed specifically at persuading the chair of foreign languages, if she hadn't first immersed herself in truth-seeking research that convinced her that ASL was indeed a distinct language. Nor are we saying that her second argument was better than her first. Both fulfilled their purposes and met the needs of their intended audiences. Both involved truth seeking and persuasion, but the first focused primarily on subject matter whereas the second focused primarily on audience.

ARGUMENT AND THE PROBLEM OF TRUTH

The tension that we have just examined between truth seeking and persuasion raises one of the oldest issues in the field of argument: Is the arguer's first obligation to truth or to winning the argument? And just what is the nature of the truth to which arguers are supposed to be obligated? To this second question we now turn.

When Does Argument Become Propaganda?
The Debate between Socrates and Callicles

One of the first great debates on the issue of truth versus victory occurs in Plato's dialogue the *Gorgias,* in which the philosopher Socrates takes on the rhetorician Callicles.

Socrates was a great philosopher known to us today primarily through his student Plato, whose "dialogues" depict Socrates debating various friends and antagonists. Socrates' stated goal in these debates was to "rid the world of error." In dialogue after dialogue, Socrates vanquishes error by skillfully leading people through a series of questions that force them to recognize the inconsistency and implausibility of their beliefs. He was a sort of intellectual judo master who takes opponents' arguments the way they want to go until they suddenly collapse.

Callicles is a shadowy figure in history. We know him only through his exchange with Socrates—hence only through Plato's eyes. But Callicles is easily recognizable to philosophers as a representative of the Sophists, a group of teachers who schooled ancient Greeks in the fine art of winning arguments. The Sophists were a favorite, if elusive, target of both Socrates and Plato. Indeed, opposition to the Sophists' approach to life lies at the core of Platonic philosophy.

Having said all that, let's turn to the dialogue. Early in the debate, Socrates is clearly in control. He easily—too easily, as it turns out—wins a couple of preliminary rounds against some less determined Sophists before confronting Callicles. But in the long and arduous debate that follows, it's not at all clear that Socrates wins. In fact, one of the points being made in the *Gorgias* seems to be that philosophers committed to "clarifying" and discovering truth may occasionally have to sacrifice winning the debate in the name of their higher ends. Although Plato makes an eloquent case for enlightenment as the goal of argument, he may well contribute to the demise of this noble principle if he should happen to lose. Unfortunately, it appears that Socrates can't win the argument without sinning against the very principle he's defending.

The effectiveness of Callicles as a debater lies in his refusal to allow Socrates *any* assumptions. In response to Socrates' concern for virtue and justice, Callicles responds dismissively that such concepts are mere conventions, invented by the weak to protect themselves from the strong. Indeed, the power to decide what's "true" belongs to the winner of the debate. For Callicles, a truth that never wins is no truth at all because it will soon disappear.

Based on what we've said up to this point about our belief in argument as truth seeking, you might guess that our sympathies are with Socrates. To a great extent they are. But Socrates lived in a much simpler world than we do, if by "simple" we mean a world where the True and the Good were, if not universally agreed-on notions, at least ones around which a clear consensus formed. For Socrates, there was one True Answer to any important question. Truth resided in the ideal world of forms, and through philosophic rigor humans could transcend the changing, shadowlike world of everyday reality to perceive the world of universals where Truth, Beauty, and Goodness resided.

Callicles, however, rejects the notion that there is only one possible truth at which all arguments will necessarily arrive. For Callicles, there are different degrees of truth and different kinds of truths for different situations or cultures. In raising the whole nettlesome question—How "true" is a "truth" that you can't get anyone to agree to?—Callicles is probably closer to the modern world than is Plato. Let's expand on Callicles' view of truth by examining some contemporary illustrations.

What Is Truth? The Place of Argument in Contemporary Life

Although the debate between Socrates and Callicles appears to end inconclusively, many readers over the centuries conceded the victory to Socrates almost by default. Callicles was seen as cheating. The term *sophistry* came to be synonymous with trickery in argument. The Sophists' relativistic beliefs were so repugnant to most people that they refused to grant any merit to the Sophists' position. In our century, however, the Sophists have found a more sympathetic readership, one that takes some of the questions they raised quite seriously.

In the twentieth century, absolute, demonstrable truth is seen by many thinkers, from physicists to philosophers, as an illusion. Some would argue that truth is merely a product of human beings' talking and arguing with each other. These thinkers say that when considering questions of interpretation, meaning, or value one can never tell for certain whether an assertion is true—not by examining the physical universe more closely or by reasoning one's way toward some Platonic form or by receiving a mystical revelation. The closest one can come to truth is through the confirmation of one's views from others in a community of peers. "Truth" in any field of knowledge, say these thinkers, is simply an agreement of knowledgeable people in that field.

To illustrate the relevance of Callicles to contemporary society, suppose for the moment that we wanted to ask whether sexual fidelity is a virtue. A Socratic approach would assume a single, real Truth about the value of sexual fidelity, one that could be discovered through a gradual peeling away of wrong answers. Callicles, meanwhile, would assume that sexual morality is culturally relative; hence, he might point out all the societies in which monogamous fidelity for one or both sexes is not the norm. Clearly, our world is more like Callicles'. We are all exposed to multiple cultural perspectives directly and indirectly. Through television, newspapers, travel, and education we experience ways of thinking and valuing that are different from our own. It is difficult to ignore the fact that our personal values are not universally shared or even respected. Thus, we're all faced with the need to justify our views in such a diverse society.

It should be clear, then, that when we speak of the truth-seeking aim of argument, we mean not the discovery of an absolute "right answer" but the willingness to think through the complexity of an issue and to consider respectfully a wide range of views. The process of argument allows social groups, through the thoughtful exchange of ideas, to seek the best solution to a problem. The value of argument is its ability to help social groups make decisions in a rational and humane way without resorting to violence or to other assertions of raw power.

A SUCCESSFUL PROCESS OF ARGUMENTATION: THE WELL-FUNCTIONING COMMITTEE

We have said that neither the fist-banging speaker nor the college debate team represents our ideal image of argument. The best image for us, as we have implied, is a well-functioning small group seeking a solution to a problem. In professional life such small groups usually take the form of committees.

We use the word *committee* in its broadest sense to indicate all sorts of important work that grows out of group conversation and debate. The Declaration of Independence is essentially a committee document with Thomas Jefferson as the chair. Similarly, the U.S. Supreme Court is in effect a committee of nine judges who rely heavily, as numerous books and articles have demonstrated, on small-group decision-making processes to reach their judgments and formulate their legal briefs.

To illustrate our committee model for argument, let's briefly consider the workings of a university committee on which coauthor John Ramage once served, the University Standards Committee. The Arizona State University (ASU) Standards Committee plays a role in university life analogous to that of the Supreme Court in civic life. It's the final court of appeal for ASU students seeking exceptions to various rules that govern their academic lives (such as registering under a different catalog, waiving a required course, or being allowed to retake a course for a third time).

The Standards Committee is a large committee, comprising nearly two dozen members who represent the whole spectrum of departments and offices across campus. Every two weeks, the committee meets for two or more hours to consider between twenty and forty appeals. The issues that regularly come before the committee draw forth all the argumentative strategies discussed in detail throughout this text. For example, all of the types of claims discussed in Part Three regularly surface during committee deliberations. The committee deals with definition issues ("Is math anxiety a 'learning disability' for purposes of exempting a student from a math requirement? If so, what criteria can we establish for math anxiety?"); cause/consequence issues ("What were the causes of this student's sudden poor performance during spring semester?" "What will be the consequences of approving or denying her appeal?"); resemblance issues ("How is this case similar to an earlier case that we considered?"); evaluation issues ("Which criteria should take precedence in assessing this sort of appeal?"); and proposal issues ("Should we make it a policy to allow course X to substitute for course Y in the General Studies requirements?").

On any given day, the committee's deliberations showed how dialogue can lead to clarification of thinking. On many occasions, committee members' initial views shifted as they listened to opposing arguments. Unlike some committees, this committee made many decisions, the consequences of which were not trivial for the people involved. Because of the significance of these outcomes, committee members were more willing than they otherwise might have been to concede a point to another member in the name of reaching a better decision and to view their deliberations as an ongoing process of negotiation rather than a series of win-lose debates.

To give you firsthand experience at using argument as a process of clarification, we conclude this chapter with an actual case that came before the University Standards Committee. We invite you to read the following letter, pretending that you are a member of the University Standards Committee, and then proceed to the exercises that follow.

Petition to Waive University Mathematics Requirement

Standards Committee Members,

1   I am a 43-year-old member of the Pawnee Tribe of Oklahoma and a very nontraditional student currently pursuing Justice Studies at the Arizona State University (ASU) College of Public Programs. I entered college as the first step toward completion of my goal—becoming legal counsel for my tribe, and statesman.

2   I come before this committee in good faith to request that ASU suspend, in my special case, its mathematics requirement for undergraduate degree completion so I may enter the ASU College of Law during Fall 1993. The point I wish to make to this committee is this: I do not need algebraic skills; I will never use algebra in my intended profession; and, if forced to comply with ASU's algebra requirement, I will be needlessly prevented from graduating in time to enter law school next fall and face an idle academic year before my next opportunity in 1994. I will address each of these points in turn, but a few words concerning my academic credentials are in order first.

3   Two years ago, I made a vow of moral commitment to seek out and confront injustice. In September of 1990, I enrolled in college. Although I had only the benefit of a ninth grade education, I took the General Equivalency Diploma (GED) examination and placed in the top ten percent of those, nationwide, who took the test. On the basis of this score I was accepted into Scottsdale Community College (SCC). This step made me the first in my entire family, and practically in my tribe, to enter college. During my first year at SCC I maintained a 4.0 GPA, I was placed on the President's list twice, was active in the Honors Program, received the Honors Award of Merit in English Humanities, and was conferred an Honors

Scholarship (see attached) for the Academic year of 1991–1992 which I declined, opting to enroll in ASU instead.

At the beginning of the 1991 summer semester, I transferred to ASU. I chose to grad-   4
uate from ASU because of the courses offered in American Indian studies, an important field ignored by most other Universities but necessary to my commitment. At ASU I currently maintain a 3.6 GPA, although my cumulative GPA is closer to 3.9. I am a member of the Honors and Justice Colleges, was appointed to the Dean's List, and awarded ASU's prestigious Maroon and Gold Scholarship twice. My academic standing is impeccable. I will enter the ASU College of Law to study Indian and criminal law during the Fall of 1993—if this petition is approved. Upon successful completion of my juris doctorate I will return to Oklahoma to become active in the administration of Pawnee tribal affairs as tribal attorney and advisor, and vigorously prosecute our right to sovereignty before the Congress of the United States.

When I began my "college experience," I set a rigid time schedule for the completion   5
of my goal. By the terms of that self-imposed schedule, founded in my belief that I have already wasted many productive years, I allowed myself thirty-five months in which to achieve my Bachelor of Science degree in Justice Studies, for indeed justice is my concern, and another thirty-six months in which to earn my juris doctorate—summa cum laude. Consistent with my approach to all endeavors, I fell upon this task with zeal. I have willingly assumed the burden of carrying substantial academic loads during fall, spring and summer semesters. My problem now lies in the fact that in order to satisfy the University's math requirement to graduate I must still take MAT-106 and MAT-117. I submit that these mathematics courses are irrelevant to my goals, and present a barrier to my fall matriculation into law school.

Upon consideration of my dilemma, the questions emerged: Why do I need college al-   6
gebra (MAT-117)? Is college algebra necessary for studying American Indian law? Will I use college algebra in my chosen field? What will the University gain or lose, from my taking college algebra—or not? I decided I should resolve these questions.

I began my inquiry with the question: "Why do I need college algebra (MAT-117)?" I   7
consulted Mr. Jim _____ of the Justice College and presented this question to him. He referred to the current ASU catalog and delineated the following answer: I need college algebra (1) for a minimum level of math competency in my chosen field, and (2) to satisfy the university math requirement in order to graduate. My reply to the first answer is this: I already possess ample math skills, both practical and academic; and, I have no need for algebra in my chosen field. How do I know this? During the spring 1992 semester at ASU I successfully completed introductory algebra (MAT-077), scoring the highest class grade on one test (see attached transcript and test). More noteworthy is the fact that I was a machine and welding contractor for fifteen years. I used geometry and algebra commonly in the design of many welded structures. I am proficient in the use of Computer Assisted Design (CAD) programs, designing and drawing all my own blueprints for jobs. My blueprints and designs are always approved by city planning departments. For example, my most recent job consisted of the manufacture, transportation and installation of one linear mile of anodized, aluminum handrailing at a luxury resort condo on Maui, Hawaii. I applied extensive use of math to calculate the amount of raw materials to order, the logistics of mass

production and transportation for both men and materials from Mesa to Maui, the job site installation itself, and cash flow. I have successfully completed many jobs of this nature—all without a mathematical hitch. As to the application of math competency in my chosen field, I can guarantee this committee that there will not be a time in my practice of Indian law that I will need algebra. If an occasion ever occurs that I need algebra, I will hire a mathematician, just as I would an engineer if I need engineering, or a surgeon if I need an operation.

8   I then contacted Dr. _____ of the ASU Mathematics Department and presented him with the same question: "Why do I need college algebra?" He replied: (1) for a well-rounded education; (2) to develop creative thinking; and (3) to satisfy the university math requirement in order to graduate. Responding to the first answer, I have a "well-rounded education." My need is for a specific education in justice and American Indian law. In fact, I do not really need the degree to practice Indian law as representative of my tribe, just the knowledge. Regarding the second, I do not need to develop my creative thinking. It has been honed to a keen edge for many years. For example, as a steel contractor, I commonly create huge, beautiful and intricate structures from raw materials. Contracting is not my only experience in creative thinking. For twenty-five years I have also enjoyed the status of being one of this country's foremost designers and builders of racebikes. Machines I have designed and brought into existence from my imagination have topped some of Japan and Europe's best engineering efforts. To illustrate this point, in 1984 I rode a bike of my own design to an international victory over Honda, Suzuki, Laverda, BMW and Yamaha. I have excelled at creative thinking my entire life—I called it survival.

9   Expanding on the question of why I need college algebra, I contacted a few friends who are practicing attorneys. All responded to my question in similar manner. One, Mr. Billy _____, Esq., whose law firm is in Tempe, answered my two questions as follows: "When you attended law school, were there any courses you took which required algebra?" His response was "no." "Have you ever needed algebra during the many years of your practice?" Again, his response was "no." All agreed there was not a single occasion when they had need for algebra in their professional careers.

10   Just to make sure of my position, I contacted the ASU College of Law, and among others, spoke to Ms. Sierra _____. I submitted the question "What law school courses will I encounter in which I will need algebra?" The unanimous reply was, they knew of none.

11   I am not proposing that the number of credit hours I need for graduation be lowered. In fact, I am more than willing to substitute another course or two in its place. I am not trying to get out of anything hard or distasteful, for that is certainly not my style. I am seeking only to dispose of an unnecessary item in my studies, one which will prevent me from entering law school this fall—breaking my stride. So little holds up so much.

12   I agree that a young adult directly out of high school may not know that he needs algebraic skills. Understandably, he does not know what his future holds—but I am not that young adult. I claim the advantage. I know precisely what my future holds and that future holds no possibility of my needing college algebra.

13   Physically confronting injustice is my end. On reservations where government apathy allows rapacious pedophiles to pose as teachers; in a country where a million and a half American Indians are held hostage as second-rate human beings whose despair results in a

suicide, alcohol and drug abuse rate second to no other people; in prisons where helpless inmates are beaten like dogs by sadistic guards who should be the inmates—this is the realm of my chosen field—the disenfranchised. In this netherworld, algebra and justice exist independently of one another.

In summary, I am convinced that I do not need college algebra for a minimum level of math competency in my chosen field. I do not need college algebra for a well rounded education, nor to develop my creative thinking. I do not need algebra to take the LSAT. I do not need algebra for any courses in law school, nor will I for any purpose in the practice of American Indian law. It remains only that I need college algebra in order to graduate. 14

I promise this committee that ASU's integrity will not be compromised in any way by approving this waiver. Moreover, I assure this committee that despite not having a formal accreditation in algebra, I will prove to be nothing less than an asset to this University and its Indian community, both to which I belong, and I will continue to set a standard for integrity, excellence and perseverance for all who follow. Therefore, I ask this committee, for all the reasons described above, to approve and initiate the waiver of my University mathematics requirement. 15

[Signed: Gordon Adams]

▼ FOR CLASS DISCUSSION

1. Before class discussion, decide how you would vote on this issue. How persuasive is Gordon Adams's letter? Should Adams be exempted from the math requirement?

2. Working in small groups or as a whole class, pretend that you are the University Standards Committee and arrive at a group decision on whether to exempt this student from the math requirement.

3. After the discussion, write for several minutes in a journal or notebook describing how your thinking evolved during the discussion. Did any of your classmates' views cause you to rethink your own? Class members should share with each other their descriptions of how the process of argument led to the clarification of their own thinking.

CONCLUSION

In this chapter we have explored some of the complexities of argument, showing you why we believe that argument is a matter not of fist banging or of win-lose debate but of finding, through a process of rational inquiry, the best solution to a problem. What is our advice for you at the close of this introductory chapter? Briefly, it is to accept both responsibilities of argument: truth seeking and persuasion. To argue responsibly, you should seek out a wide range of views, especially ones different from your own, and treat those views as rationally defensible, paying special attention to the reasons and evidence on which they rest.

Our goal in this text is to help you learn skills of argument. If you choose, you can use these skills cynically to argue any side of any issue. But we hope you choose to use these skills in the service of your deepest beliefs—beliefs that you discover or clarify through open-minded inquiry. Thus we hope that on some occasions you will modify your position on an issue while writing a rough draft (a sure sign that the process of arguing has complicated your views). If our culture sets you adrift in pluralism, argument can help you take a stand, to say, "These things I believe." In this text we will not pretend to tell you what position to take on any given issue. But if this text helps you define and defend your beliefs—to say, "Here are the reasons that I consider choice A better than choice B, and why you ought to share my view"—then we'll consider it a success.

2   Reading Arguments

WHY READING ARGUMENTS
IS IMPORTANT FOR WRITERS

In the previous chapter we explained how reading and writing arguments is a social phenomenon growing out of people's search for the best answers to important questions. In this chapter we'll focus on the first half of that social dynamic—the thoughtful reading of arguments.

Much of the advice we offer about reading applies equally to listening. In fact, it is often helpful to think of reading as a conversation. We like to tell students that a college library is not so much a repository of information as a discussion frozen in time until you as reader bring it to life. Those books and articles, stacked neatly on library shelves, or stored in Web sites or databases, are arguing with each other, carrying on a great extended conversation. As you read, you bring those conversations to life. And when you write in response to your reading, you enter those conversations.

SUGGESTIONS FOR IMPROVING
YOUR READING PROCESS

Before we offer specific strategies for reading arguments, let's examine some general reading strategies applicable to most complex texts.

1. *Slow down:* Ads for speed-reading courses misleadingly suggest that the best readers are the fastest readers. They're not. Expert readers adjust their reading speed to the complexity of the text and to their purpose for reading and often read complex texts several times. They hold confusing passages in suspension, hoping that their confusion will be dispelled later in the text. They interact with the text in the margins, often extensively and vigorously.

2. *Get the dictionary habit:* When you can't tell a word's meaning from context, look it up—but not necessarily right away. One strategy is to make tick marks next to troublesome words and look them up when you come to a resting place so as not to break your concentration.

3. *Lose your highlighter/find your pen:* Relying on yellow highlighters makes you too passive. Next time you get the urge to highlight a passage, write in the margin *why* you think it's important. Use the margins to note new points or major evidence, to mark particularly strong or weak points, to jot down summaries of major points or connections to other texts, to ask questions. Don't just color the pages.

4. *Reconstruct the rhetorical context:* Train yourself to ask "Who is this author? To whom is he or she writing? Why? What's the occasion?" Writers are real people writing for a real purpose in a specific context. Knowing these specifics will help you make sense of the writing.

5. *Continue conversing with a text after reading:* Soon after reading, complete the following statements in a journal: "The most significant question this essay raises is. . . ." "The most important thing I learned from this essay is. . . ." "I agree with the author about. . . ." "But I disagree about. . . ."

6. *Try "translating" difficult passages:* Translate difficult passages into your own words. Doing so may not yield up the author's intended meaning, but it will force you to focus on the precise meaning of the words and help you to discover the source of your confusion.

STRATEGIES FOR READING ARGUMENTS: AN OVERVIEW

The preceding strategies work for a variety of texts. In what follows, we focus on reading strategies specific to arguments. All our strategies are grounded in the social nature of argument and the assumption that every argument is one voice in a larger conversation. We recommend, thus, the following sequence of strategies:

1. Read as a believer.
2. Read as a doubter.
3. Consider alternative views, and analyze sources of disagreement.
4. Use disagreement productively to prompt further investigation.

Let's now explore each of these strategies in turn.

STRATEGY 1: READING AS A BELIEVER

When you read as a believer, you practice what psychologist Carl Rogers calls *empathic listening*. Empathic listening requires you to see the world through the author's eyes, to adopt temporarily the author's beliefs and values, and to suspend your skepticism and biases long enough to hear what the author is saying.

Because empathic listening is such a vital skill, we will invite you shortly to try it on a controversial op-ed piece by conservative columnist George Will on the subject of equal pay for men and women. First, though, here is some background.

Each year, the federal government, using data collected by the Census Bureau and other sources, publishes wage data showing earnings broken down by state, region, profession, ethnicity, gender, and other categories. One of the most controversial statistics is the wage gap between the average earnings of men and women. The figure widely published in 1999, based on 1996 census data, was that women, on average, earn 74 cents to a man's dollar. Many advocacy groups argue for legislation or other government intervention to end the wage gap. As an example of such an advocacy group, see the Web page (Figure 2.1) from the site of the nation's largest labor organization, the AFL-CIO (American Federation of Labor and Congress of Industrial Organizations). This site aims to persuade workers to join the cause of pay equity for women.

Supporters of pay equity proposals generally have two areas of concern: First, they desire "equal pay for equal work," so that female mechanics receive the same pay as male mechanics and female college professors the same pay as male college professors. Second, they desire "equal pay for comparable work." The concept "comparable worth" means that jobs held mostly by women, such as social workers, should pay the same wages as comparable jobs held mostly by men, such as parole officers. Comparable worth would be measured by such criteria as the training and education required for entry into the field, the levels of stress and responsibility demanded by the work, and the social value of the work.

As you can imagine, opinion is deeply divided over the issue of pay equity.

▼ FOR CLASS DISCUSSION

Working individually or in groups, respond to the following questions.

1. Do you think the pay gap between women and men is a small, moderate, or major social and economic problem? Why?

2. What do you think are the causes of the pay gap between men and women?

3. Suppose you are on a task force to determine the comparable worth of jobs, particularly those held primarily by men versus those held primarily by women. Do you think an elementary teacher with an M.A. degree should earn

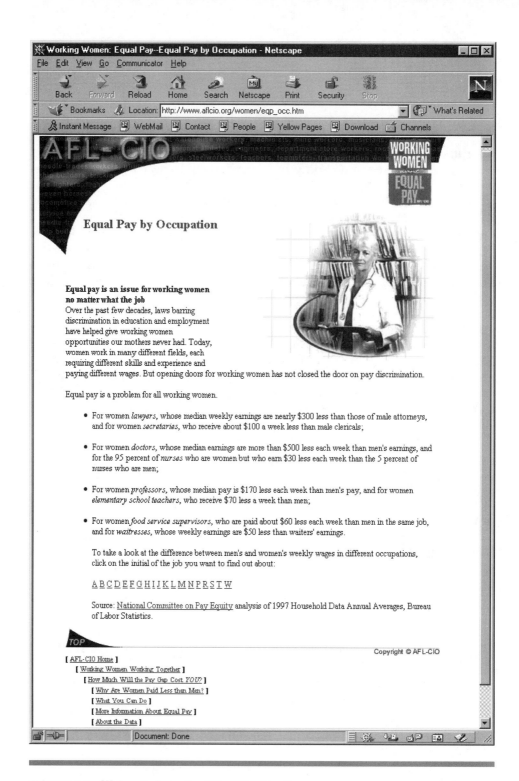

The web page shown contains:

Working Women: Equal Pay--Equal Pay by Occupation - Netscape

File Edit View Go Communicator Help

Back Forward Reload Home Search Netscape Print Security Stop

Bookmarks Location: http://www.aflcio.org/women/eqp_occ.htm   What's Related

Instant Message WebMail Contact People Yellow Pages Download Channels

AFL-CIO   WORKING WOMEN EQUAL PAY

Equal Pay by Occupation

Equal pay is an issue for working women no matter what the job

Over the past few decades, laws barring discrimination in education and employment have helped give working women opportunities our mothers never had. Today, women work in many different fields, each requiring different skills and experience and paying different wages. But opening doors for working women has not closed the door on pay discrimination.

Equal pay is a problem for all working women.

- For women *lawyers*, whose median weekly earnings are nearly $300 less than those of male attorneys, and for women *secretaries*, who receive about $100 a week less than male clericals;

- For women *doctors*, whose median earnings are more than $500 less each week than men's earnings, and for the 95 percent of *nurses* who are women but who earn $30 less each week than the 5 percent of nurses who are men;

- For women *professors*, whose median pay is $170 less each week than men's pay, and for women *elementary school teachers*, who receive $70 less a week than men;

- For women *food service supervisors*, who are paid about $60 less each week than men in the same job, and for *waitresses*, whose weekly earnings are $50 less than waiters' earnings.

To take a look at the difference between men's and women's weekly wages in different occupations, click on the initial of the job you want to find out about:

A B C D E F G H I J K L M N P R S T W

Source: National Committee on Pay Equity analysis of 1997 Household Data Annual Averages, Bureau of Labor Statistics.

TOP   Copyright © AFL-CIO

[AFL-CIO Home]
[Working Women Working Together]
[How Much Will the Pay Gap Cost *YOU*?]
[Why Are Women Paid Less than Men?]
[What You Can Do]
[More Information About Equal Pay]
[About the Data]

Document: Done

FIGURE 2.1 Web page from the AFL-CIO Web site

more or less than an accountant with a B.A. degree? Do you think a secretary with an A.A. degree should earn more or less than an auto mechanic with an A.A. degree?

4. Who, if anyone, should be responsible for establishing fair pay: businesses and employers alone? the government?

Now that you have some background on the pay equity issue, you are ready to read George Will's argument.

Lies, Damned Lies, and . . .

George F. Will

With the Dow Average nearing a fifth digit, Americans are cheerful. However, soon the   1
women's division of the Great American Grievance Industry will weigh in, saying women remain trapped beneath the "glass ceiling" and in the "pink ghetto." Brace yourself for a blizzard of statistics purporting to prove that women are suffering a "wage gap" primarily caused by discrimination that requires government actions like affirmative action, quotas and set-asides.

But a counterblizzard has blown in from Diana Furchtgott-Roth and Christine Stolba,   2
authors of *Women's Figures: An Illustrated Guide to the Economic Progress of Women in America.* Furchtgott-Roth is a fellow at The American Enterprise Institute and Stolba is a historian living in Washington, and both had better mind their manners. Feminists are not famous for their sense of humor and may frown at the authors' dedication of their book to their husbands "who have always appreciated our figures."

The National Committee On Pay Equity and other participants in the theatrics of Equal   3
Pay Day will not appreciate the figures Furchtgott-Roth and Stolba marshal. The premise of Equal Pay Day is that women work from Jan. 1 until early April essentially for no pay because women earn only 74 cents for every dollar men earn. That uninformative number is the basis for the allegation that the average woman loses approximately $420,000 in wages and benefits during her working life. The 74 cents factoid is prima facie proof of "the demeaning practice of wage discrimination," according to President Clinton, who opposes everything demeaning to women.

Furchtgott-Roth and Stolba argue that the 74 cents statistic is the product of faulty   4
methodology that serves the political agenda of portraying women as victims needing yet more government intervention in the workplace. The authors demonstrate that income disparities between men and women have been closing rapidly and that sex discrimination, which has been illegal for 30 years, is a negligible cause of those that remain, which are largely the result of rational personal choices by women.

Between 1960 and 1994 women's wages grew 10 times faster than men's, and today,   5
among people 27 to 33, women who have never had a child earn about 98 cents for every

dollar men earn. Children change the earnings equations. They are the main reason that meaningful earnings contrasts must compare men and women who have similar experiences and life situations. Earnings differentials often reflect different professional paths that are cheerfully chosen because of different preferences, motivations, and expectations.

6   The "adjusted wage gap," adjusted for age, occupation, experience, education and time in the work force, is primarily the product of personal choices women make outside the work environment. Eighty percent of women bear children and 25 percent of working women work part-time, often to accommodate child rearing. Many women who expect to have children choose occupations where job flexibility compensates for somewhat lower pay, and occupations (e.g., teaching) in which job skills deteriorate slower than in others (e.g., engineering). And it is not sex discrimination that accounts for largely male employment in some relatively high-paying occupations (e.g., construction, oil drilling and many others) which place a premium on physical strength. (Workers in some such occupations pay a price: the 54 percent of all workers who are male account for 92 percent of all job-related deaths.)

7   Still, between 1974 and 1993 women's wages have been rising relative to men's in all age groups, and most dramatically among the youngest workers. The rise would be more dramatic if many women did not make understandable decisions to favor family over higher pay and more rapid job advancement purchased by 60-hour weeks on the fast track.

8   Some victimization theorists say the fast track is pointless for women because they are held down by the "glass ceiling" that limits their rise in business hierarchies. In 1995 the government's Glass Ceiling Commission (the propagandistic title prejudged the subject) saw proof of sex discrimination in the fact that women are only 5 percent of senior managers at Fortune 1000 industrial and Fortune 500 service companies. But Furchtgott-Roth and Stolba note that typical qualifications for such positions include an M.B.A. and 25 years' work experience. The pool of women with those qualifications is small, not because of current discrimination but because of women's expectations in the 1950s and 1960s. In 1970 women received only 4 percent of all M.B.A. degrees, 5 percent of law degrees.

9   Which lends support to the optimistic "pipeline" theory: women are rising in economic life as fast as they pour from the educational pipeline—which is faster than men. Since 1984 women have outnumbered men in undergraduate and graduate schools. Women are receiving a majority of two-year postsecondary degrees, bachelor's and master's degrees, almost 40 percent of M.B.A degrees, 40 percent of doctorates, more than 40 percent of law and medical degrees. Education improves economic opportunities—and opportunities encourage education, which has higher rewards for women than for men because men without college degrees or even high-school diplomas can get those high-paying, physically demanding—and dangerous—jobs.

10   The supposed "pink ghetto" is where women are, in the Glass Ceiling Commission's words, "locked into" low-wage, low-prestige, dead-end jobs. Such overheated rhetoric ignores many women's rational sacrifices of pay and prestige for job flexibility in occupations in which skills survive years taken off for raising children. Women already predominate in the two economic sectors expected to grow fastest in the near future, service/trade/retail and finance/insurance/real estate.

The 74 cents statistic and related propaganda masquerading as social science are arrows   11
in the quivers of those waging the American left's unending struggle to change the American premise, which stresses equality of opportunity, not equality of outcomes. Furchtgott-Roth and Stolba have better figures.

Summary Writing as a Way of Reading to Believe

Now that you have finished the article, ask yourself how well you "listened" to it. If you listened well, you should be able to write a summary of Will's argument in your own words. A *summary* (also called an *abstract*, a *précis*, or a *synopsis*) presents only a text's major points and eliminates supporting details. Writers often incorporate summaries of other writers' views into their own arguments, either to support their own claims or to represent opposing arguments that they intend to refute. Summaries can be any length, depending on the writer's purposes, but they usually range from several sentences to one or two paragraphs.

Practicing the following steps should help you be a better summary writer.

Step 1: Read the argument first for general meaning. Don't judge it; just follow the writer's meaning, trying to see the issue from the writer's perspective. Try to adopt the writer's values and belief system.

Step 2: Read the argument slowly a second and a third time, writing in the margins brief *does* and *says* statements for each paragraph (or group of closely connected paragraphs). A *does* statement identifies a paragraph's function, such as "summarizes an opposing view," "introduces a supporting reason," or "gives an example." A *says* statement summarizes a paragraph's content. What follows are our *does* and *says* statements for the first five paragraphs of Will's article.

DOES/SAYS ANALYSIS OF WILL'S ARTICLE

Paragraph 1: *Does:* Introduces issue by summarizing the wage gap argument that Will opposes. *Says:* Although most Americans are cheerful about the boom economy, the "American Grievance Industry" will soon complain that women suffer a wage gap that will require government intervention.

Paragraph 2: *Does:* Introduces two authors whose research debunks the wage gap argument *Says:* Diana Furchtgott-Roth and Christine Stolba provide a very different interpretation of the data on men's and women's wages.

Paragraph 3: *Does:* Summarizes the wage gap argument of the National Committee on Pay Equity. *Says*: According to the National Committee on Pay Equity, women earn only 74 cents for every dollar that men earn, so the average woman loses $420,000 in wages over a career, thus proving wage discrimination.

Paragraph 4: *Does:* Summarizes the counterargument of Diana Furchtgott-Roth and Christine Stolba. *Says:* The 74 cents "factoid" is not proof of wage discrimination, the pay gap has been closing rapidly, and whatever pay gap remains can be explained by women's personal career choices.

Paragraph 5: *Does:* Further develops this argument by focusing on the impact on children. *Says:* Women's pay has risen ten times faster than men's since 1960, and childless women ages twenty-seven to thirty-three earn 98 percent of men's wages; having children makes the difference, causing women to choose different career paths.

FOR CLASS DISCUSSION

Working individually or in groups, make *does* and *says* statements for the remaining paragraphs in Will's article.

Step 3: Examine your *does* and *says* statements to determine the major sections of the argument, and create a list of major points and subpoints. If you are visually oriented, you may prefer to make a flowchart or diagram of the article.

Step 4: Turn your list, flowchart, or diagram into a prose summary. Typically, writers do this in one of two ways. Some start by joining all their *says* statements into a lengthy paragraph-by-paragraph summary and then prune it. Others start with a one-sentence summary of the argument's thesis and major supporting reasons and then gradually flesh it out with more supporting ideas.

Step 5: Revise your summary until it is the desired length and is sufficiently clear, concise, and complete. When you incorporate a summary of someone else's argument into your own essay, you must distinguish that author's words and ideas from your own by using *attributive tags* (expressions like "Will says," "according to Will," or "Will further explains"), by putting any directly borrowed language in quotation marks, and by citing the original author using appropriate conventions for documenting sources.*

As illustrations, we will show you our summaries of Will's article—a one-paragraph version and a single-sentence version. In the one-paragraph version we illustrate the MLA documentation system, in which page numbers for direct quotations are placed in parentheses after the quotation and complete biblio-

---

*The most frequently used documentation systems in academic writing are those of the Modern Language Association (MLA) and the American Psychological Association (APA). Both are explained in Appendix 2, "A Concise Guide to Evaluating and Documenting Sources."

graphic information is placed in a Works Cited list at the end of the paper. See Appendix 2 for a complete explanation of the MLA and APA documentation systems.

ONE-PARAGRAPH SUMMARY OF WILL'S ARGUMENT

Identification of author and source

Insertion of brief quotation; MLA documentation style shows page number in parentheses

Attributive tag

Main claim of the article

Attributive tag

Attributive tag

Attributive tag with transition

Another short quotation

Attributive tag

Attributive tag

In a recent *Newsweek* editorial entitled "Lies, Damned Lies and . . . ," conservative columnist George Will questions the claim that women, in earning 74 cents to a man's dollar, are victims of gender-based wage discrimination that "requires government actions like affirmative action, quotas and set-asides" (23). Citing a recent book by Diana Furchtgott-Roth and Christine Stolba, Will argues that the 74 cents statistic is a "factoid" (23) that indicates personal career choices, not wage discrimination. Arguing that the wage gap is rapidly closing and has virtually disappeared for childless women between ages 27 and 33, Will claims that the remaining wage gap results from women's sacrificing pay and prestige for flexible jobs that allow time off for child raising. Women's dramatic increases in pay, Will asserts, would be even more dramatic if women desiring children didn't drop out of the fast track. Will then examines the objection made by "victimization theorists" (24) that the absence of high-level women executives in Fortune 1000 companies reveals a glass ceiling. He rebuts this argument by claiming that women haven't occupied professional jobs long enough to gain the experience and qualifications to attain upper-level positions, a situation that will soon end now that half of advanced degrees are earned by women. Will concludes that the 74 cents statistic is mere propaganda aimed at changing the traditional American value of equal opportunity into the leftist value of equal outcomes. (236 words)

Will's article cited completely in MLA documentation format; in a formal paper the Works Cited list begins on a new page.

Work Cited

Will, George F. "Lies, Damned Lies and . . ." *Newsweek* 29 Mar. 1999: 84. Rpt. in John D. Ramage, John C. Bean, and June Johnson. *Writing Arguments: A Rhetoric with Readings.* Concise ed., 2nd ed. Needham: Allyn, 2001. 23–25.

ONE-SENTENCE SUMMARY OF WILL'S ARGUMENT

In a recent *Newsweek* editorial, conservative columnist George Will argues that the supposed wage gap between men and women is the result not of wage discrimination but of women's rational choices to sacrifice the pay and prestige of fast-track careers for flexible jobs that allow time off for child raising. (50 words)

Whether you write a very short summary or a more detailed one, your goal should be to come as close as possible to a fair, accurate, and balanced condensation of the author's argument and to represent the relationships among the parts fairly and accurately. We don't want to pretend that summary writing is easy; often it's not, especially if the argument is complex and if the author doesn't explicitly highlight his or her thesis and main supporting reasons. Nonetheless, being able to summarize the arguments of others in your own words is an important skill for arguers.

Suspending Doubt: Willing Your Own Belief in the Writer's Views

Summarizing an argument is only the first step in your effort to believe it. You must also suspend doubt and will yourself to adopt the writer's view. Suspending doubt is easy if you already agree with the author. But if an author's views affront your own values, then "believing" can be a hard but valuable exercise. By struggling to believe strange, threatening, or unfamiliar views, we can grow as learners and thinkers.

To believe an author, search your mind for personal experiences, values, and beliefs that affirm his or her argument. Here is how one female student wrote a journal entry trying to believe Will's argument.

JOURNAL ENTRY SHOWING STUDENT'S ATTEMPT TO BELIEVE WILL

When I first read the Web page from the AFL-CIO I was outraged at the low pay women got. I thought that this was outright discrimination against women. I thought of all the money that women lost during their careers because men automatically got more pay than women just because people don't think women's work is worth as much. But then when I read George Will I saw that maybe there was another explanation. It is really true that many women worry how they are going to balance a career with having children, and I can see how women might seek out jobs that don't demand 80-hour workweeks and that give them some flexibility in hours so that they can spend more time with their children. Although I think dads ought to make the same sacrifices, I can see how women are more likely to focus on family issues. So if enough women are opting for less prestigious jobs, then the average wages of all women would be lower. It's a shame that just women rather than men have to sacrifice their careers for children, but I can see Will's point that their lower earnings are a result of personal choices rather than discrimination.

STRATEGY 2: READING AS A DOUBTER

Reading as a believer is only half of being a powerful reader. You must also read as a doubter by raising objections, asking questions, expressing skepticism, and withholding assent. In the margins of the text, as a doubter, you add a new layer of notes demanding more proof, doubting evidence, challenging the author's assumptions and values, and so forth.

▼ FOR CLASS DISCUSSION

Return to Will's article, reading it skeptically. Raise questions, offer objections, express doubts. Then, working as a class or in small groups, list all your doubts about Will's argument.

Now that you've doubted Will's article, compare your doubts to some of those raised by our students:

- Will implies that mainly feminists believe that a gender wage gap exists. Who exactly is protesting the gender wage gap?

- What is the background of the two authors—Diana Furchgott-Roth and Christine Stolba? What biases do they bring to their research?

- What is the source of Will's claim that in the last thirty years women's wages have been rising ten times faster than men's? The AFL-CIO Web page doesn't agree at all with this claim. We wonder what jobs and careers he is describing.

- Will automatically assumes that if a job is flexible it ought to pay less. What's wrong with good-paying jobs also being flexible?

- Will assumes that if a job is dangerous it ought to pay more (he mentions construction and other occupations). What about athletic-shoe sweatshops in Asia and Mexico where women workers are exposed to dangerous chemicals? By Will's argument, they ought to be making a mint.

- Will assumes a two-parent family in which the father has the main career. He completely ignores mothers who must work and single mothers who can't afford to take time off from work and who must pay for childcare.

- He also ignores working-class women. His optimistic picture involves college-educated women who are willing to forgo having children.

These are only some of the objections that might be raised against Will's argument. Perhaps you and your classmates have other objections that are equally important. Our point is that you should practice "doubting" an argument as well as "believing" it. Both skills are essential. *Believing* helps you expand your view of the world or modify your arguments and beliefs in response to others. *Doubting* helps protect you from becoming overpowered by others' arguments and teaches you to stand back, consider, and weigh points carefully.

STRATEGY 3: SEEKING OUT ALTERNATIVE VIEWS AND ANALYZING SOURCES OF DISAGREEMENT

If you were an arbitrator, you wouldn't think of settling a dispute between A and B on the basis of A's testimony alone. You would insist on hearing B's side of the story. By the same token, you can't fairly evaluate an argument detached from the controversy out of which it arose or isolated from the alternative views to which it speaks. You must seek out those views.

When analyzing disagreements among various points of view, you'll find they typically fall into two categories: (1) disagreement about the facts or reality of the case and (2) disagreements about underlying beliefs, values, or assumptions. Let's consider each in turn.

Disagreement about Facts or Reality

Theoretically, a fact is a piece of empirical data on which everyone agrees. Often, however, one person's "fact" is another person's misconception. Note how the "facts" are contested in these cases:

- In arguing whether silver-mercury amalgam tooth fillings should be banned, dental researchers disagree on the amount of mercury vapor released by older fillings. They also disagree on how much mercury vapor has to be present before it is harmful.

- In arguing what to do about the problem of illegitimacy, disputants might agree that the illegitimacy rate is rising but disagree about the cause of this phenomenon. Disagreeing about causes, they also disagree about solutions to the problem.

Disagreements about Values, Beliefs, or Assumptions

A second source of disagreement concerns differences in values, beliefs, or assumptions.

- Persons A and B may agree that a huge tax on gasoline would cut down on the consumption of petroleum. They may agree further that the world's supply of petroleum will eventually run out. Thus A and B agree at the level of facts. But they may disagree about whether the United States should enact a huge gas tax. Person A may support a tax increase to conserve oil, whereas person B may oppose it, perhaps because B believes that scientists will find alternative energy sources before the petroleum runs out or because B believes that the short-term harm of such a tax outweighs distant benefits.

Sometimes disagreements about assumptions present themselves as disagreements about definitions or analogies.

- Social theorist A and social theorist B might disagree about whether the covers of some women's magazines, such as *Cosmopolitan*, are pornographic. This disagreement turns on the definition of *pornography*, with different definitions reflecting different underlying values and beliefs.

- Person A and Person B might disagree on whether it is ethically acceptable for Down's syndrome children to undergo plastic surgery to correct some of the facial abnormalities associated with this genetic condition. Person A supports the surgery, arguing it is analogous to any other cosmetic surgeries done to improve appearance. Person B argues against such surgery, saying that the motivation for the surgery is analogous to the racial self-hatred of some minority persons who have tried to change their ethnic appearance and become lily white. (The latter analogy argues that Down's syndrome is nothing to be ashamed of and that persons should take pride in their difference.)

❖ FOR CLASS DISCUSSION

As we discussed in Chapter 1, we live in a pluralistic world in which many differing systems of values and beliefs compete for our allegiance. It is not surprising, therefore, that people disagree on the issue of pay equity. What follows is a syndicated column by journalist Ellen Goodman, written about the same time as George Will's *Newsweek* piece. Read Goodman's column carefully. Then, working as a whole class or in small groups, answer the following questions:

1. To what extent do Will and Goodman disagree about the basic facts concerning men's and women's wages?

2. In what ways are the disagreements between Will and Goodman related to their differing values, beliefs, and underlying assumptions?

A New Campaign for Pay Equity
Ellen Goodman

Somewhere in the recesses of my desk drawer there is a battered old pink pin bearing the message: 59 cents. This was not the price of the pin. It was the price of being a working woman circa 1969.   1

When these pins first began to appear at political conferences and conventions, women were earning 59 cents for every male dollar. Today, after 30 years of change, guess what? Women are earning 74 cents for every male dollar.   2

We have, in short, made economic progress at roughly half a cent a year. And before you choke over this breakneck pace, consider that three-fifths of the "progress" in closing the gender gap has come from men's falling wages, not women's rising wages.   3

4   Somehow or other the unsexy issue of the paycheck—equal pay for the same or equivalent work—dropped off the economic agenda. But it never left the minds of women. In surveys, women workers went on rating pay equity as "very important," and a third said they didn't have it. These are the same women who worry about balancing work and family, but many said, if we get a fair paycheck, we'll work it out.

5   Now, without a whole lot of fanfare, the issue of pay equity is back.

6   Remember that moment in the State of the Union address when the president told Congress to "make sure women and men get equal pay by strengthening enforcement of the equal pay laws"? To everyone's surprise he got a bipartisan Standing O. Since then the president proposed a $14 million equal pay initiative with most of the money going to better enforcement of the existing laws.

7   Now, as spring rolls in, new legislation for pay equity is being planted in 24 state-houses. This campaign has a two-part strategy. Part One: Get the old laws enforced. Part Two: Expand the notion of equal pay to include work of equal value.

8   As for Part One, if you have any doubts that the old laws aren't enforced enough, click onto the depressing union Web page, www.aflcio.org/women/. There's a lot of bad news.

9   The gender gap between male and female accountants is $201 a week. The gap between bartenders is $48. And, to pick another occupation out of a hat, the gap between male and female reporters and editors—ahem—is $163. The Web site will also help you figure out your own lifetime net loss.

10   As for Part Two, if you have any doubts that the old laws are too narrow, even if women were paid equally for the same job, most don't hold the same jobs. The jobs held primarily by women are "worth less" than the ones held primarily by men. That's true even if they involve roughly the same skills, effort, responsibility and working conditions.

11   For this reason, a 911 dispatcher is paid less in many places than an emergency operator at the Fire Department. A social worker is paid less than a probation officer. And in some states we have the tale of two nursery workers, one working with plants, the other with children. Guess who gets paid more?

12   Underlying the new campaign for pay equity are attitudes that are changing faster than wages. When the 59-cent button first appeared, it was assumed that any woman who wanted to get paid "like a man" had to do a "man's job."

13   At the Center for Policy Alternatives, Linda Tarr-Whelan says, "In this economy we have a diminished sense that the work women do with people is worth the same amount as the work men do with machines and dollars." Many are finally asking why "women's jobs" should be "worth less"?

14   For a long time, the glib excuse for the gender values gap has been market values: "the marketplace." Now it's being reframed as a matter of fairness and discrimination.

15   Not surprisingly, the legislative campaign will begin at the state level—where the percentage of women legislators is twice as high as in Congress—and build momentum before it goes to Washington.

16   In the meantime, there is a figure from the new survey to keep in mind: $200 billion. That's the amount families of working women lose every year to the gender gap. At that rate, half a cent a year just won't hack it.

Writing an Analysis of a Disagreement

A common writing assignment in argument courses asks students to analyze the sources of disagreement between two or more writers who take different positions on an issue. In writing such an analysis, you need to determine whether the writers disagree primarily about facts/reality, about values, or about both. To illustrate an analysis of a disagreement, we've constructed the following model: our own brief analysis of the sources of disagreement between Will and Goodman. We've written it as a short, formal paper following the MLA documentation style.

An Analysis of the Sources of Disagreement between Will and Goodman

The op-ed pieces of George Will and Ellen Goodman on the gender pay gap show disagreements of both fact and value. Will and Goodman agree that there is a gender wage gap reflected in the statistic that women earn only 74 cents to a man's dollar. However, they disagree about the causes of this pay gap. Goodman attributes the gap to gender discrimination in the workplace, whereas Will attributes it to women's personal choices in opting for flexible jobs that permit time off for child raising. Will therefore calls the 74 cents statistic a meaningless "factoid" rather than a meaningful fact.

This basic disagreement about cause explains each author's choice of data for framing the issue. Goodman accepts the statistics disseminated on the AFL-CIO Web site. She believes that women have made little progress in closing the wage gap in the last thirty years and argues that "three-fifths of the 'progress' in closing the gender gap has come from men's falling wages, not women's rising wages" (31). Goodman sees discrimination operating at two levels—in the disparate wages paid to men and women in the same jobs and in the lower worth placed on women's jobs.

In contrast, Will's selection of data paints an optimistic picture of women's progress. Drawing statistics from Furchgott-Roth and Stolba, Will asserts that the 74 cents figure is not accurate for all women, citing instead the data that women's wages grew ten times faster than men's in the last thirty years and arguing that "today, among people 27 to 33, women who have never had a child earn about 98 cents for every dollar men earn" (23–24). Thus Goodman and Will disagree on which "facts" are significant. Their selection of data creates different views of reality.

Will's and Goodman's different views of the facts reflect deep differences in values. Will, a political conservative, upholds the free market and opposes "government actions like affirmative action, quotas and set-asides" (23). Will claims that the American left is trying "to change the American premise, which stresses equality of opportunity, not equality of outcomes" (25). Underneath Will's belief that women "cheerfully" opt for lower-paying jobs in order to raise children is a belief in the two-parent, nuclear family and in traditional gender roles that make child rearing primarily the mother's responsibility. In contrast, as a political liberal, Goodman sees the gender wage gap as an unfair, discriminatory situation that should be corrected by government. Moreover, she sees it as a problem for men and for families as well as for women.

5   To convey their values, Will and Goodman adopt the breezy, somewhat flippant tone typical of many op-ed pieces. Will's frequent use of the phrase "women's figures" as well as his statements that women are making up the problem ("victimization theorists") and that feminists like to complain ("the Great American Grievance Industry") suggests anger directed at feminists rather than concern for the social consequences of low-paying jobs. Goodman's piece is also a little sarcastic. She impatiently clarifies women's "economic progress" as a pay increase of "roughly half a cent a year" and quips, "And before you choke over this breakneck pace [. . .]" (31). Both Will and Goodman choose tones that risk alienating readers who don't agree with them even as they invite readers who share their values to joke with them.

6   Not surprisingly, both Will's and Goodman's different interpretations of facts and their different values lead to different proposals for action. Believing that women are making progress through higher education and more professional experience, Will asserts that the gender wage gap is correcting itself. In contrast, Goodman calls for immediate political action and change. She is concerned with working-class jobs as well as professional, white-collar careers and supports enactment of new laws to "expand the notion of equal pay to include work of equal value" (32).

7   In sum, Will and Goodman disagree about both facts and values.

Works Cited

Goodman, Ellen. "A New Campaign for Pay Equity." *Buffalo News* 16 Mar. 1999: 3B. Rpt. in John D. Ramage, John C. Bean, and June Johnson. *Writing Arguments: A Rhetoric with Readings.* Concise ed., 2nd ed. Needham: Allyn, 2001. 31–32.

Will, George F. "Lies, Damned Lies and . . ." *Newsweek* 29 Mar. 1999: 84. Rpt. in John D. Ramage, John C. Bean, and June Johnson. *Writing Arguments: A Rhetoric with Readings.* Concise ed., 2nd ed. Needham: Allyn, 2001. 23–25.

STRATEGY 4: USING DISAGREEMENT PRODUCTIVELY TO PROMPT FURTHER INVESTIGATION

Our fourth strategy—using disagreement productively to prompt further investigation—is both a powerful strategy for reading arguments and a bridge toward constructing your own arguments. Our goal is to suggest ways to help you proceed when the experts disagree.

When confronted with conflicting positions, you must learn to cope with ambiguity. If there were no disagreements, of course, there would be no need for argument. It is important to realize that experts can look at the same data, can analyze the same arguments, can listen to the same authorities, and still can reach different conclusions. Seldom will one expert's argument triumph over another's in a field of dissenting claims. Accepting ambiguity enables you to delve deeply into an issue and to resist easy answers.

As you sort through conflicting viewpoints, your goal is not to identify one of them as "correct" but to ask what is the best solution to the problem being debated here. You may eventually decide that one of the current viewpoints is indeed the best solution. Or you may develop a synthesis that combines strengths from several divergent viewpoints. In either case, you will emerge from the process with an enlarged, informed understanding. You will have developed the ability to remain intellectually flexible while listening to alternative viewpoints. Most important, you will have learned how to avoid falling into valueless relativism. Responding productively to disagreement thus becomes part of your preparation for writing ethically responsible arguments.

To try to illustrate the process of responding to disagreements, we now show you how we responded to the disagreement between Will and Goodman over pay equity.

Seeking Out Sources of Facts and More Complete Versions of Alternative Views

After analyzing the sources of disagreement between Will and Goodman (see our sample essay on pages 33–34), we next attempted to use these disagreements productively by striving for a more complete understanding of alternative views. We began by pursuing the sources cited by Will and Goodman. We needed to determine whether the book by Furchtgott-Roth and Stolba cited by Will or the data compiled by the AFL-CIO (American Federation of Labor and the Congress of Industrial Organizations) cited by Goodman seemed more reliable and persuasive. We also hoped to determine if there is a majority position among commentators.

Our searching for sources helped us see a pattern in the views of experts. We discovered that Will's perspective is endorsed by the American Enterprise Institute (a conservative think tank of which Furchtgott-Roth is a fellow) and by the Senate Republican Committee. Because conservatives tend to favor free markets, these endorsements seemed understandable. Numerous other organizations, however, believe that the gender pay gap is a serious problem: the Bureau of Labor Statistics, the Institute for Women's Policy Research, Catalyst (a women's research group), and the National Committee on Pay Equity. Furthermore, the results of the AFL-CIO's 1997 "Ask a Working Woman" survey, which strongly argues that a gender pay gap exists, are presented very clearly in the AFL-CIO Web site (www.aflcio.org). Because these organizations are aligned with labor or with women's advocacy groups, they understandably favor proactive policies to boost wages of low-pay workers.

However, these pro-labor groups did provide strong evidence to confirm the reality of a gender pay gap. These sources gave extensive national and state data, based on what seemed to us factual information about wages, to show that a wage gap exists, that it varies by state, and that the gap is bigger for women of color.

Our search for fuller understanding inspired us to seek out information on the Fair Pay Act and the Paycheck Fairness Act currently before Congress to see how the legislators propose to deal with this problem. We discovered that pro-business commentators think that new laws could lead to costly litigation as women sue for back pay and could lead to government micro-management of corporations. These concerns are valid, but we also found that one main goal of the legislation is to encourage corporations and institutions to self-audit for internal equity in hiring and in establishing equitable policies for evaluations for salaries, promotions, and benefits.

We were also drawn to arguments that framed the gender pay gap as an issue affecting women, men, children, and families. The families of working women, and particularly of single mothers, are suffering the most from the inequity in wages of wives and mothers. These sources persuasively widened their concerns to show that equal pay for women affects children's security, health care, the poverty rate, domestic violence, Social Security, pensions, and family stability. The issue thus has enormous social repercussions.

Determining What Values Are at Stake for You in the Issue and Articulating Your Own Values

In responding to disagreement, you need to articulate your own values and to try to justify them by explaining the reasons you hold them. The authors of this text, for example, tend to support the need for greater pay equity and question Will's emphasis on women's choices as a complete explanation for lower pay for women. We know that for many women and families, working isn't a choice, it is a necessity. We have seen that women often sacrifice salaries and advancements when they have to take time off for children and that these choices are not always "cheerfully" made, as Will claims, but involve agonizing conflicts between job and family. Thinking about the fairness of pay reminds us that the United States has the highest poverty rate, the highest rate of children in poverty, and the biggest disparity of income distribution among industrialized nations. Therefore, we tend to favor government policies that boost the earnings of people at the bottom of the economic ladder.

Considering Ways to Synthesize Alternative Views

As a final step in your evaluation of conflicting sources, you should consider what you have gained from the different perspectives. How do the alternative views modify each other or otherwise "speak to each other"? If conflicting views don't lead to a synthesis, how do the different perspectives at least lead to an informed, enlarged vision of the issue?

What valuable points could we take from the opposing stands on this topic if we were to write our own argument on pay equity? What perspective could we synthesize from the free-market optimism of Will and the need for reform voiced by Goodman? Will claims that more women are earning college and graduate degrees and that these qualifications will equip them for better jobs; basically, he argues, the situation for women is improving and any inequalities will fix themselves. Yet Goodman believes that rigorous enforcement of pay equity laws *and* the enactment of new ones are needed. Could an argument on pay equity acknowledge the progress that Will cites and the urgency of the problems that Goodman discusses? We concluded that an informed position would need to recognize the economic progress of college-educated, professional women willing to forgo childbearing, while at the same time pointing out the injustice of persistently low wages for women in working-class jobs. Our goal would be to find ways to connect the pay equity problem to issues of family and poverty.

When you try to synthesize points from conflicting positions, as we did here, you experience the dialectical nature of argument, questioning and modifying positions in response to new perspectives. We cannot claim that the position we are tentatively formulating on the pay equity issue is the right one. We can claim only that it is a reasonable and responsible one in light of the available facts and our own values. We have tried to show how the process of responding to disagreement— coping with ambiguity, pursuing researched answers to questions about fact and value, articulating your own values, and seeking possible syntheses—launches you on the path to becoming a responsible writer of arguments.

CONCLUSION

This chapter has explained why reading arguments is crucially important to writers of argument and has offered suggestions for improving your own reading process. We have suggested four main strategies for deep reading: (1) Read as a believer. (2) Read as a doubter. (3) Consider alternative views and analyze sources of disagreement. (4) Use disagreement productively to prompt further investigation. This chapter has also shown you how to summarize an article and incorporate summaries into your own writing through the use of attributive tags.

In the next chapter we turn from the reading of arguments to the writing of arguments, suggesting ways that you can generate ideas for arguments, structure your arguments, and improve your own writing processes.

3   Writing Arguments

As the opening chapters suggest, when you write an argument, you try to achieve two goals: (1) to persuade your audience toward your stance on an issue and (2) to see the issue complexly enough so that your stance reflects an ethical consideration of conflicting views. Because managing these tasks takes time, the quality of any argument depends on the quality of the thinking and writing processes that produced it. In this chapter, we suggest ways that you can improve these processes. We begin by looking at the social contexts that produce arguments, asking who writes arguments and why. We then present some writing tips based on the composing practices of experienced writers. Finally we describe nuts-and-bolts strategies for generating ideas and organizing an argument for an intended audience, concluding with two sets of exploratory exercises that can be adapted to any kind of argumentative task.

WHO WRITES ARGUMENTS AND WHY?

To help you see how writers operate in a social context—how they are spurred to write by a motivating occasion and by a desire to change the views of particular audiences—we begin by asking you to consider more fully who writes arguments.

In the classical period of ancient Greece and Rome, when the discipline of rhetoric was born, arguers usually made speeches before deliberative bodies. Arguers today, however, can present their views in a wide range of media and genres: speeches at public hearings, at committee meetings, or on talk radio; letters to legislators, bosses, or newspaper editors; professional proposals, marketing plans, or workplace memos; white papers advising lawmakers on issues; posters and pamphlets advocating a cause; e-mail letters or posts to chat rooms or personal Web sites; paid advertisements—even T-shirts and bumper stickers. Experienced writers and media specialists have even more options: freelance articles, books, syndicated columns, and TV documentaries. If we asked who in our culture actually writes arguments—let's say, for example, arguments on pay equity—a partial list would include lobbyists and advocacy groups, legislators, people in businesses and corporations, employment and corporate lawyers and judges, media commentators, professional freelance or staff writers, scholars and academics, and average citizens.

As a student, you are already a member of two of these groups—"scholars and academics" and "average citizens." Moreover, as a professional-in-training, you have the opportunity to practice the kinds of arguments written by other groups on our list, whether advocacy arguments or inquiry-based research pieces. You might publish your writing as letters to the editor or as guest editorials, present your arguments at undergraduate research conferences, write persuasive letters to legislators, submit proposals to decision makers in the workplace, or post your arguments on Web sites.

What all these writers have in common is a deep engagement with their issues. They share a strong belief that an issue matters, that decisions have consequences, and that the stakes are often high. You can engage an issue either by having a position to advocate or by seeking to clarify your stand. What is important to note is how fluid a writer's position can be along this continuum ranging from "advocate" to "inquirer." An advocate, while writing an argument, might discover an issue's complexity and be drawn into inquiry. Likewise, an inquirer, in the course of studying an issue, might clarify her thinking, establish a strong claim, and become an advocate. It is also possible to write arguments from any position on the continuum: You can be a tentative advocate as well as an avidly committed one, or you can be a cautious skeptic. You can even remain an inquirer by arguing that no proposed solution to a problem is yet adequate.

So how do you become engaged? We suggest that you immerse yourself in the arguments of the communities to which you belong—your classroom community, your dorm or apartment community, your work community, your civic communities—and look for points of entry into these conversations: either places where you can take a stand or places where you are puzzled and uncertain. By opening yourself to the conversations of your culture, and by initiating these conversations when you encounter situations you would like to change, you will be ready to write arguments.

LEARNING FROM EXPERTS: TIPS FOR IMPROVING YOUR WRITING PROCESS

Once you are motivated to write, you can improve your arguing ability if you know something about the writing processes of experienced writers. Too often inexperienced writers cut this process short, producing undeveloped arguments that don't speak effectively to the needs of the intended audience. Although no two writers follow the same process, we can describe the evolution of an argument in a loose way and offer tips for making your writing processes more effective. You should regard the writing process we are about to describe as recursive, meaning that writers often loop back to earlier phases by changing their minds on an issue, by throwing out a draft and starting over, or by going back to do more research late in the process.

Starting Point: Most writers of arguments start with a problem they want to solve or a claim they want to assert. At the outset, they may pose questions such as these: Who are the interested parties in this conversation? What are the causes of disagreement? What is the best way to solve the problem being debated? Who is the audience that must be persuaded? What is the best means of persuading that audience? Often a specific occasion spurs them to write. They feel hooked.

Tips for Starting the Process

- In many cases arguers are motivated to write because they find situations in their lives that they want to change. You can often focus on argument by asking yourself who has the power to make the changes you desire. How can you craft an argument that connects your desired changes to this audience's beliefs and values? What obstacles in your audience's environment might constrain that audience from action? How can these obstacles be overcome? This rhetorical focus—identifying the decision makers who have the power to change a situation and looking at the constraints that keep them from action—can give you a concrete sense of audience and clarify how your argument might proceed.

- In a college context you may sometimes have only a secondary occasion for writing—an assignment due date rather than an issue that hooks you. In such cases you can use the exploratory exercises described later in this chapter. These exercises help you inventory issues within the communities to which you belong, find points of engagement, and articulate the values and consequences that are at stake for you. Knowing why an issue matters to you can help you make it matter to others.

- Discuss issues with friends and classmates. Talking about ideas in small groups may help you discover claims that you want to make or issues that you find significant yet perplexing. By questioning claims and presenting multiple points of view, groups can help you understand points of disagreement on an issue.

Exploration, Research, and Rehearsal: To discover, refine, and support their claims, writers typically research their issues carefully, trying to understand arguments on all sides, to resolve disagreements about facts or reality, to clarify their own values, and to identify the beliefs and values of their audience. While researching their issues, writers often discover that their own views evolve. During research, writers often do exploratory writing in online chat rooms, e-mail exchanges, or a writer's journal, sometimes drafting whole pieces of an argument.

Tips for Exploring, Researching, and Rehearsing

- When you research an issue, focus on your rhetorical context. You need to research the issue itself, but also the values and beliefs of your targeted audience, and the obstacles in your audience's social environment that might prevent audience members from acting on your claim or adopting your beliefs.

- As you explore divergent views on your issue through library or Internet research or through interviews and field research, pay particular attention to why your views may be threatening to others. Later chapters in this text explain strategies for overcoming audience resistance.

- As you take notes on your research and imagine ways of shaping an argument for an intended audience, try some of the visual techniques suggested later in this chapter. Many writers find that idea maps and tree diagrams help them brainstorm for ideas and visualize structure.

- Stay in conversation with others. Active discussion of your issue—especially with persons who don't agree with you—is a powerful way to explore an argument and find the best means of persuasion. As you talk through your argument, note where listeners look confused or skeptical and where they question your points. Skeptics may find holes in your reasoning, argue from different values, surprise you by conceding points you thought had to be developed at length, and challenge you by demanding more justification of your claim.

Writing a First Draft: At some point in the process, a writer's attention shifts temporarily away from gathering data and probing an issue to composing a first draft. The act of writing a draft forces deep and focused thinking, which may then send the writer back to do more research and exploration. Effective first drafts are likely to be jumbled, messy, and full of gaps. Ideas appear at the point the writer thought of them rather than where readers need them. The writer's tone and style may be inappropriate, needed evidence may be entirely missing, the audience's beliefs and values may not be adequately addressed, and the whole draft may be confusing to an outside reader. Moreover, writers may discover that their own views are still shifting and unstable. Nevertheless, such drafts are a crucial first step. They get your ideas onto paper and give you material to work with.

Tips for Writing a First Draft

- Try lowering your expectations. If you get blocked, keep writing. Don't worry about grammar, correctness, or polish. Just get ideas on paper.

- Rehearse your ideas orally. Working in pairs with another student, talk through your argument orally before you write it down. Make a scratch outline first to prompt you as you talk. Then let your partner question you to help you flesh out your argument with more details.

- For a first draft, try following the template for a "classical argument" described on pages 51–53. This strategy will help you consider and respond to opposing views as well as clarify the reasons and evidence that support your own claim.

- Do the exploration tasks entitled "Set 2: Exploration and Rehearsal" (pp. 55–57) prior to writing a first draft. These exercises will help you brainstorm most of the ideas you'll need for an initial draft.

Revising through Multiple Drafts: After completing a first draft, you now have materials out on the table to work with. Most writers need multiple drafts to convert an early draft into a persuasive finished product. They also often need to return to the earlier stage of exploration and research now that writing a draft has revealed gaps in their arguments or provided a clearer understanding of their audience.

Tips for Revising

- Don't manicure your drafts; rebuild them. Cross out whole paragraphs and rewrite them from scratch. Move blocks of text to new locations. Make a mess. Inexperienced writers often think of revision as polishing and correcting rather than as making substantial changes (what writing teachers call "global revision"). Revising means to rethink your whole argument. Some writers even throw away the first draft and start fresh.

- Improve your mechanical procedures. We recommend that you revise off double-spaced hard copy rather than off the computer screen. Leave lots of space between lines and in margins on your drafts so that you have room to draw arrows and make pencil or pen deletions and inserts. When your draft becomes too messy, keyboard your changes back into the computer. If you manage all your drafts on computer, you may find that copying to a new file for each new draft gives you more freedom to experiment with changes (since you can always recover an earlier draft).

- As you revise, think of your audience. Many first drafts show why the writer believes his or her claim but not why the intended audience should believe it or act on it. How can you hook into your audience's beliefs and values using audience-based rather than writer-based reasons? Look also at the obstacles or constraints that keep your audience from adopting your beliefs or acting on your claim. How can you address those constraints in your revision?

- As you revise, also consider the image of yourself conveyed in your tone and style. Do you want to come across as angry? As sarcastic? As conciliatory and sympathetic? Also, to what extent do you want to appeal to audience members' emotions and imagination as well as to their logical intellects? These concerns are discussed in Chapter 7 under the headings *ethos* and *pathos.*

- Exchange drafts with classmates. Ask classmates where your argument is not persuasive, where your tone is offensive, where they have doubts, where your writing is unclear or undeveloped. Ask your classmates to role-play members of your intended audience. Explain the values and beliefs of this audience and the constraints members face. Let your classmates give you their reactions and advice. Classmates also can help you meet your readers' needs for effective organization, development, and style.

- Loop back to do more exploration and research. Writing is a recursive process during which writers frequently loop back to earlier stages. Revising your first draft may involve considerably more research and exploration.

Editing for Style, Impact, and Correctness: Writers now polish their drafts, rephrasing sentences, finding the precise word, and establishing links between sentences. At this point, you should turn to surface features such as spelling, punctuation, and grammar as well as to the appearance and form of the final manuscript.

Tips for Editing

- Read your draft out loud. Your ear can often pick up problems that your eye missed.

- Use your computer's spell check program. Remember, however, that spell checkers won't pick up mistakes with homonyms like *to/two/too, here/hear,* or *affect/effect.* Be skeptical of computerized grammar checkers, which cannot "read" with human intelligence but can only mechanically count, sort, and match. Your instructor can guide you on what grammar checkers can and cannot do.

- Use a good handbook for up-to-date advice on usage, punctuation, style, and manuscript form.

- Ask a classmate or friend to proofread your paper.

- Be prepared to loop back again to earlier stages. Sometimes thinking of a better way to word a sentence uncovers larger problems of clarity and meaning requiring you to rewrite a whole section of your argument.

USING EXPLORATORY WRITING TO DISCOVER IDEAS AND DEEPEN THINKING

What follows is a compendium of strategies to help you discover and explore ideas. None of these strategies works for every writer. But all of them are worth trying. Each requires practice, so don't give up on the strategy if it doesn't work at first. We recommend that you keep your exploratory writing in a journal or in easily identified files in your word processor so you can review it later and test the "staying power" of ideas produced by the different strategies.

Freewriting or Blind Writing

Freewriting is useful at any stage of the writing process. When you freewrite, you put pen to paper and write rapidly *nonstop*, usually ten to fifteen minutes at a stretch. The object is to think of as many ideas as possible without stopping to edit your work. On a computer, freewriters often turn off the monitor so that they can't see the text being produced. Such "blind writing" frees the writer from the urge to edit or correct the text and simply lets ideas roll forth. Some freewriters or blind writers achieve a stream-of-consciousness style, recording their ideas at the very moment they bubble into consciousness, stutters and stammers and all. Others produce more focused chunks, though without clear connections among them. You will probably find your initial reservoir of ideas running out in three to five minutes. If so, force yourself to keep writing or typing. If you can't think of anything to say, write "relax" or "I'm stuck" over and over until new ideas emerge.

Here is an example of a freewrite from a student named Stephen, exploring his thoughts on the question "What can be done about the homeless?" (He eventually wrote the proposal argument found on pages 228–36.)

> Let's take a minute and talk about the homeless. Homeless homeless. Today on my way to work I passed a homeless guy who smiled at me and I smiled back though he smelled bad. What are the reasons he was out on the street? Perhaps an extraordinary string of bad luck. Perhaps he was pushed out onto the street. Not a background of work ethic, no place to go, no way to get someplace to live that could be afforded, alcoholism. To what extent do government assistance, social spending, etc, keep people off the street? What benefits could a person get that stops "the cycle"? How does welfare affect homelessness, drug abuse programs, family planning? To what extent does the individual have control over homelessness? This question of course goes to the depth of the question of how community affects the individual. Relax, relax. What about the signs that I see on the way to work posted on the windows of businesses that read, "please don't give to panhandlers it only promotes drug abuse etc" a cheap way of getting homeless out of the way of business? Are homeless the natural end of unrestricted capitalism? What about the homeless people who are mentally ill? How can you maintain a living when

haunted by paranoia? How do you decide if someone is mentally ill or just laughs at society? If one can't function obviously. How many mentally ill are out on the street? If you are mentally ill and have lost the connections to others who might take care of you I can see how you might end up on the street. What would it take to get treatment? To what extent can mentally ill be treated? When I see a homeless person I want to ask, How do you feel about the rest of society? When you see "us" walk by how do you think of us? Do you possibly care how we avoid you.

FOR CLASS DISCUSSION

Individual task: Choose one of the following controversial claims (or another chosen by your instructor) and freewrite your response to it for five or ten minutes. **Group task:** Working in pairs, in small groups, or as a whole class, share your freewrite with classmates. Don't feel embarrassed if your freewrite is fragmentary or disjointed. Freewrites are not supposed to be finished products; their sole purpose is to generate a flow of thought. The more you practice the technique, the better you will become.

1. A student should report a fellow student who is cheating on an exam or plagiarizing an essay.
2. States should legalize marriages between homosexuals.
3. Companies should not be allowed to enforce English-only policies in the workplace.
4. For grades 1 through 12, the school year should be extended to eleven months.
5. Violent video games such as Mortal Kombat should be made illegal.

Idea Mapping

Another good technique for exploring ideas is *idea mapping*. When you make an idea map, draw a circle in the center of the page and write some trigger idea (a broad topic, a question, or working thesis statement) in the center of the circle. Then record your ideas on branches and subbranches extending from the center circle. As long as you pursue one train of thought, keep recording your ideas on the branch. But when that line of thinking gives out, start a new branch. Often your thoughts jump back and forth between branches. That's a major advantage of "picturing" your thoughts; you can see them as part of an emerging design rather than as strings of unrelated ideas.

Idea maps usually generate more ideas, though less well-developed ones, than freewrites. Writers who practice both techniques report that each strategy causes them to think about their ideas very differently. When Stephen, the freewriter on homelessness, created an idea map (see Figure 3.1), he was well into an argument disagreeing with a proposal by columnist Charles Krauthammer advocating the confinement of the homeless mentally ill in state mental hospitals. Stephen's idea map helped him find some order in his evolving thoughts on homelessness and his reasons for disagreeing with Krauthammer.

✔ FOR CLASS DISCUSSION

Choose a controversial issue—national, local, or campus—that's interesting to the class. The instructor will lead a class discussion on the issue, recording ideas on an idea map as they emerge. Your goal is to appreciate the fluidity of idea maps as a visual form of idea generation halfway between an outline and a list.

Playing the Believing and Doubting Game

The believing/doubting game* is an excellent way to imagine views different from your own and to anticipate responses to those views. As a believer, your role is to be wholly sympathetic to an idea, to listen carefully to it, and to suspend all disbelief. You must identify all the ways in which the idea might appeal to different audiences and all the reasons for believing the idea. The believing game is easy so long as you already accept an idea. But when dealing with ideas that strike you as shaky, false, or threatening, you will find that the believing game can be difficult, even frightening.

The doubting game is the opposite of the believing game. As a doubter, your role is to be judgmental and critical, to find faults with an idea. You do your best to find counterexamples and inconsistencies that undermine the idea. It is easy to play the doubting game with ideas you reject. Doubting ideas you've invested in can be threatening.

When you play the believing and doubting game with an assertion, simply write two different chunks, one chunk arguing for the assertion (the believing game) and one chunk opposing it (the doubting game). Freewrite both chunks, letting your ideas flow without censoring. Or, alternatively, make an idea map with believing and doubting branches.

Here is how one student played the believing and doubting game as part of a class discussion about the following classified ad seeking young college women to be egg donors for an infertile couple:

Infertile professional couple seeks egg-donor for artificial insemination. Donor should be slim, athletic, blue-eyed with 1400 SATs or better. $50,000 and all medical

---

*A term coined by Peter Elbow, *Writing without Teachers* (New York: Oxford UP, 1973), 147–90.

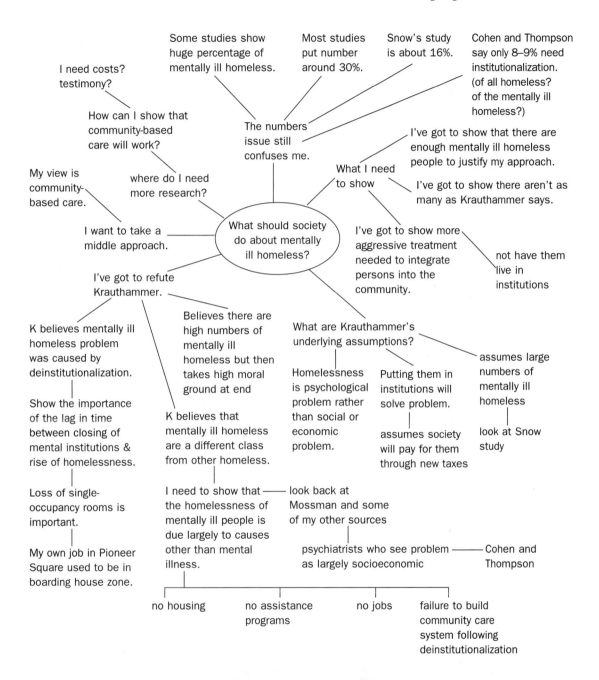

FIGURE 3.1   Stephen's initial idea map on the issue "What should society do about the mentally ill homeless?"

expenses. Must be discrete and willing to sign documents giving up all legal rights to a baby that might be produced.

This student is responding to the assertion "Recent advances in reproductive technology, including the use of egg donors, are good for society."

BELIEVING EXAMPLE

The latest advances in reproductive technology are good for society. Up until now, infertile couples had only adoption to turn to if they wanted a child. Using egg donation enables the parents to feel like real parents because the mother does carry the child. The parents can be a bit more selective about the child they get because egg donors are carefully screened. I think egg donors are more stable and safe than women who carelessly or accidentally get pregnant and give up their babies for adoption. Egg donors can be smart, healthy young women, such as college students. These young women also get an opportunity to make some money. Another point is that women can preserve some of their own eggs from their youth and actually have a child much later in life when they are ready for such a commitment. I can see how egg donation can help infertile couples, young women, and older women.

DOUBTING EXAMPLE

While egg donation sounds promising, I think the supporters of it often leave out the dark side and the moral implications. The process is changing having babies from a natural experience to a completely commercial one. Eggs are bought and judged like any other product. The high prices reaching even tens of thousands of dollars mean that only rich couples will be able to afford the process. The fact that the preferred egg donors have common traits (are Ivy League students, are tall, blonde, and blue eyed) only serves to increase a certain elitism. The donor part has pitfalls too. I can understand the attraction of the large sums of money, but the medical process is not easy. The young women must take fertility drugs and injections to boost their egg production. These drugs may have side effects and long-term complications. I wouldn't want my girlfriend to undergo this process.

Although this writer condemns these medical advances in reproductive technology, he does a good job of trying to sympathize with women who are involved in them. Playing the believing and doubting game has helped him see the issue more complexly.

❧ FOR CLASS DISCUSSION

Return to the five controversial claims in the For Class Discussion exercise on page 45. **Individual task:** Choose one of the claims and play the believing and doubting game with it by freewriting for five minutes trying to believe the claim and then for five minutes trying to doubt the claim. Or, if you prefer, make an idea map by creating a believing spoke and a doubting spoke off the main hub. Instead of freewriting, enter ideas onto your idea map, moving back and forth between believing and doubting. **Group task:** Share what you produced with members of your group or with the class as a whole.

Repeat the exercise with another claim.

Brainstorming for Pro and Con *Because* Clauses

This activity is similar to the believing and doubting game in that it asks you to brainstorm ideas for and against a controversial assertion. In the believing and doubting game, however, you simply freewrite or make an idea map on both sides of the issue. In this activity, you try to state your reasons for and against the proposition as *because* clauses. The value of doing so is discussed in depth in Chapter 4, which shows how a claim with *because* clauses can form the core of an argument.

Here is an example of how you might create *because* clauses for and against the claim "The recent advances in reproductive technology, including the use of egg donors, are good for society."

PRO

The recent advances in reproductive technology, including the use of egg donors, are good for society

- because children born using this technology are really wanted and will be given loving homes
- because this technology overcomes infertility, a medical disorder that can destroy marriages
- because curing this disorder will support marriages and create loving families
- because this technology restores to parents some measure of control over their reproductive capabilities

CON

The recent advances in reproductive technology, including the use of egg donors, are dangerous to society

- because this technology could lead to situations in which persons have no idea to whom they are genetically related
- because the technology might harm persons such as the egg donors who do not know what the long-term consequences of tampering with their reproductive systems through the use of fertility drugs might be

- because using donor eggs is equivalent to "special ordering" children who may not live up to the parents' expectations (to be smart, tall)

- because the expense of reproductive technology (especially when it results in multiple births) is too large for individuals, insurance companies, or the state to bear

FOR CLASS DISCUSSION

Generating *because* clauses like these is an especially productive discussion activity for groups. Once again return to the five controversial claims in the For Class Discussion exercise on page 45. Select one or more of these claims (or others provided by your instructor) and, working in small groups, generate pro and con *because* clauses supporting and attacking the claim. Share your group's *because* clauses with those of other groups.

Brainstorming a Network of Related Issues

The previous exercise helps you see how certain issues can provoke strong pro-con stances. Occasionally in civic life, an issue is presented to the public in just such a pro-con form, as when voters are asked to approve or disapprove a referendum or when a jury must decide the guilt or innocence of a defendant. But in most contexts, the argumentative situation is more open-ended and fluid.

You can easily oversimplify an issue by reducing it to two opposing sides. Most issues are embedded in a network of subissues, side issues, and larger issues, and seeing an issue in pro-con terms can often blind you to other ways to join a conversation. For example, a writer might propose the middle ground between adversarial positions, examine a subissue in more depth, connect an issue to a related side issue, or redefine an issue to place it in a new context.

Consider, for example, the assertion about reproductive technology. Rather than arguing for or against this claim, a writer might focus on reproductive technology in a variety of other ways:

- Who should determine the ethics of reproductive technology? Families? Doctors? Government?

- How can risky physical outcomes such as multiple births (mothers carrying seven and eight babies) be avoided?

- What effect will the new reproductive technologies have on concepts of motherhood and family?

- In case of divorce, who has legal rights to frozen embryos and other genetic material?

- Will reproductive technology lead to control over the sex and genetic makeup of children? Should it?

- What is the difference between paying someone to donate a kidney (which is illegal) and paying a woman to donate her eggs (which is currently legal)?

- Many adopted children want to seek out their birth mothers. Would children born from donated eggs want to seek out their genetic mothers?

- Who should pay for reproductive technology?

❖ FOR CLASS DISCUSSION

Working as a whole class or in small groups, choose one or more of the controversial assertions on page 45. Instead of arguing for or against them, brainstorm a number of related issues (subissues, side issues, or larger issues) on the same general subject.

SHAPING YOUR ARGUMENT: USING CLASSICAL STRUCTURE AS AN INITIAL GUIDE

We turn now from discovery strategies to organizing strategies. As you begin drafting, you need some sort of plan. How elaborate that plan is varies considerably from writer to writer. Some writers plan extensively before writing; others write extensively before planning. But somewhere along the way all writers must develop a structure.

In making an initial plan, writers often rely on knowledge of typical argument structures to guide their thinking. One of the oldest models is the *classical argument*—so called because it follows a pattern recommended by ancient rhetoricians. In traditional Latin terminology, classical argument has the following parts: the *exordium* (which gets the audience's attention); the *narratio* (which provides needed background); the *propositio* (which introduces the speaker's proposition or thesis); the *partitio* (which forecasts the main parts of the speech); the *confirmatio* (which presents arguments supporting the proposition); the *confutatio* (which refutes opposing views); and the *peroratio* (which sums up the argument, calls for action, and leaves a strong last impression). Classical arguments are often best suited for undecided or neutral audiences (See Chapter 8).

In slightly homelier terms (see Figure 3.2), writers of classical argument typically begin with a dramatic story or a startling statistic that commands attention. Then they focus the issue, often by stating it directly as a question and perhaps by briefly summarizing opposing views. Next, they contextualize the issue by providing needed background, explaining the immediate context, or

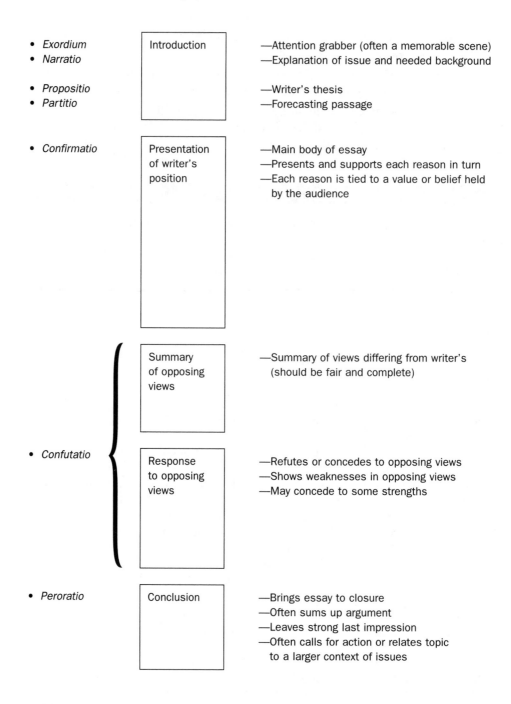

- *Exordium* | Introduction | —Attention grabber (often a memorable scene)
- *Narratio* | | —Explanation of issue and needed background

- *Propositio* | | —Writer's thesis
- *Partitio* | | —Forecasting passage

- *Confirmatio* | Presentation of writer's position | —Main body of essay
  | | | —Presents and supports each reason in turn
  | | | —Each reason is tied to a value or belief held by the audience

- *Confutatio* | Summary of opposing views | —Summary of views differing from writer's (should be fair and complete)

  | | Response to opposing views | —Refutes or concedes to opposing views
  | | | —Shows weaknesses in opposing views
  | | | —May concede to some strengths

- *Peroratio* | Conclusion | —Brings essay to closure
  | | | —Often sums up argument
  | | | —Leaves strong last impression
  | | | —Often calls for action or relates topic to a larger context of issues

FIGURE 3.2   Diagram of a classical argument

defining key terms. They conclude the introduction by presenting the thesis and forecasting the argument's structure.

Next, in usually the longest part of the classical argument, writers present the major reasons and evidence supporting their thesis, typically trying to develop reasons that appeal to their audience's values and beliefs. Often, each reason is developed in its own section. Each section opens with a statement of the reason, which is then supported with evidence or chains of other reasons. Along the way, writers guide their readers with appropriate transitions.

Subsequently, alternative views are summarized and critiqued. (Some writers put this section *before* the presentation of their own argument.) If opposing arguments consist of several parts, writers may either (1) summarize all opposing arguments before responding or (2) summarize and respond one part at a time. Writers may respond to opposing views either by refuting them or by conceding their strengths but shifting to a different field of values where these strengths are less decisive. Finally, in their conclusion, writers will sum up their argument, often calling for some kind of action, thereby creating a sense of closure and leaving a strong final impression.

For all its strengths, the classical argument may not always be your best model. In some cases, for example, delaying your thesis or ignoring alternative views may be justified (see Chapter 8). Even in these cases, however, the classical argument is a useful planning tool. Its call for a thesis statement and a forecasting statement in the introduction helps you see the whole of your argument in miniature. And by requiring you to summarize and consider opposing views, classical argument alerts you to the limits of your position and to the need for further reasons and evidence. Moreover, the classical argument is a particularly persuasive mode of argument when you address a neutral or undecided audience.

USING EXPLORATORY WRITING TO DISCOVER IDEAS AND DEEPEN THINKING: TWO SETS OF EXPLORATORY TASKS

The following tasks use exploratory writing to help you generate ideas. The first set of tasks helps you gather ideas early in a writing project either by helping you think of issues to write about or by deepening and complicating your response to readings. The second set of tasks helps you think about your ideas systematically before you compose a first draft.

Set 1: Starting Points

Task 1: Make an Inventory of the Communities to Which You Belong: What Issues Arise in Those Communities?

All of us belong to a variety of communities. For example, you have a classroom community for each course you are taking. Each club or organization has its own community, as does the community where you live (dorm, apartment, your family). Beyond these small communities, you have your campus community and beyond that your city, state, region, nation, and world communities. You may also belong to a work or job community, to a church/mosque/synagogue community, or to communities related to your hobbies or avocations.

The occasion for argument grows out of your life in these communities—your desire to make a difference on some issue that divides or troubles the community. As an arguer, you might tackle a big issue in your world community (What is the best way to prevent destruction of rain forests?) or a small issue in your dorm (Should quiet hours be enforced?). In your classroom community, you might tackle a practical problem (What should the instructor do about persons coming in late?) or intellectual issues in the discipline itself (Was Hamlet really mad? Is Freud's view of dreams defensible?).

For this task, make a list of the communities to which you belong. Then brainstorm controversies in these communities—issues that are being debated or that you would like to see debated. You might find one or more of the following "trigger questions" helpful:

- Persons in my dorm (at work, in the state legislature, at the United Nations) disagree about . . . .

- Our campus (this dorm, my hometown, our state, our country) would be a better place if . . . .

- Something that really makes me mad about this campus (my apartment life, city government, our society) is . . . .

- In the career I hope to pursue, X is a serious problem that needs to be addressed.

- Person X believes . . . ; however, I believe . . . .

Task 2: Make an Inventory of Issues That Interest You

The previous task can overwhelm students with the sheer number of issues that surround them. Once you broaden out to the large communities of city, state, nation, and world, the numbers of issues multiply rapidly. Moreover, each large issue has numerous subissues. For this task make an inventory of ten to fifteen possible issues that you would like to explore more deeply and possibly write about. Share your list with classmates, adding their ideas to yours.

Task 3: Choose Several Areas of Controversy for Exploration

For this task, choose two or three possible controversies from the Task-2 list and explore them through freewriting or idea mapping. Try responding to the following questions: (a) What is my position on this issue and why? (b) What are opposing or alternative positions on this issue? (c) Why do people disagree about this issue? (Do they disagree about the facts of the case? About underlying values, assumptions, and beliefs?) (d) To argue a position on this issue, what evidence do I need to find, and what further research will be required?

Task 4: Choose a Local Issue and Explore Its Rhetorical Context

For this task choose a local issue (some situation that you would like to see changed on your campus, in your place of work, or in your town or city) and explore its rhetorical context. (a) What is the situation you would like to change? (b) Who has the power to change that situation? (c) What are the values and beliefs of these decision makers? (d) What obstacles or constraints may prevent these decision makers from acting on your desires? (e) What reasons and evidence would exert the most pressure on these decision makers? (How can you make acting on your proposal a good thing for them?)

Task 5: Identify and Explore Issues That Are Problematic for You

A major assignment often given in argument courses is to write a research-based argument on an issue or problem initially puzzling to you. Perhaps you don't know enough about the issue (for example, establishing international controls on pesticides), or perhaps the issue draws you into an uncomfortable conflict of values (for example, assisted suicide, legalization of drugs, noncriminal incarceration of sexual predators). Your goal for this task is to identify several issues about which you are undecided, to choose one, and to explore your current uncertainty. Why can't you make up your mind on this issue?

Task 6: Deepen Your Response to Readings

This task requires you to read a collection of arguments on an issue and to explore them thoughtfully. As you read the arguments assigned by your instructor, annotate the margins with believing and doubting notes as explained in Chapter 2. Then respond to one or more of the following prompts, using freewriting or idea mapping:

- Why do the writers disagree? Are there disagreements about facts? About underlying values, beliefs, and assumptions?
- Identify "hot spots" in the readings—passages that evoke strong agreement or disagreement, anger, confusion, or any other memorable response—and explore your reaction to these passages.
- Explore the evolution of your thinking as you read and later review the essays. What new questions have they raised? How did your thinking change? Where do you stand now and why?
- If you were to meet one of the authors on a plane or at a ball game, what would you say to him or her?

Set 2: Exploration and Rehearsal

The following tasks are designed to help you once you have chosen a topic and begun to clarify your thesis. While these tasks may take two or more hours to complete, the effort pays off by helping you produce a full set of ideas for your rough draft. We recommend using these tasks each time you write a paper for this course.

Task 1

What issue do you plan to address in this argument? Try wording the issue as a one-sentence question. Reword your question in several different ways because each version will frame the issue somewhat differently. Then put a box around your best version of the question.

Task 2

Now write out your tentative answer to the question. This will be your beginning thesis statement or claim. Put a box around this answer. Next write out one or more different answers to your question. These will be alternative claims that a neutral audience might consider.

Task 3

Why is this a controversial issue? Is there insufficient evidence to resolve the issue, or is the evidence ambiguous or contradictory? Are definitions in dispute? Do the parties disagree about basic values, assumptions, or beliefs?

Task 4

What personal interest do you have in this issue? What are the consequences for you if your argument succeeds or doesn't succeed? How does the issue affect you? Why do you care about it? (Knowing why you care about it might help you get your audience to care about it.)

Task 5

Who is the audience that you need to persuade? If your argument calls for an action, who has the power to act on your claim? Can you address these persons of power directly? Or do you need to sway others (such as voters) to exert pressure on persons in power? With regard to your issue, what are the values and beliefs of the audience you are trying to sway?

Task 6

What obstacles or constraints in the social or physical environment prevent your audience from acting on your claim or accepting your beliefs? What are some ways these obstacles can be overcome? If these obstacles cannot be overcome, should you change your claim?

Task 7

In this task you will rehearse the main body of your paper. Using freewriting or idea mapping, think of the main reasons and evidence you could use to sway your intended audience. Brainstorm everything that comes to mind that might help you support your case. Because this section will eventually provide the bulk of your argument, proceed rapidly without worrying whether your argument makes sense. Just get ideas on paper. As you generate reasons and evidence, you are likely to discover gaps in your knowledge. Where could your argument be bolstered by additional data such as statistics, examples, and expert testimony? Where and how will you do the research to fill these gaps?

Task 8

Now reread what you wrote for Tasks 5 and 6, in which you examined your audience's perspective. Role playing that audience, imagine all the counterarguments audience members might make. Where does your claim threaten them or oppose their values? What are the obstacles or constraints in their environment that they are likely to point to. ("I'd love to act on your claim, but we just don't have the money" or "If we grant your request, it will set a bad precedent.") Brainstorm all the objections your audience might raise to your argument.

Task 9

How can you respond to those objections? Take them one by one and brainstorm possible responses.

Task 10

Explore again why this issue is important. What are its broader implications and consequences? What other issues does it relate to? Thinking of possible answers to these questions may prove useful when you write your introduction or conclusion.

WRITING ASSIGNMENTS FOR CHAPTERS 1–3

OPTION 1: *An Argument Summary*   Write a 250-word summary of an argument selected by your instructor. Then write a one-sentence summary of the same argument. Use as models the summaries of George Will's argument on pay equity in Chapter 2 (p. 27).

OPTION 2: *An Analysis of Sources of Disagreement in a Controversy*   Using as a model the analysis of the controversy between Will and Goodman on pay equity in Chapter 2 (pp. 33–34), write an analysis of the sources of disagreement in any two arguments that take differing views on the same issue.

OPTION 3: *Propose a Problem for a Major Course Project*   An excellent major project for an argument course is to research an issue about which you are initially undecided. Your final essay for the course could be an argument in which you take a stand on this issue. Choose one of the issues you listed in Task 5 on page 55 (issues that are problematic for you), and make this issue a major research project for the course. During the term keep a log of your research activities and be ready, in class discussion or in writing, to explain what kinds of arguments or evidence turned out to be most persuasive in helping you take a stand.

For this assignment, write a short letter to your instructor identifying the issue you have chosen and explain why you are interested in it and why you can't make up your mind at this time.

Principles
of Argument

4   The Core of an Argument

A Claim with Reasons

THE RHETORICAL TRIANGLE

Before we examine the structure of arguments, we should explain briefly their social context, which can be visualized as a triangle with interrelated points labeled *message, writer/speaker,* and *audience.* Effective arguments consider all three points on this *rhetorical triangle.* As we will see in later chapters, when you alter one point of the triangle (for example, when you change the audience for whom you are writing), you often need to alter the other points (by restructuring the message itself and perhaps by changing the tone or image you project as writer/speaker). We have created a series of questions based on the "rhetorical triangle" to help you plan, draft, and revise your argument (see Figure 4.1).

Each point on the triangle in turn corresponds to one of the three kinds of persuasive appeals that ancient rhetoricians named *logos, ethos,* and *pathos.*

Logos (Greek for "word") refers primarily to the internal consistency and clarity of the message and to the logic of its reasons and support. The impact of *logos* on an audience is referred to as its *logical appeal.*

Ethos (Greek for "character") refers to the credibility of the writer/speaker. *Ethos* is often conveyed through the tone and style of the message, through the care with which the writer considers alternative views, and through the writer's investment in his or her claim. In some cases, it's also a function of the writer's reputation for honesty and expertise independent of the message. The impact of *ethos* on an audience is referred to as its *ethical appeal* or *appeal from credibility.*

Our third term, *pathos* (Greek for "suffering" or "experience") is often associated with emotional appeal. But *pathos* appeals more specifically to our audience's

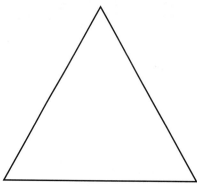

Message
(LOGOS: *How can I make the argument
internally consistent and logical?
How can I find the best reasons and
support them with the best evidence?*)

Audience
(PATHOS: *How can I make the reader
open to my message? How can I best
appeal to my reader's values and
interests? How can I engage my
reader emotionally and imaginatively?*)

Writer or Speaker
(ETHOS: *How can I present myself
effectively? How can I enhance my
credibility and trustworthiness?*)

FIGURE 4.1   The rhetorical triangle

imaginative sympathies—their capacity to feel and see what the writer feels and sees. Thus, when we turn the abstractions of logical discourse into a palpable and immediate story, we are making a pathetic appeal. Appeals to *logos* and *ethos* can further intellectual assent to our claim, but appeals to *pathos* engage imagination and feelings, moving the audience to deeper appreciation of the argument's significance.

In Part Two, we treat all three elements of the rhetorical triangle in detail. Although all three terms overlap, Chapters 4, 5, and 6 focus primarily on *logos,* and Chapters 7 and 8 focus primarily on *ethos* and *pathos.*

Given this background on the rhetorical triangle, let's turn now to *logos*—the logic and structure of arguments.

ISSUE QUESTIONS AS THE ORIGINS OF ARGUMENT

At the heart of any argument is a controversial question, or issue question, that gives rise to alternative answers. Any topic area, such as "criminal rights" or "health care," has embedded within it a number of issue questions. Thus the topic area "abortion" gives rise to issue questions such as "Should abortion be legal?" "Should the federal government underwrite the cost of abortion?" and "When does a fetus become a human being?" Each of these issue questions opens up one strand of the complex debate on abortion.

Difference between an Issue Question and an Information Question

Of course, not all questions are issue questions. Some may simply call for more information, not argument. Keeping this distinction in mind, consider the following two questions:

How does the abortion rate in the United States compare with the rate in Sweden? If the rates are different, why?

On the surface, both seem like noncontroversial information questions. But the latter could be an issue question if reasonable people disagreed on the answer. Thus, one person might attribute Sweden's higher abortion rate to the absence of a large Catholic or conservative Protestant population. But a second might attribute the higher rate to Sweden's generous national health coverage or to differences in sex education in the schools. In this case, the *why* question provokes alternative points of view rather than a simple informational answer.

To determine if a given question is an issue question or an information question, examine the role it calls you to play in relation to your audience. If the question asks you to be a teacher providing new information or knowledge, then it is probably an information question. But if the question asks you to be an advocate, persuading your audience toward your point of view in a controversy, then it is probably an issue question. Sometimes context will determine if a given question is an issue question or an information question. Consider the following examples:

- How does a diesel engine work? (Almost surely an information question, posed by an audience of learners who regard you as a teacher.)
- What is the most cost-effective way to produce diesel fuel from crude oil? (This would be an information question if experts agreed on the answer and you were teaching this knowledge to new learners. But if experts disagreed—imagine a roomful of petroleum engineers seeking ways to reduce the production costs of diesel fuel—it would be an issue question.)
- Should the tax on diesel fuel be reduced? (A slam-dunk issue question sure to provoke controversy in almost any context.)

▼ FOR CLASS DISCUSSION

Working as a class or in small groups, decide whether the following questions are information questions or issue questions. Some questions could be either, depending on the context. For such questions, create a hypothetical context that justifies your choice.

1. What percentage of single-parent families receives welfare support?
2. Should the United States eliminate welfare support for unwed mothers?
3. Are chiropractors legitimate health professionals?
4. How does chiropractic treatment of illness differ from a medical doctor's treatment?
5. What is the effect of violent TV shows on children?

DIFFERENCE BETWEEN A GENUINE ARGUMENT AND A PSEUDO-ARGUMENT

While every argument features an issue question with alternative answers, not every dispute over answers is a rational argument. Rational arguments require two additional factors: (1) reasonable participants who operate within the conventions of reasonable behavior and (2) potentially shareable assumptions that can serve as a starting place or foundation for the argument. Lacking one or both of these conditions, disagreements remain stalled at the level of pseudo-arguments.

Pseudo-Arguments: Fanatical Believers and Fanatical Skeptics

A reasonable argument assumes the possibility of growth and change; disputants may modify their views as they acknowledge strengths in an alternative view or weaknesses in their own. Such growth becomes impossible—and argument degenerates to pseudo-argument—when disputants are fanatically committed to their positions. Consider the case of the fanatical believer or the fanatical skeptic.

Fanatical believers believe their claims are true because they say so, period. They may cite some authoritative text—the Bible, the *Communist Manifesto,* or *The Road Less Traveled*—but in the end it's their narrow and quirky reading of the text or their faith in the author (which others might not share) that underlies their argument. Disagreeing with a fanatical believer is like ordering the surf to quiet down. The only response is another crashing wave.

The fanatical skeptic, in contrast, dismisses the possibility of proving anything. So what if the sun has risen every day of recorded history? That's no proof that it will rise tomorrow. Short of absolute proof, which never exists, fanatical skeptics accept nothing. In a world where the most we can hope for is increased audience adherence to our ideas, the fanatical skeptic demands an ironclad logical demonstration of our claim's rightness. In the presence of fanatical believers or skeptics, then, genuine argument is impossible.

Another Source of Pseudo-Arguments: Lack of Shared Assumptions

A reasonable argument is difficult to conduct unless the participants share common assumptions on which the argument can be grounded. Like axioms in geometry, these shared assumptions serve as the starting point for the argument. Consider the following conversation, in which Randall refuses to accept Rhonda's assumptions.

RHONDA: Smoking should be banned because it causes cancer.

RANDALL: So it causes cancer. What's so bad about that?

RHONDA: Don't be perverse, Randy. Cancer causes suffering and death.

RANDALL: Rhonda, my dear girl, don't be such a twinkie. Suffering and death are just part of the human condition.

RHONDA: But that doesn't make them desirable, especially when they can be avoided.

RANDALL: Perhaps in particular cases they're avoidable for a while, but in the long run, we all suffer and we all die, so who cares if smoking causes what's inevitable anyway?

This, we would suggest, is a doomed argument. Without any shared assumptions (for example, that cancer is bad, that suffering should be minimized and death delayed), there's no "bottom" to this argument, just an endless regress of reasons based on more reasons. While calling assumptions into question is a legitimate way to deepen and complicate our understanding of an issue, the unwillingness to accept any assumption makes argument impossible.

While our smoking example may be a bit heavy handed, less obvious variants of this debate happen all the time. Whenever we argue about purely personal opinions—opera is boring, soccer is better than baseball, pizza is tastier than nachos—we're condemned to a bottomless dispute. Because there are no common criteria for "boring" or "better" or "tastier," we can't put our claims to any common test. We can only reassert them.

Of course, reasonable arguments about these disputes become possible once common assumptions are established. For example, a nutritionist could argue that pizza is better than nachos because it provides a better balance of nutrients per calorie. Such an argument can succeed if the disputants accept the nutritionist's assumption that "a better balance of nutrients per calorie" is a criterion for "better." But if one of the disputants responds, "Nah, nachos are better than pizza because nachos taste better," then he makes a different assumption—"My sense of taste is better than your sense of taste." This is a wholly personal standard, an assumption that others are unable to share.

FOR CLASS DISCUSSION

The following questions can all be answered in alternative ways. However, not all of them will lead to reasonable arguments. Try to decide which questions will lead to reasonable arguments and which will lead only to pseudo-arguments.

1. Is Spike Lee a good film director?
2. Is postmodern architecture beautiful?
3. Should cities subsidize professional sports venues?
4. Is this abstract oil painting by a monkey smearing paint on a canvas a true work of art?
5. Are nose rings and tongue studs attractive?

FRAME OF AN ARGUMENT: A CLAIM SUPPORTED BY REASONS

In writing an argument, you take a position on an issue and support it with reasons and evidence. You state your position in the form of a claim, which functions as the thesis statement of your argument. A claim should provide a one-sentence answer to the issue question. Your task, then, is to make a claim and support it with reasons and evidence, which together comprise your argument's framework.

What Is a Reason?

A reason is a claim used to support another claim. Reasons are usually linked to their claims with words like *because, thus, since, consequently,* and *therefore* to underscore their logical connection.

Let's take an example. In one of our classes, a female naval ROTC student ignited a heated discussion by suggesting that women not be allowed to serve on submarines. The ensuing discussion expanded into a more general debate about women's fitness to serve in combat units. Here are frameworks the class developed for two alternative positions on this issue.

One View

CLAIM: Women should be barred from military combat units.

REASON 1: Most women lack the strength and endurance needed for combat.

REASON 2: Serving in combat isn't necessary for female soldiers' career advancement.

REASON 3: Female soldiers would hurt morale by introducing sexual jealousy into combat units.

REASON 4: Pregnancy or need to care for infants would render women unreliable soldiers.

REASON 5: Women haven't been socialized into warrior roles and thus would be more reluctant than males to kill the enemy.

Alternative View

CLAIM: Women should be allowed to serve as combat soldiers.

REASON 1: Millions of women do have the strength and endurance to serve in combat roles.

REASON 2: Female combat soldiers would offer a positive role model to young women and help society overcome harmful gender stereotyping.

REASON 3: Serving in combat would open up new career advancement opportunities for female soldiers.

REASON 4: Simple justice demands that women be allowed to serve in combat units.

Formulating a list of reasons in this way breaks your persuasive task into a series of more manageable subtasks. Thus, in the first view given, five possible lines of support are laid out. A writer might use all five or select only two or three, depending on which would most persuade the intended audience. Each line of reasoning would compose a distinct section of the argument.

For example, one section of an argument opposing women in combat might open with the following sentence: "Women should be excluded from combat units because they lack strength or endurance necessary for combat roles." The writer thereby assumes the burden of showing that women can't meet the prescribed physical requirements for combat duty. Further, the writer may also need to support the unstated assumption underlying this reason—namely, that meeting these physical requirements is a necessary condition for combat effectiveness.

The writer could develop each section of the argument in the same way. After a clear statement of the reason to be developed, the writer would offer evidence or chains of reasons in support. Depending on the intended audience, the writer might also articulate and support assumptions underlying the reason.

We can summarize the gist of this section as follows: The frame of an argument consists of a claim (the thesis statement of the essay), which is supported by one or more reasons, which are in turn supported by evidence or sequences of further reasons.

Advantages of Expressing Reasons in *Because* Clauses

Chances are that when you were a child the word *because* contained magical explanatory powers:

DOROTHY: I want to go home now.

TOMMY: Why?

DOROTHY: Because.

TOMMY: Because why?

DOROTHY: Just because.

Somehow *because* seemed decisive. It persuaded people to accept your view of the world; it changed people's minds. Later, you discovered that *because* only introduced your arguments and that it was the reasons following *because* that made the difference. But for most of us the word retains some residual magic and is persuasive in and of itself.

Of course, there are many other ways to express the logical connection between a reason and a claim. Our language is rich in ways of stating *because* relationships:

- Women shouldn't be allowed to join combat units because they don't have the strength or endurance for combat roles.

- Women don't have the strength or endurance for combat roles. Therefore women should not be allowed to join combat units.

- Women don't have the strength or endurance for combat roles, so they should not be allowed to join combat units.

- One reason why women should not be allowed to join combat units is that they don't have the strength or endurance for combat roles.

But even though logical relationships can be stated in various ways, writing out one or more *because* clauses remains the most succinct way to clarify an argument for oneself. We therefore suggest that sometime in the writing process you create a *working thesis statement* that summarizes your main reasons as *because* clauses attached to your claim.* Some writers compose their working thesis statement before they write their rough draft. Others discover their thesis as they write. Still others compose their working thesis statement in mid-draft in order to rein in an argument headed off in too many directions. Some wait until the very end, using their thesis statement to check the unity of the final product.

No matter when you write your working thesis statement, you will find doing so both thought provoking and frustrating. On the plus side, composing *because* clauses can be a powerful discovery tool, causing you to think of many different kinds of arguments to support your claim. But often it is difficult to wrestle your ideas into *because* clauses, which sometimes seem to be overly tidy for the complex network of ideas you are trying to work with. In the end, though, constructing a scale-model version of your argument in your working thesis statement is immensely helpful and worth the effort.

FOR CLASS DISCUSSION

Try the following group exercise to help you see how writing *because* clauses can be a discovery procedure.

Divide into small groups. Each group member should contribute an issue that he or she might like to explore. Discussing one person's issue at a time, help each member develop a claim supported by several reasons. Express each reason as a *because* clause. Then write out the working thesis statement for each person's argument by attaching the *because* clauses to the claim. Finally, try to create *because* clauses in support of an alternative claim for each issue. Recorders should select two or three working thesis statements from the group to present to the class as a whole.

APPLICATION OF THIS CHAPTER'S PRINCIPLES TO YOUR OWN WRITING

In Chapter 2, we discussed the difficulties of summarizing various types of arguments. Generally, an argument is easiest to summarize when the writer places the thesis in the introduction and uses explicit transitions to highlight the argument's reasons and structural frame. Such arguments are said to have

---

*A working thesis statement for an argument opposing women in combat units might look like this: *Women should not be allowed to join combat units because they lack the strength, endurance, and "fighting spirit" needed in combat; because being pregnant or having small children would make them unreliable for combat at a moment's notice; and because women's presence would hurt morale of tight-knit combat units.* (A working thesis statement for an argument supporting women in combat is found on pp. 70–71.)

You might choose not to put a bulky thesis statement like this into your essay itself. A working thesis statement offers a behind-the-scenes way to summarize your argument for yourself, so that you can see it whole and clear.

a *self-announcing structure* because they announce their thesis (and sometimes supporting reasons) and forecast their shape at the outset. Self-announcing arguments typically follow the conventional format of classical argument discussed in Chapter 3. The invention strategies set forth in this chapter—generating parallel *because* clauses and nutshelling them in a working thesis statement—lead naturally to a classical argument with a self-announcing structure. Each *because* clause, together with its supporting evidence, becomes a separate section of the argument.

An argument with an *unfolding structure,* in contrast, is considerably harder to summarize. In an unfolding structure, the thesis is delayed until the end or is unstated and left to be inferred by the reader from a narrative that may be both complex and subtle. As we explain in Chapter 8, unfolding structures can be especially effective when dealing with hostile audiences or with troubling or tangled issues. In contrast, classical arguments are often best for neutral or undecided audiences weighing alternative views on a clearcut issue.*

In our own classes, we ask students initially to write arguments with self-announcing structures, thereby forcing them to articulate their arguments clearly to themselves and helping them to master the art of organizing complex ideas. Later in the course, we invite them to experiment with structures that unfold their meanings in subtler, more flexible ways.

In writing classical arguments, students often ask how much of the argument to summarize in the introduction. Consider the following options. You might announce only your claim:

Women should be allowed to join combat units.

Or you could also predict a series of parallel reasons:

Women should be allowed to join combat units for several reasons.

Or you could forecast the actual number of reasons:

Women should be allowed to join combat units for four reasons.

Or you could forecast the whole argument:

Women should be allowed to join combat units because they are physically capable of doing the job; because the presence of women in combat units would

---

*Instead of the terms *self-announcing* and *unfolding,* rhetoricians sometimes use *closed form* and *open form. A closed-form structure* tells the reader in advance where the argument is headed. Choosing a closed form, which forecasts the structure in the introduction, obligates the writer to follow through with that structure in a straightforward, undeviating way. In contrast, an *open-form structure* is like a story or narrative, keeping the reader in suspense about the argument's final destination.

weaken gender stereotypes; because opening combat units to women would expand their military career opportunities; and because doing so would advance the cause of civil rights.

These are not, of course, your only options. If you choose to delay your thesis until the end (a typical kind of unfolding argument), you might place the issue question in the introduction without giving away your own position:

Is the nation well served by allowing women to join combat units?

No formula can tell you how much of your argument to forecast in the introduction. In Chapters 7 and 8 we discuss how forecasting or withholding your thesis affects your *ethos*. We also show how a delayed thesis argument may be a better option for hostile audiences. It is clear at this point, though, that the more you forecast, the clearer your argument is to your reader, whereas the less you forecast, the more surprising your argument will be. The only general rule is this: Readers sometimes feel insulted by too much forecasting. In writing a self-announcing argument, forecast only what is needed for clarity. In short arguments readers often need only your claim. In longer arguments or in especially complex ones, readers appreciate your forecasting the complete structure of the argument (claim with reasons).

APPLICATION OF THIS CHAPTER'S PRINCIPLES TO THE READING OF ARGUMENTS

When you read a complex argument that lacks explicit forecasting, it is often hard to discern its structural core, to identify its claim, and to sort out its reasons and evidence. The more "unfolding" its structure, the harder it is to see exactly how the writer makes his or her case. Moreover, extended arguments often contain digressions and subarguments. Thus there may be dozens of small interlinked arguments going on inside a slowly unfolding main argument.

When you feel yourself getting lost in an unfolding structure, try converting it to a self-announcing structure. (It might help to imagine that the argument's author must state the argument as a claim with *because* clauses. What working thesis statement might the writer construct?) Begin by identifying the writer's claim. Then ask yourself: What are the one, two, three, or four main lines of argument this writer puts forward to support that claim? State those arguments as *because* clauses attached to the claim. Then compare your *because* clauses with your classmates'. You can expect disagreement—indeed, that disagreement can enrich your understanding of a text—because the writer has left it to you to infer her intent. You should, however, find considerable overlap in your responses. Once you have converted the support for the claim to *because* clauses and reached consensus on them, you will find it much easier to analyze the writer's reasoning, underlying assumptions, and use of evidence.

CONCLUSION

This chapter has introduced you to the rhetorical triangle and its key concepts: *logos, ethos,* and *pathos.* It has also shown how arguments originate in issue questions, how issue questions differ from information questions, and how arguments differ from pseudo-arguments. At the heart of this chapter we explained that the frame of an argument is a claim supported by reasons. As you generate reasons to support your own arguments, it is often helpful to articulate them as *because* clauses attached to the claim. Finally, we explained how you can apply the principles of this chapter to your own writing and reading of arguments.

In the next chapter we will see how to support a reason by examining its logical structure, uncovering its unstated assumptions, and planning a strategy of development.

5 The Logical Structure of Arguments

In Chapter 4 you learned that the core of an argument is a claim supported by reasons and that these reasons can often be stated as *because* clauses attached to a claim. In the present chapter we examine the logical structure of arguments in more depth.

AN OVERVIEW OF *LOGOS:* WHAT DO WE MEAN BY THE "LOGICAL STRUCTURE" OF AN ARGUMENT?

As you will recall from our discussion of the rhetorical triangle, *logos* refers to the strength of an argument's support and its internal consistency. *Logos* is the argument's logical structure. But what do we mean by "logical structure"?

First of all, what we *don't* mean by logical structure is the kind of precise certainty you get in a philosophy class in formal logic. Logic classes deal with symbolic assertions that are universal and unchanging, such as "If all ps are qs and if r is a p, then r is a q." This statement is logically certain so long as p, q, and r are pure abstractions. But in the real world, p, q, and r turn into actual things, and the relationships among them suddenly become fuzzy.

For example, p might be a class of actions called "sexual harassment," and q could be the class "actions that justify dismissal from a job." If r is the class "telling off-color stories," then the logic of our p–q–r statement suggests that telling off-color stories (r) is an instance of sexual harassment (p), which in turn is an action justifying dismissal from one's job (q). Now, most of us would agree that sexual harassment is a serious offense that might well justify dismissal from a job. In turn,

73

we might agree that telling off-color stories, if the jokes are sufficiently raunchy and are inflicted on an unwilling audience, constitutes sexual harassment. But few of us would want to say categorically that all people who tell off-color stories are harassing their listeners and ought to be fired. Most of us would want to know the particulars of the case before making a final judgment.

A key difference, then, between formal logic and real-world argument is that real-world arguments are not grounded in abstract, universal statements. Rather, as we shall see, they must be grounded in beliefs, assumptions, or values granted by the audience. A second important difference is that in real-world arguments these beliefs, assumptions, or values are often unstated. So long as writer and audience share the same assumptions, then it's fine to leave them unstated. But if these underlying assumptions aren't shared, the writer has a problem. To illustrate the nature of this problem, consider one of the arguments we introduced in the last chapter.

> Women should be allowed to join combat units because the image of women in combat would help eliminate gender stereotypes.

On the face of it, this is a plausible argument. But the argument is persuasive only if the audience agrees with the writer's assumption that it is a good thing to eliminate gender stereotyping.

The writer assumes that gender stereotyping (for example, seeing men as the fighters who are protecting the women and children back home) is harmful and that society would be better off without such fixed gender roles. But what if you believed that some gender roles are biologically based, divinely intended, or otherwise culturally essential and that society should strive to maintain these gender roles rather than dismiss them as "stereotypes"? If such were the case, you might believe as a consequence that our culture should socialize women to be nurturers, not fighters, and that some essential trait of "womanhood" would be at risk if women served in combat. If these were your beliefs, the argument wouldn't work for you because you would reject its underlying assumption. To persuade you with this line of reasoning, the writer would have to show not only how women in combat would help eliminate gender stereotypes but also why these stereotypes are harmful and why society would be better off without them.

The previous core argument ("Women should be allowed to join combat units because the image of women in combat would help eliminate gender stereotypes") is what the Greek philosopher Aristotle would call an enthymeme. An *enthymeme* is an incomplete logical structure that depends for its completeness on one or more unstated assumptions (values, beliefs, principles) that serve as the starting point of the argument. The successful arguer, said Aristotle, is the person who knows how to formulate and develop enthymemes so that the argument is rooted in the audience's values and beliefs.

To clarify the concept of the enthymeme, let's go over this same territory again more slowly, examining what we mean by "incomplete logical structure." The original claim with *because* clause is an enthymeme. It combines a claim ("Women should be allowed to join combat units") with a reason expressed as a *because* clause ("because the image of women in combat would help eliminate gender stereotypes"). To render this enthymeme logically complete, you must supply an unstated assumption—that gender stereotypes are harmful and should be eliminated. If your audience accepts this assumption, then you have a starting place on which to build an effective argument. If your audience doesn't accept this assumption, then you must supply another argument to support it, and so on until you find common ground with your audience. To sum up:

1. Claims are supported with reasons. You can usually state a reason as a *because* clause attached to a claim (see Chapter 4).

2. A *because* clause attached to a claim is an incomplete logical structure called an enthymeme. To create a complete logical structure from an enthymeme, the unstated assumption (or assumptions) must be articulated.

3. To serve as an effective starting point for the argument, this unstated assumption should be a belief, value, or principle that the audience grants.

Let's illustrate this structure by putting the previous example—plus a new one—into schematic form.

INITIAL ENTHYMEME:	Women should be allowed to join combat units because the image of women in combat would help eliminate gender stereotypes.*
CLAIM:	Women should be allowed to join combat units.
STATED REASON:	because the image of women in combat would help eliminate gender stereotypes
UNSTATED ASSUMPTION:	Gender stereotypes are harmful and should be eliminated.
INITIAL ENTHYMEME:	Cocaine and heroin should be legalized because legalization would eliminate the black market in drugs.
CLAIM:	Cocaine and heroin should be legalized.
STATED REASON:	because legalization would eliminate the black market in drugs
UNSTATED ASSUMPTION:	An action that eliminates the black market in drugs is good.

---

*Most arguments have more than one *because* clause or reason in support of the claim. Each enthymeme thus develops only one line of reasoning, one piece of your whole argument.

FOR CLASS DISCUSSION

Working individually or in small groups, identify the claim, stated reason, and unstated assumption that complete each of the following enthymemic arguments.

EXAMPLE:

Rabbits make good pets because they are gentle.

CLAIM:	Rabbits make good pets.
STATED REASON:	because they are gentle
UNSTATED ASSUMPTION:	Gentle animals make good pets.

1. We should not choose Joe as committee chairperson because he is too bossy.
2. Buy this stereo system because it has a powerful amplifier.
3. Drugs should not be legalized because legalization would greatly increase the number of drug addicts.
4. Practicing the piano is good for kids because it teaches discipline.
5. Welfare benefits for unwed mothers should be eliminated because doing so will greatly reduce the nation's illegitimacy rate.
6. Welfare benefits for unwed mothers should not be eliminated because these benefits are needed to prevent unbearable poverty among our nation's most helpless citizens.
7. We should strengthen the Endangered Species Act because doing so will preserve genetic diversity on the planet.
8. The Endangered Species Act is too stringent because it severely damages the economy.
9. The doctor should not perform an abortion in this case because the mother's life is not in danger.
10. Abortion should be legal because a woman has the right to control her own body. (This enthymeme has several unstated assumptions behind it. See if you can recreate all the missing premises.)

ADOPTING A LANGUAGE FOR DESCRIBING ARGUMENTS: THE TOULMIN SYSTEM

Understanding a new field usually requires us to learn a new vocabulary. For example, if you were taking biology for the first time, you'd spend days memorizing dozens of new terms. Luckily, the field of argument requires us to learn a mere handful of new terms. A particularly useful set of argument terms, one we'll be using throughout the rest of this text, comes from philosopher Stephen Toulmin. In the 1950s, Toulmin rejected the prevailing models of argument based on formal logic in favor of a very audience-based courtroom model.

Toulmin's courtroom model differs from formal logic in assuming that (1) all assertions and assumptions are contestable by "opposing counsel" and (2) all final "verdicts" about the persuasiveness of alternative arguments will be rendered by a neutral third party, a judge or jury. Keeping in mind the "opposing counsel" forces us to anticipate counterarguments and to question our assumptions. Keeping in mind the judge and jury reminds us to answer opposing arguments fully, without rancor, and to present positive reasons for supporting our case as well as negative reasons for disbelieving the alternative views. Above all else, Toulmin's model reminds us not to construct an argument that appeals only to those who already agree with us, and it helps arguers tailor arguments to their audiences.

The system we use for analyzing arguments combines Toulmin's system with Aristotle's concept of the enthymeme. The purpose of this system is to provide writers with economical language for articulating the structure of argument and, in the process, to help them anticipate their audience's needs. More particularly, this system helps writers see enthymemes—in the form of a claim with *because* clauses—as the core of their argument and see the other structural elements from Toulmin as strategies for elaborating and supporting that core.

This system builds on the one you have already been practicing. We simply need to add a few more key terms from Toulmin. The first key term is Toulmin's *warrant*, the name we will now use for the unstated assumption that turns an enthymeme into a complete logical structure. For example:

INITIAL ENTHYMEME:	Women should be allowed to join combat units because the image of women in combat would help eliminate gender stereotypes.
CLAIM:	Women should be allowed to join combat units.
STATED REASON:	because the image of women in combat would help eliminate gender stereotypes
WARRANT:	Gender stereotypes are harmful and should be eliminated.
INITIAL ENTHYMEME:	Cocaine and heroin should be legalized because legalization would eliminate the black market in drugs.
CLAIM:	Cocaine and heroin should be legalized.
STATED REASON:	because legalization would eliminate the black market in drugs
WARRANT:	An action that eliminates the black market in drugs is good.

Toulmin derives his term *warrant* from the concept of a warranty or guarantee. The warrant is the value, belief, or principle that the audience has to hold if the soundness of the argument is to be guaranteed or warranted. We sometimes make similar use of this word in ordinary language when we say "That is an unwarranted conclusion."

But arguments need more than claims, reasons, and warrants. These are simply one-sentence statements—the frame of an argument, not a developed argument. To flesh out our arguments and make them convincing, we need what Toulmin calls *grounds* and *backing*. Grounds are the evidence you use to support your *because* clause (your stated reason). Toulmin suggests that grounds are "what you have to go on" in an argument—the facts, data, statistics, testimony, or examples you use to support your reason. It sometimes helps to think of grounds as the answer to a "How do you know that . . . ?" question prefixed to your stated reason. (How do you know that letting women into combat units would help eliminate gender stereotypes? How do you know that legalizing drugs will end the black market?) Here is how grounds fit into our emerging argument schema:

CLAIM:	Women should be allowed to join combat units.
STATED REASON:	because the image of women in combat would help eliminate gender stereotypes
GROUNDS:	data and evidence showing that a chief stereotype of women is that they are soft and nurturing whereas men are stereotyped as tough and aggressive; images of women in combat gear packing rifles, driving tanks, firing machine guns from a foxhole, or radioing for artillery support would shock people into seeing women not as "soft and nurturing" but as equal to men.
CLAIM:	Cocaine and heroin should be legalized.
STATED REASON:	because legalization would eliminate the black market in drugs
GROUNDS:	data and evidence showing how legalizing cocaine and heroin would eliminate the black market (statistics, data, and examples showing the size of the current black market and explaining why legalization would eliminate it)

In many cases, successful arguments require just these three components: a claim, a reason, and grounds. If the audience already accepts the unstated assumption behind the reason (the warrant), then the warrant can safely remain in the background unstated and unexamined. But if there is a chance that the audience will question or doubt the warrant, then the writer needs to back it up by providing an argument in its support. *Backing* is the argument that supports the warrant. Backing answers the question "How do you know that . . . ?" or "Why do you believe that . . . ?" prefixed to the warrant. (Why do you believe that gender stereotyping is harmful? Why do you believe that ending the black market is good?) Here is how *backing* is added to our schema:

WARRANT: Gender stereotypes are harmful and should be eliminated.

BACKING: arguments showing how the existing stereotype of soft and nurturing women and tough and aggressive men is harmful to both men and women (examples of how the stereotype keeps men from developing their nurturing sides and women from developing autonomy and power; examples of other benefits that come from eliminating gender stereotypes including a more egalitarian society, no limits on what persons can pursue, deeper respect for both sexes)

WARRANT: An action that eliminates the black market in drugs is good.

BACKING: an argument supporting the warrant by showing why the benefits of eliminating the black market outweigh the social cost of legalizing drugs (statistics and examples about the ill effects of the black market, data on crime and profiteering, evidence that huge profits make drug dealing more attractive than ordinary jobs, the high cost of crime created by the black market, the cost to taxpayers of waging the war against drugs, the high cost of prisons to house incarcerated drug dealers, etc.)

Finally, Toulmin's system asks us to imagine how a resistant audience would try to refute our argument. Specifically, this adversarial audience might challenge our reason and grounds, our warrant and backing, or both. In the case of the argument supporting women in combat, an adversary might offer one or more of the following rebuttals:

CONDITIONS OF REBUTTAL

Rebutting the reasons and grounds: evidence that letting women join combat units wouldn't overcome gender stereotyping (very few women would want to join combat units; those who did would be considered freaks; most girls would still identify with Barbie doll models, not with female infantry)

Rebutting the warrant and backing: arguments showing it is important to maintain gender role differences because they are biologically based, divinely inspired, or otherwise important culturally; women should be nurturers and mothers, not fighters; essential nature of "womanhood" sullied by putting women in combat

Likewise, a skeptical audience might rebut the legalization of drugs argument in one or more of the following ways:

CONDITIONS OF REBUTTAL

Rebutting the reasons and grounds: evidence that legalizing drugs might not end the black market (perhaps taxes would keep prices high or constraints on buyers would send them to the streets rather than to federal drugstores; or perhaps new designer drugs would be developed and sold on the black market)

Rebutting the warrant and backing: arguments showing that the costs of eliminating the black market by legalizing drugs outweigh the benefits (an unacceptably high number of new drug users and addicts; a catastrophic increase in health care costs because of increased drug use; harm to the social structure from increased acceptance of drugs; high social costs to families and communities associated with addiction or erratic behavior during drug-induced "highs")

Toulmin's final term, used to limit the force of a claim and indicate the degree of its probable truth, is *qualifier.* The qualifier reminds us that real-world arguments almost never prove a claim. We may add words like *very likely, probably,* or *maybe* to indicate the strength of the claim we are willing to draw from our grounds and warrant. Thus if your grounds or warrant can be rebutted, you will have to qualify your claim. For example, you might say, "Except in rare cases, women should not be allowed in combat units," or "With full awareness of the potential dangers, I suggest that legalizing drugs may be the best way to eliminate the social costs of the black market."

FOR CLASS DISCUSSION

Working individually or in small groups, imagine that you have to write arguments developing the ten enthymemes listed in the For Class Discussion exercise on page 76. Use the Toulmin schema to help you determine what you need to consider when developing each enthymeme. As an example, we have applied the Toulmin schema to the first enthymeme.

ORIGINAL ENTHYMEME: We should not choose Joe as committee chairperson because he is too bossy.

CLAIM: We should not choose Joe as committee chair.

STATED REASON: because he is too bossy

GROUNDS: various examples of Joe's bossiness; testimony about

CONDITIONS OF REBUTTAL: *Rebuttal of reason and grounds:* Perhaps Joe isn't really bossy (counterevidence of Joe's cooperativeness and kindness, testimony that Joe is easy to work with, etc.).

his bossiness from people who have worked with him

WARRANT: Bossy people make bad committee chairs.

BACKING: arguments showing that other things being equal, bossy people tend to bring out the worst rather than the best in those around them; bossy people tend not to ask advice, make bad decisions, etc.

Rebuttal of the warrant and backing: Perhaps bossy people sometimes make good chairpersons (arguments showing that at times a group needs a bossy person who can make decisions and get things done). Perhaps Joe has other traits of good leadership that outweigh his bossiness (evidence that, despite his bossiness, Joe has many other good leadership traits such as high energy, intelligence, and charisma).

QUALIFIER: In most circumstances, bossy people make bad committee chairs.

USING TOULMIN'S SCHEMA TO DETERMINE A STRATEGY OF SUPPORT

Having introduced you to Toulmin's terminology for describing the logical structure of arguments, we can turn directly to a discussion of how to use these concepts for developing your own arguments. As we have seen, the claim, supporting reasons, and warrant form the frame for a line of reasoning. The majority of words in an argument, however, are devoted to grounds and backing—the supporting sections that develop the argument frame. Generally these supporting sections take one of two forms: either (1) *evidence* such as facts, examples, case studies, statistics, and testimony from experts or (2) a *sequence of reasons*—that is, further conceptual argument. The Toulmin schema can help you determine what kind of support your argument needs. Let's look at each kind of support separately.

Evidence as Support

It's often easier for writers to use evidence rather than sequences of reasons for support because using evidence entails moving from generalizations to specific details—a basic organizational strategy that most writers practice regularly. Consider the following hypothetical case. A student, Ramona, wants to write a complaint letter to the head of the philosophy department about a philosophy professor, Dr. Choplogic, whom Ramona considers incompetent. Ramona plans to develop two different lines of reasoning: first, that Choplogic's courses are disorganized and, second, that Choplogic is unconcerned about students. Let's look briefly at how she can develop her first main line of reasoning, which is based on the following enthymeme:

Dr. Choplogic is an ineffective teacher because his courses are disorganized.

The grounds for this argument will be evidence that Choplogic's courses are disorganized. Using the Toulmin schema, Ramona lists under "grounds" all the evidence she can muster that Choplogic's courses are disorganized. Here is how this argument might look when placed into written form:

A LINE OF ARGUMENT DEVELOPED WITH EVIDENCE

Claim and reason	One reason why Dr. Choplogic is ineffective is that his courses are poorly organized. I have had him for two courses—Introduction to Philosophy and Ethics—and both were disorganized. He never gave us a syllabus or explained his grading system. At the beginning of the course he wouldn't tell us how many papers he would require, and he never seemed to know how much of the textbook material he planned to cover. For Intro he told us to read the whole text, but he covered only half of it in class. A week before the final I asked him how much of the text would be on the exam and he said he hadn't decided. The Ethics class was even more disorganized. Dr. Choplogic told us to read the text, which provided one set of terms for ethical arguments, and then he told us he didn't like the text and presented us in lecture with a wholly different set of terms. The result was a whole class of confused, angry students.
Grounds (evidence in support of reason)	

As you can see, Ramona has plenty of evidence to support her contention that Choplogic is disorganized. But how effective is this argument as it stands? Is this all she needs? The Toulmin schema also encourages Ramona to examine the warrant, backing, and conditions of rebuttal for this argument. She believes that no one can challenge her reason and grounds—Choplogic is indeed a disorganized teacher. But she recognizes that some people might challenge her warrant ("Disorganized teachers are ineffective"). A supporter of Dr. Choplogic might say that some teachers, even though they are hopelessly disorganized, might nevertheless do an excellent job of stimulating thought and discussion. Moreover, such teachers might possess other valuable traits that outweigh their disorganization. Ramona therefore decides to address these concerns by adding another section to this portion of her argument.

CONTINUATION OF RAMONA'S ARGUMENT

Backing for warrant (shows why disorganization is bad)	Dr. Choplogic's lack of organization makes it difficult for students to take notes, to know what to study, or to relate one part of the course to another. Moreover, students lose confidence in the teacher because he doesn't seem to care enough to prepare for class.

Response to conditions of rebuttal   In Dr. Choplogic's defense, it might be thought that his primary concern is involving students in class discussions or other activities to teach us thinking skills or get us involved in philosophical discussions. But this isn't the case. Students rarely get a chance to speak in class. We just sit there listening to rambling, disorganized lectures.

This section of her argument backs the warrant that disorganized teachers are ineffective and anticipates some of the conditions for rebuttal that an audience might raise to defend Dr. Choplogic. Throughout her draft, Ramona has supported her argument with evidence. Although Ramona takes her evidence from personal experience, in other cases evidence might come primarily from reading and research. Chapter 6 is devoted to a more detailed discussion of evidence in arguments.

Sequence of Reasons as Support

So far we have been discussing how reasons can be supported with evidence. Often, however, reasons require for their support further conceptual arguing rather than empirical data. Reasons of this kind must be supported with a sequence of other reasons. Consider, for example, a writer proposing a mandatory death penalty for convicted serial killers. Let's assume that this writer, living in a state where the death penalty is legal but seldom used, is angry that a recently convicted serial killer was sentenced to life imprisonment. His claim, along with his main supporting reason, is as follows:

CLAIM: The law should mandate capital punishment for serial killers.

STATED REASON: Serial killings belong in a class of their own, that of exceptionally heinous crimes.

WARRANT: Crimes that are exceptionally heinous deserve a more severe punishment than other crimes.

To make this argument, the writer can use empirical evidence to show that serial killing is heinous (data about the grisliness of the crimes). But the main thrust of the argument requires something more. The writer must show that serial killing is *exceptionally* heinous, an argument requiring a sequence of further reasons. Why should the law single out serial killers for a mandatory death sentence but not other murderers? Since all murders are heinous, what is unique about those committed by serial killers that justifies executing them while letting other murderers get by with lesser sentences? To support his stated reason and gain acceptance for his warrant that a different order of crime deserves a different order of punishment, the writer must establish the peculiarity of serial killings. To distinguish serial killings from other murders, the writer develops the following list of potential reasons:

- Serial killers have murdered more than one person, usually many; the crime is multiple.
- Serial murders are calculated crimes, often requiring extensive planning that goes far beyond the mere "intent" required in first-degree murder cases.
- Serial murders typically involve torture of at least some of the victims in order to satisfy the serial killer's deep need not just to kill but to dominate his victims.
- The repetitious nature of the crime indicates that serial killers cannot be rehabilitated.
- The repetitious nature of the crime also means that the chances of mistakenly executing a defendant, which are minuscule to begin with, are virtually nonexistent with serial killers.

Having developed a list of reasons for singling out serial killers, the writer is ready to draft this part of his argument. Here is a portion of the argument, picking up after the writer has used evidence (in the form of gruesome narratives) to demonstrate the heinous nature of serial murders.

A LINE OF ARGUMENT DEVELOPED WITH A SEQUENCE OF REASONS

These stories show the heinous nature of serial murders. "But aren't all murders heinous?" someone might ask. What makes serial murders exceptionally heinous? Why single these criminals out for a mandatory death sentence while leaving the fate of other murderers to the discretion of judges and juries?

Serial murders represent a different order of crime from other murders and belong in a class of exceptionally heinous crimes. First, serial murderers have killed more than one person, sometimes as many as twenty or thirty. Moreover, these killings are ruthless and brutal. Typically they involve torture of at least some of the victims to satisfy the serial killer's deep need not just to kill but also to humiliate and dominate his victims. Whereas most killers kill for a motive such as greed, jealousy, or momentary rage, the serial killer derives pleasure from killing. Serial killers are particularly frightening because they use their rational intelligence to plot their attack on their next victim. Their crimes are calculated, often involving extensive planning that goes beyond the mere "intent" required for other first-degree murder convictions. The very repetition of this crime indicates that serial killers cannot be rehabilitated. Lastly, when the serial killer is finally caught, he has left behind so many signature marks that it is virtually impossible to execute the wrong person. This frequent objection to capital punishment—that an innocent person may be executed—isn't an issue with serial killers, who differ substantially from other criminals.

As you can tell, this section is considerably more complex than one that simply cites data as evidence in support of a reason. Here the writer must use a sequence of reasons to make his point, showing all the ways that serial killers' crimes belong in a class of their own and thus should be punished differently. Certainly, this argument is not definitive and rests on the cumulative persuasiveness of the reasons themselves, but such an argument is considerably more compelling than simply asserting your claim without elaboration. Although developing a line of argument with a sequence of reasons is harder than using empirical evidence, many arguments will require this kind of support.

FOR CLASS DISCUSSION

1. Working individually or in small groups, consider ways you could use evidence from personal experience to support the stated reason in each of the following partial arguments:
   a. Another reason to oppose a state sales tax is that it is so annoying.
   b. Professor X should be rated down on his (her) teaching because he (she) doesn't design homework effectively to promote real learning.
   c. Professor X is an outstanding teacher because he (she) generously spends so much time outside of class counseling students with personal problems.

2. Try to create a sequence-of-reasons argument to support the warrants in the three partial arguments listed in item 1. The warrants for each argument are stated below.
   a. Support this warrant: "We should oppose taxes that are annoying."
   b. Support this warrant: "The effective design of homework to promote real learning is an important criterion for rating teachers."
   c. Support this warrant: "Time spent counseling students with personal problems is an important criterion for rating teachers."

3. Using Toulmin's conditions of rebuttal, work out a strategy for refuting the stated reasons, the warrants, or both in each of the three preceding arguments.

CONCLUSION

Chapters 4 and 5 have provided an anatomy of argument. They have shown that the core of an argument is a claim with reasons that usually can be summarized in one or more *because* clauses attached to the claim. Often, it is as important to support the unstated premises in your argument as it is to support the stated ones. In order to plan out an argument strategy, arguers can use the Toulmin schema, which helps writers discover grounds, warrants, and backings for their arguments and to test them through conditions for rebuttal. Finally, we saw how stated reasons and warrants are supported through the use of evidence or through sequences of other reasons. In the next chapter we will look more closely at the uses of evidence in argumentation.

6 Evidence in Arguments

In the previous chapter, we examined two basic ways to support arguments: through reasons supported by evidence and through reasons supported by a sequence of other reasons. In this chapter we return to a discussion of evidence—how to find, use, and evaluate it. We focus on four categories of evidence: (1) data from personal experience—either from memory or from observations; (2) data from interviews, surveys, and questionnaires; (3) data from reading, especially library research; and (4) numerical or statistical data. At the end of the chapter, we discuss how to evaluate evidence in order to use it fairly, responsibly, and persuasively.

USING EVIDENCE FROM PERSONAL EXPERIENCE

Your own life can be the source of supporting evidence in many arguments. You can draw examples from your own experience or tell your experiences as narratives to illustrate important points. Personal examples and narratives can build bridges to readers who often find personal experience more engaging and immediate than dry lists of facts or statistics. Moreover, when readers sense a writer's personal connection to and investment in an issue, they are more likely to find the writer's position creditable.

Using Personal Experience Data Collected from Memory

Many arguments can be supported extensively, sometimes even exclusively, by information gathered from personal experience or recalled from memory. Here, for example, is how a student used personal experience to help support her argument that foreign language instruction in the United States should be started in elementary school. In the following passage she supports one of her reasons: Young children can learn foreign languages faster than adults.

> We need to start foreign language training early because young children can pick up a language much faster than adults. This truth is exemplified by the experience of several of my family members. In 1993, my uncle was transferred to Switzerland by his employer. A small village named Ruthi in northeastern Switzerland became the new home of my uncle, his wife, and their two young boys, ages six and nine. To add to the difficulty of the move, no one in the family spoke German. Their experience with language acquisition ended up being a textbook case. The youngest child was able to learn German the fastest; the older child also picked it up, but not as quickly. By contrast, my uncle and aunt, who were in their early forties, could not learn the language at all. This same pattern was repeated several years later when they were transferred again, this time to Japan.

The personal examples in this paragraph support the writer's point that foreign language instruction should begin as early as possible in a child's schooling.

Using Personal Experience Data Collected from Observations

For other arguments you can gather evidence through personal observations, as in the following example:

> The intersection at 5th and Montgomery is particularly dangerous. Traffic volume on Montgomery is so heavy that pedestrians almost never find a comfortable break in the flow of cars. On April 29, I watched fifty-seven pedestrians cross this intersection. Not once did cars stop in both directions before the pedestrian stepped off the sidewalk onto the street. Typically, the pedestrian had to move into the street, start tentatively to cross, and wait until a car finally stopped. On fifteen occasions, pedestrians had to stop halfway across the street, with cars speeding by in both directions, waiting for cars in the far lanes to stop before they could complete their crossing.

USING EVIDENCE FROM INTERVIEWS, SURVEYS, AND QUESTIONNAIRES

In addition to direct observations, you can gather evidence by conducting interviews, taking surveys, or passing out questionnaires.

Conducting Interviews

Interviewing people is a useful way not only to gather expert testimony and important data but also to learn about alternative views. To conduct an effective interview, you must have a clear sense of purpose, prepare in advance, be punctual, and respect your interviewee's time.

When you use interview data in your own writing, put quotation marks around any direct quotations. Except when unusual circumstances might require anonymity, identify your source by name and indicate his or her title or credentials—whatever will convince the reader that this person's remarks are to be taken seriously. Here is how one student used interview data to support an argument against carpeting dorm rooms.

> Finally, university-provided carpets will be too expensive. According to Robert Bothell, Assistant Director of Housing Services, the cost will be $300 per room for the carpet and installation. The university would also have to purchase more vacuum cleaners for the students to use. Altogether, Bothell estimated the cost of carpets to be close to $100,000 for the whole campus.

Using Surveys or Questionnaires

Still another form of field research data can come from surveys or questionnaires. Sometimes an informal poll of your classmates can supply evidence persuasive to a reader. One of our students, in an argument supporting public transportation, asked every rider on her bus one morning the following two questions:

> Do you enjoy riding the bus more than commuting by car? If so, why?

She was able to use her data in the following paragraph:

> Last week I polled forty-eight people riding the bus between Bellevue and Seattle. Eighty percent said they enjoyed riding the bus more than commuting by car, while 20 percent preferred the car. Those who enjoyed the bus cited the following reasons in this order of preference: It saved them the hassle of driving in traffic; it gave them time to relax and unwind; it was cheaper than paying for gas and parking; it saved them time.

More formal research can be done through developing and distributing questionnaires. Plan your questionnaire carefully, write nonambiguous questions, and keep it short. Type it neatly so that it looks clean, uncluttered, and easy to complete. At the head of the questionnaire you should explain its purpose. Your tone should be courteous and, if possible, you should offer the reader some motivation to complete the questionnaire.

USING EVIDENCE FROM READING

Although you can base some arguments on evidence from personal experience or from questionnaires and interviews, most arguments require research evidence gleaned from reading: books, magazines, journals, newspapers, government documents, Internet sources, chat groups, specialized encyclopedias and almanacs, corporate bulletins, and so forth. When you use research data from reading, it often takes one or more of the following forms: facts and examples, summaries of research studies, and testimony.

Facts and Examples

A common way to incorporate evidence from reading is to cite facts and examples. Here is how one student writer argues that plastic food packaging and Styrofoam cups aren't necessarily damaging to the environment.

> It's politically correct today to scorn plastic food wrapping and Styrofoam cups. But in the long run these containers may actually help the environment. According to Tierney, a typical household in countries that don't use plastic food wrapping produces one-third more garbage from food spoilage than do U.S. households. Those plastic wrappers on foods allow us to buy foods in small quantities and keep them sterile until use. Tierney also claims that plastic packaging requires far less energy to produce than does paper or cardboard and is lighter to transport (27). Similarly, he claims that the energy costs of producing a ceramic coffee mug and of washing it after each use make it less environmentally friendly than throwaway Styrofoam cups (44).

Knowing that experts can disagree about what is a "fact," this writer attributes her evidence to Tierney ("Tierney claims . . . ") rather than stating Tierney's claims baldly as facts and simply citing him in parentheses. (This writer is using the Modern Language Association documentation style: The numbers in parentheses are page numbers in the Tierney article where the cited information can be found. At the end of her paper, she will provide complete bibliographic information about the Tierney source on her Works Cited page. See Appendix 2, "A Concise Guide to Evaluating and Documenting Sources.")

Summaries of Research

An argument can often be supported by summarizing research studies. Here is how a student writer used a summary statement to support his opposition to mandatory helmet laws for motorcycle riders:

> However, a helmet won't protect against head injury when one is traveling at normal traffic speeds. According to a U.S. Department of Transportation study, "There is no evidence that any helmet thus far, regardless of cost or design, is capable of rejecting impact stress above 13 mph" ("Head Injuries" 8).

Testimony

Research data can also take the form of *testimony*, an expert's opinion that you cite to help bolster your case. Testimony, which we might call secondhand evidence, is often blended with other kinds of data. Using testimony is particularly common wherever laypersons cannot be expected to be experts. Thus, you might cite an authority on the technical feasibility of cold fusion, the effects of alcohol on fetal tissue development, or the causes of a recent airplane crash. Here is how a student writer used testimony to bolster an argument on global warming:

> We can't afford to wait any longer before taking action against global warming. At a recent Senate hearing of the Subcommittee on Environmental Pollution, Senator Chafee warned: "There is a very real possibility that man—through ignorance or indifference or both—is irreversibly altering the ability of our atmosphere to [support] life" (qtd. in Begley 64). At this same hearing, Robert Watson of the National Aeronautics and Space Administration (which monitors the upper atmosphere) claimed: "Global warming is inevitable—it's only a question of magnitude and time" (qtd. in Begley 66).

Here the writer uses no factual or statistical data that global warming is occurring; rather, she cites the testimony of experts.

USING NUMERICAL DATA AND STATISTICS

Among the most pervasive kinds of evidence in modern arguments are numerical data and statistics. Many of us, however, are understandably mistrustful of numerical data. "There are three kinds of lies," we have all heard: "lies, damned lies, and statistics."

Those who gather, use, and analyze numerical data have their own language for degrees of data manipulation. *Teasing* and *tweaking* data are usually legitimate attempts to portray data in a better light; *massaging* data may involve a bit of subterfuge but is still within acceptable limits. When the line is crossed and manipulation turns into outright, conscious misrepresentation, however, we say the data have been *cooked*—an unsavory fate for data and people alike. If we are to use data responsibly and protect ourselves from others' abuses of them, it's important for us to understand how to analyze them. In this section we examine ways to use numerical data both responsibly and persuasively.

Using Graphics for Effect

Any time a writer presents numerical data pictorially, the potential for enhancing the rhetorical presence of the argument, or of manipulating the audience outright, increases markedly. By *presence*, we mean the immediacy and impact of the material. For example, raw numbers and statistics, in large doses, are likely to dull people's minds and perplex them. But numbers turned into pictures are very immediate. Graphs, charts, and tables help an audience see at a glance what long strings of statistics can only hint at.

We can have markedly different effects on our audience according to how we design and construct a graphic. For example, by coloring one variable prominently and enlarging it slightly, a graphic artist can greatly distort the importance of that variable. Although such depictions may carry warnings that they are "not to scale," the visual impact is often more memorable than the warning.

One of the subtlest ways of controlling an audience's perception of a numerical relationship is the way you assign values to the horizontal x-axis and vertical y-axis of a line graph. Consider, for example, the graph in Figure 6.1 depicting the monthly net profits of an ice-cream sandwich retailer. When you look at this graph, you might think that Bite O' Heaven's net profits are shooting heavenward. But if you were considering investing in an ice-cream sandwich franchise, you would want to consider how the graph was constructed.

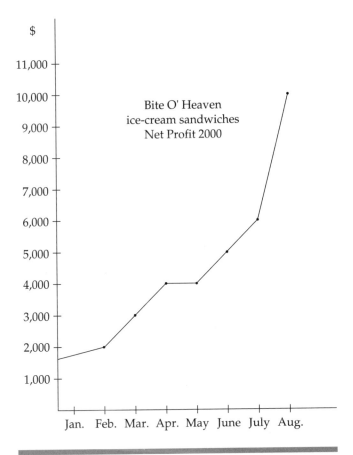

FIGURE 6.1   A line graph that distorts the data

One can easily distort or overstate a rate of change on a graph. Although Figure 6.1 does represent the correct quantities, the designer's choice of increments on the vertical axis leads to a wildly exaggerated depiction of success. If the Bite O' Heaven folks had chosen a larger increment—say, $5,000 instead of $1,000—the company's rise in profitability would look like the graph in Figure 6.2.

Another way to create a rhetorical effect with a line graph is to vary the scope of time it covers. Note that Figures 6.1 and 6.2 cover net sales from January through August. What do you think the sales figures for this company might typically be from September through December?

▼ FOR CLASS DISCUSSION

In small groups, create a line graph for Bite O' Heaven's net profits for a whole year based on your best estimates of when people are most likely to buy ice-cream sandwiches. Then draw graphs showing net profits, quarter by quarter, over a three-year period to represent the following conditions:

1. Bite O' Heaven maintains a stable market share with no increase or decrease in the rate of profits over the three years.

2. Bite O' Heaven increases its market share, and each year is more profitable than the preceding one.

3. Bite O' Heaven loses market share, and each year is leaner than the previous one.

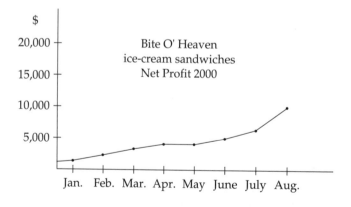

FIGURE 6.2   A line graph that more accurately depicts the data

Using Numbers Strategically

As we have suggested, your choice and design of a graphic can markedly affect your audience's perception of your subject. But you can also influence your audience through the kinds of numbers you use: raw numbers versus percentages, raw numbers versus "adjusted" numbers (for example, wages "adjusted for inflation"), or a statistical presentation versus a narrative one. The choice always depends on the audience you're addressing and the purpose you want to achieve.

One of the most common choices writers have to make is whether to cite raw numbers or to cite percentages or rates. In some cases, a raw number will be more persuasive than a percentage. If you were to say that the cost of attending a state college will increase at a rate 15 percent greater than the Consumer Price Index over the next decade, most audiences would be lost—few would know how to translate that percentage into terms they could understand. But if you were to say that in the year 2007 the cost of attending a state college for one year will be about $21,000, you would surely grab your audience's attention. So, if you were a financial planner trying to talk a young couple into saving money for their children's college education, you would be more inclined to use the raw number rather than the percentage increase. But if you were a college administrator trying to play down the increasing costs of college to a hostile legislator, you might well use the percentage increase rather than the raw number.

In turn, how you state raw numbers can markedly increase or decrease their impact on an audience. For example, to say that newspapers consume huge amounts of wood pulp is mildly interesting. To say that publication of the *New York Times* requires 248 million tons of pulp each year is even more impressive. To say that publication of just one Sunday edition of the *New York Times* requires the cutting of 75,000 trees is mind-boggling. Again, translate the number into what is most meaningful to your audience and the impact you wish to have on that audience.

WRITING YOUR OWN ARGUMENT: USING EVIDENCE PERSUASIVELY

Once you have arrived at a position on an issue, often after having written a draft that enables you to explore and clarify your own views, you need to select the best evidence possible and to use it persuasively. Whether your evidence comes from research or from personal experience, the following guidelines may be helpful.

When Possible, Select Your Data from Sources Your Reader Trusts

Other things being equal, choose data from sources you think your reader will trust. After immersing yourself in an issue, you will get a sense of who the participants in a conversation are and what their reputations tend to be. You need to know the political biases of sources and the extent to which a source has a financial or personal investment in the outcome of a controversy. When the controversy about the greenhouse effect first struck the national consciousness, two prolific writers on the subject were Carl Sagan and Dixie Lee Ray. Both writers held Ph.D. degrees in science, and both had national reputations for speaking out in the popular press on technical and scientific issues. Carl Sagan, however, was an environmentalist, while Dixie Lee Ray tended to support business and industry. To some audiences, neither of these writers was as persuasive as more cautious and less visible scientists who published primarily in scientific journals. Similarly, citing a conservative magazine such as *Reader's Digest* is not likely to be persuasive to liberal audiences, and citing a Sierra Club publication probably would not be pursuasive to conservatives.

Increase Persuasiveness of Factual Data by Ensuring Recency, Representativeness, and Sufficiency

Other things being equal, choose data that are recent, representative, and sufficient. The more your data meet these criteria, the more persuasive they are.

Recency: Although some timeless issues don't depend on recent evidence, most issues, especially those related to science and technology or to current political and economic issues, depend on up-to-date information. Make sure your supporting evidence is the most recent you can find.

Representativeness: Supporting examples are more persuasive when the audience believes they are typical examples instead of extreme cases or rare occurrences. Ensuring representativeness is an especially important concern of statisticians, who seek random samples to avoid bias toward one point of view. Seeking representative examples helps you guard against irresponsible use of data.

Sufficiency: One of the most common reasoning fallacies, called *hasty generalization* (see p. 254), occurs when a person leaps to a sweeping generalization based on only one or two instances. The criterion of sufficiency (which means having enough examples to justify your point) helps you guard against hasty generalization. In our experience, lack of sufficiency occurs frequently in personal experience arguments.

In Citing Evidence, Distinguish Fact from Inference or Opinion

In citing research data, you should be careful to distinguish facts from inferences or opinions. A *fact* is a noncontroversial piece of data that is verifiable through observation or through appeal to communally accepted authorities. Although the distinction between a fact and an inference is a fuzzy one philosophically, at a pragmatic level all of the following can loosely be classified as facts:

The Declaration of Independence was signed in 1776.

An earthquake took place in San Francisco on the opening day of the World Series in 1989.

The amount of carbon dioxide in the atmosphere has increased by 7 percent since 1955.

An *inference,* in contrast, is an interpretation or explanation of the facts that may be reasonably doubted. This distinction is important because, when reading as a doubter, you often call into question a writer's inferences. If you treat these inferences as facts, you are likely to cite them as facts in your own arguments, thereby opening yourself up to easy rebuttal. For the most part, inferences should be handled as testimony rather than as fact.

> **WEAK:** Flohn informs us that the warming of the atmosphere will lead to damaging droughts by the year 2035. [treats Flohn's inference as a fact about global warming]
>
> **BETTER:** Flohn interprets the data pessimistically. He believes that the warming of the atmosphere will lead to damaging droughts by the year 2035. [makes it clear that Flohn's view is an inference, not a fact]

CONCLUSION

Good arguers use evidence effectively. As we have seen, evidence includes facts, examples, statistics, testimony, and other forms of data, and it can come from personal experience as well as from reading and research. It is important to select data from sources that your reader will trust, to ensure the recency, representativeness, and sufficiency of your evidence, and to distinguish between facts and inference.

WRITING ASSIGNMENTS FOR CHAPTERS 4–6

OPTION 1: *A Microtheme That Supports a Reason with Personal Experience Data*
Write a one- or two-paragraph argument in which you support one of the following enthymemes, using evidence from personal experience. Most of your microtheme should support the stated reason with personal experience data. However, also include a brief passage supporting the implied warrant. The opening sentence of your microtheme should be the enthymeme itself, which serves as the thesis statement for your argument.

1. Reading fashion magazines can be detrimental to teenage girls because such magazines can lower a girl's self-esteem.

2. Learning to surf the Web might harm your studying because it causes you to waste time.

3. Getting a part-time job in college might improve your grades because the job will teach you time management.

4. X (a teacher/professor of your choosing) is an outstanding teacher because she (he) generously spends time counseling students with personal problems.

5. Any enthymeme (a claim with *because* clause) of your choice that can be supported through personal experience. Clear your enthymeme with your instructor.

OPTION 2: *A Microtheme That Uses Evidence from Research*   The purpose of this microtheme is to help you learn how to support reasons with evidence gathered from research. The following presentation of data attempts to simulate the kinds of research evidence one might typically gather during a research project.

The situation: By means of startling "before and after" photographs of formerly obese people, the commercial diet industry heavily advertises rapid weight-loss diets that use liquids and powders or special low-calorie frozen dinners. **Your task:** Drawing on the following data, write a short argument warning people of the hazards of these diets.

Source: Representative Ron Wyden (D–Oregon), chairman of a congressional subcommittee investigating the diet industry.

- Wyden fears that diet programs now include many shoddy companies that use misleading advertisements and provide inadequate medical supervision of their clients.
- "This industry has been built almost overnight on a very shaky foundation."
- "All the evidence says that losing large amounts of weight very fast does more harm than good."
- Wyden believes that the diet industry may need to be federally regulated.

Source: Theodore B. VanItallie, M.D., a founder of the Obesity Research Center at St. Luke's Roosevelt Hospital Center in New York.

- Rapid weight-loss systems (such as liquid diets) were originally designed for morbidly obese individuals.
- For people who are only slightly overweight, rapid weight loss can be hazardous.

- When weight loss is too rapid, the body begins using lean muscle mass for fuel instead of excess fat. The result is a serious protein deficiency that can bring on heart irregularities.
- "If more than 25 percent of lost weight is lean body mass, the stage is set not only for early regain of lost weight but for a higher incidence of fatigue, hair loss, skin changes, depression and other undesirable side effects."

Source: Bonnie Blodgett, freelance writer on medical/health issues.

- Rapid weight loss may accelerate formation of gallstones. Currently 179 people are suing a major diet company because of gallstone complications while pursuing the company's diet. The company denies responsibility.
- For every five people who start a commercial weight-loss program, only one stays with it long enough to lose a significant amount of weight.
- Up to 90 percent of dieters who lose more than 25 pounds gain it all back within two years.
- Only one in fifty maintains the weight loss for seven years.
- The best way to lose weight is through increased exercise, moderate reduction of calories, and a lifelong change in eating habits.
- Unless one is grossly obese and dieting under a physician's supervision, one should strive to lose no more than 1 or 2 pounds per week.

Source: Philip Kern, M.D., in a study appearing in *The New England Journal of Medicine.*

- Rapid weight-loss programs result in the "yo-yo" syndrome—a pattern of compulsive fasting followed by compulsive bingeing.
- This pattern may upset the body's metabolism by producing an enzyme called lipoprotein lipase.
- This protein helps restore fat cells shrunken by dieting.
- It apparently causes formerly fat people to crave fatty foods, thereby promoting regain of lost weight.*

OPTION 3: *A Classical Argument*   Write a classical argument that uses at least two reasons to support your claim (classical argument is explained in detail in Chapter 3, pp. 51–53). As we explain further in Chapter 8, classical argument is particularly effective when you are addressing neutral or undecided audiences. It has a

---

*Source of these data is Bonnie Blodgett, "The Diet Biz," *Glamour* Jan. 1991: 136ff.

self-announcing or closed-form structure in which you state your claim at the end of the introduction, begin body paragraphs with clearly stated reasons, and use effective transitions throughout to keep your reader on track. In developing your argument, place your most important reason last, where it will have the greatest impact on your readers. Typically, a classical argument also summarizes anticipated objections to the writer's argument and responds to them appropriately. You can place this section either before or after you develop your main argument. (Chapter 8, pp. 120–25, gives a detailed explanation of how to respond to objections and alternative views.)

The following student essay illustrates a classical argument.

"Half-Criminals" or Urban Athletes?
A Plea for Fair Treatment of Skateboarders

David Langley (Student)

1   For skateboarders, the campus of the University of California at San Diego is a wide-open, huge, geometric, obstacle-filled, stair-scattered cement paradise. The signs posted all over campus read "No skateboarding, biking, or rollerblading on campus except on Saturday, Sunday, and Holidays." I have always respected these signs at my local skateboarding spot. On the first day of 1999, I was skateboarding here with my hometown skate buddies and had just landed a trick when a police officer rushed out from behind a pillar, grabbed me, and yanked me off my board. Because I didn't have my I. D. (I had emptied my pockets so I wouldn't bruise my legs if I fell—a little trick of the trade), the officer started treating me like a criminal. She told me to spread my legs and put my hands on my head. She frisked me and then called in my name to police headquarters.

2   "What's the deal?" I asked. "The sign said skateboarding was legal on holidays."

3   "The sign means that you can only *roll* on campus," she said.

4   But that's *not* what the sign said. The police officer gave one friend and me a warning. Our third friend received a fifty-dollar ticket because it was his second citation in the last twelve months. Like other skateboarders throughout cities, we have been bombarded with unfair treatment. We have been forced out of known skate spots in the city by storeowners and police, kicked out of every parking garage in downtown, compelled to skate at strange times of day and night, and herded into crowded skateboard parks. However, after I was searched by the police and detained for over twenty minutes in my own skating sanctuary, the unreasonableness of the treatment of skateboarders struck me. Where are skateboarders supposed to go? Cities need to change their unfair treatment of skateboarders because skateboarders are not antisocial misfits as popularly believed, because the laws regulating skateboarding are ambiguous, and because skateboarders are not given enough legitimate space to practice their sport.

Possibly because to the average eye most skateboarders look like misfits or delinquents, 5
adults think of us as criminal types and associate our skateboards with antisocial behavior.
But this view is unfair. City dwellers should recognize that skateboards are a natural reaction to the urban environment. If people are surrounded by cement, they are going to figure
out a way to ride it. People's different environments have always produced transportation
and sports to suit the conditions: bikes, cars, skis, ice skates, boats, canoes, surfboards. If we
live on snow, we are going to develop skis or snowshoes to move around. If we live in an
environment that has flat panels of cement for ground and lots of curbs and stairs, we are
going to invent an ingeniously designed flat board with wheels. Skateboards are as natural
to cement as surfboards are to water or skis to snow. Moreover, the resulting sport is as
healthful, graceful, and athletic. A fair assessment of skateboarders should respect our ele-
gant, nonpolluting means of transportation and sport, and not consider us hoodlums.

A second way that skateboarders are treated unfairly is that the laws that regulate skate- 6
boarding in public places are highly restrictive, ambiguous, and open to abusive application
by police officers. My being frisked on the UCSD campus is just one example. When I moved
to Seattle to go to college, I found the laws in Washington to be equally unclear. When a sign
says "No Skateboarding," that generally means you will get ticketed if you are caught skateboarding in the area. But most areas aren't posted. The general rule then is that you can
skateboard so long as you do so safely without being reckless. But the definition of "reckless" is up to the whim of the police officer. I visited the front desk of the Seattle East Precinct
and asked them exactly what the laws against reckless skateboarding meant. They said that
skaters are allowed on the sidewalk as long as they travel at reasonable speed and the sidewalks aren't crowded. One of the officers explained that if he saw a skater sliding down a
handrail with people all around, he would definitely arrest the skater. What if there were no
people around, I asked? The officer admitted that he might arrest the lone skater anyway and
not be questioned by his superiors. No wonder skateboarders feel unfairly treated.

One way that cities have tried to treat skateboarders fairly is to build skateboard parks. 7
Unfortunately, for the most part these parks are no solution at all. Most parks were designed
by nonskaters who don't understand the momentum or gravity pull associated with the
movement of skateboards. For example, City Skate, a park below the Space Needle in Seattle, is very appealing to the eye, but once you start to ride it you realize that the transitions
and the verticals are all off, making it unpleasant and even dangerous to skate there. The
Skate Park in Issaquah, Washington, hosts about thirty to fifty skaters at a time. Collisions
are frequent and close calls, many. There are simply too many people in a small area. The
people who built the park in Redmond, Washington, decided to make a huge wall in it for
graffiti artists to "tag" on legally. They apparently thought they ought to throw all us teenage
"half criminals" in together. At this park, young teens are nervous to skate near a gangster
"throwing up his piece," and skaters become dizzy as they take deep breaths from their
workouts right next to four or five cans of spray paint expelling toxins in the air.

Of course, many adults probably don't think skateboarders deserve to be treated fairly. 8
I have heard the arguments against skateboarders for years from parents, storeowners,
friends, police officers, and security guards. For one thing, skateboarding tears up public
and private property, people say. I can't deny that skating leaves marks on handrails and
benches, and it does chip cement and granite. But in general skateboarders help the

environment more than they hurt it. Skateboarding places are not littered or tagged up by skaters. Because skaters need smooth surfaces and because any small object of litter can lead to painful accidents, skaters actually keep the environment cleaner than the average citizen does. As for the population as a whole, skateboarders are keeping the air a lot cleaner than many other commuters and athletes such as boat drivers, car drivers, and skiers on ski lifts. In the bigger picture, infrequent repair of curbs and benches is cheaper than attempts to heal the ozone.

9   We skateboarders aren't going away so cities are going to have to make room for us somewhere. Here is how cities can treat us fairly. We should be allowed to skate when others are present as long as we skate safely on the sidewalks. The rules and laws should be clearer so that skaters don't get put into vulnerable positions that make them easy targets for tickets. I do support the opening of skate parks, but cities need to build more of them, need to situate them closer to where skateboarders live, and need to make them relatively wholesome environments. They should also be designed by skateboarders so that they are skater-friendly and safe to ride. Instead of being treated as "half criminals," skaters should be accepted as urban citizens and admired as athletes; we are a clean population, and we are executing a challenging and graceful sport. As human beings grow, we go from crawling to walking; some of us grow from strollers to skateboards.

7 Moving Your Audience

Audience-Based Reasons, *Ethos*, and *Pathos*

In Chapters 5 and 6 we discussed *logos*—the logical structure of reasons and evidence in an argument. In this chapter and the next, we show you how to make your arguments as persuasive as possible. Particularly, we show you how to connect your argument to your audience's values and beliefs (audience-based reasons), how to appear credible and trustworthy (*ethos*), and how to engage your audience's sympathies (*pathos*). In Chapter 8 we show you how to vary the tone, content, and structure of your argument, depending on whether your audience is initially sympathetic, neutral, or hostile to your views.

While all these persuasive strategies can be used cynically to manipulate an audience, we presuppose an arguer whose position is based on reasoned investigation of the evidence and on consistent and communicable values and beliefs. Our goal is to help you create arguments that are responsible, rationally sound, and persuasive.

STARTING FROM YOUR READERS' BELIEFS: THE POWER OF AUDIENCE-BASED REASONS

Whenever you ask if an argument is persuasive, the immediate rejoinder should be "Persuasive to whom?" What seems a good reason to you may not be a good reason to others. The force of a logical argument, as Aristotle showed in his explanation of enthymemes, depends on the audience's acceptance of underlying assumptions, values, or beliefs (see pp. 74–76). Finding audience-based reasons means creating arguments that are effectively rooted in your audience's values.

Difference between Writer- and Audience-Based Reasons

To illustrate the difference between writer- and audience-based reasons, consider the following hypothetical case. Suppose you believed that the government should build a dam on the nearby Rapid River—a project bitterly opposed by several environmental groups. Which of the following two arguments might you use to address environmentalists?

1. The government should build a dam on the Rapid River because the only alternative power sources are coal-fired or nuclear plants, both of which pose greater risk to the environment than a hydroelectric dam.

2. The government should build a hydroelectric dam on the Rapid River because this area needs cheap power to attract heavy industry.

Clearly, the warrant of Argument 1 ("Choose the source of power that poses least risk to the environment") is rooted in the values and beliefs of environmentalists, whereas the warrant of Argument 2 ("Growth of industry is good") is likely to make them wince. To environmentalists, new industry means more congestion, more smokestacks, and more pollution. However, Argument 2 may appeal to out-of-work laborers or to the business community, to whom new industry means more jobs and a booming economy.

From the perspective of *logos* alone, Arguments 1 and 2 are both sound. They are internally consistent and proceed from reasonable premises. But they will affect different audiences very differently. Neither argument proves that the government should build the dam; both are open to objection. Passionate environmentalists, for example, might counter Argument 1 by asking why the government needs to build any power plant at all. They could argue that energy conservation would obviate the need for a new power plant. Or they might argue that building a dam hurts the environment in ways unforeseen by dam supporters. Our point, then, isn't that Argument 1 will persuade environmentalists. Rather, our point is that Argument 1 will be more persuasive than Argument 2 because it is rooted in beliefs and values the intended audience shares.

Let's consider a second example by returning to student Gordon Adams's petition to waive the university math requirement (Chapter 1, pp. 14–17). Gordon's central argument, as you will recall, had the following core:

I should be exempted from the algebra requirement because in my chosen field of law I will have no need for algebra.

The warrant for Gordon's argument is that general education requirements should be based on career utility (that is, if a course isn't needed for a particular student's career, it shouldn't be required).

In our discussions of this case with students and faculty, students generally vote to support Gordon's request, whereas faculty members generally vote against it. And in fact, the University Standards Committee rejected Gordon's petition, thus delaying his entry into law school.

Why do faculty members and students differ on this issue? Mainly they differ because faculty members reject Gordon's warrant that general education requirements should serve students' individual career interests. Most faculty members believe that general education courses, including math, provide a base of common learning that links us to the past and teaches us modes of understanding that remain useful throughout life. Gordon's argument thus challenges one of college professors' most cherished beliefs—that the liberal arts are innately valuable. Further, it threatens his immediate audience, the committee, with a possible flood of student requests to waive other general education requirements on the grounds of their irrelevance to a particular career choice.

How might Gordon have created a more persuasive argument? In our view, Gordon might have prevailed had he accepted the faculty's belief in the value of the math requirement and argued that he had fulfilled the "spirit" of that requirement through alternative means. He could have based his argument on an enthymeme like this:

> I should be exempted from the algebra requirement because my experience as a contractor and inventor has already provided me with equivalent mathematical knowledge.

Following this audience-based approach, Gordon would drop all references to algebra's uselessness for lawyers and expand his discussion of the mathematical savvy he acquired on the job. This argument would honor faculty values and reduce faculty members' fears of setting a bad precedent. Few students are likely to have Gordon's background, and those who did could apply for a similar exemption without threatening the system. Again, this argument may not have won, but it would have gotten a more sympathetic hearing.

FOR CLASS DISCUSSION

Working in groups, decide which of the two reasons offered in each instance would be more persuasive to the specified audience. Be prepared to explain your reasoning to the class. Write out the implied warrant for each *because* clause, and decide whether the specific audience would likely grant it.

1. Audience: a beleaguered parent
   a. I should be allowed to stay out until 2 A.M. because all my friends do.
   b. I should be allowed to stay out until 2 A.M. because only if I'm free to make my own decisions will I mature.

2. Audience: people who oppose the present grading system on the grounds that it is too competitive
   a. We should keep the present grading system because it prepares people for the dog-eat-dog pressures of the business world.
   b. We should keep the present grading system because it tells students that certain standards of excellence must be met if individuals are to reach their full potential.

3. Audience: conservative proponents of "family values"
   a. Same-sex marriages should be legalized because doing so will promote public acceptance of homosexuality.
   b. Same-sex marriages should be legalized because doing so will make it easier for gay people to establish and sustain long-term stable relationships.

Finding Audience-Based Reasons: Asking Questions about Your Audience

As the preceding exercise makes clear, reasons are most persuasive when linked to your audience's values. This principle seems simple enough, yet it is easy to forget. For example, employers frequently complain about job interviewees whose first concern is what the company will do for them, not what they might do for the company. Conversely, job search experts agree that most successful job candidates do extensive background research on a prospective company so that in an interview they can relate their own skills to the company's problems and needs. Successful arguments typically grow out of similar attention to audience needs.

To find out all you can about an audience, we recommend that you explore the following questions:

1. *Who is your audience?* Your audience might be a single, identifiable person. For example, you might write a letter to your student body president arguing for a change in intramural policies, or your audience might be a decision-making body such as an influential committee. At other times your audience might be the general readership of a newspaper, church bulletin, magazine, or journal, or you might produce a flier to be handed out on street corners.

2. *How much does your audience know or care about your issue?* Are audience members currently part of the conversation on this issue, or do they need considerable background information? If you are writing to specific decision makers (for example, the administration at your college about restructuring the student orientation program), are they currently aware of the problem or issue you are addressing, and do they care about it? If not, how can you get their attention? Your answers to these questions will especially affect your introduction and conclusion.

3. *What is your audience's current attitude toward your issue?* Are members supportive of your position on the issue? Neutral or undecided? Skeptical? Strongly opposed? What other points of view besides your own will your audience be weighing? In Chapter 8 we will explain how your answers to these questions can help you decide the structure, content, and tone of your argument.

4. *What will be your audience's likely objections to your argument?* What weaknesses will members find? What aspects of your position will be most threatening to them and why? How are your basic assumptions, values, or beliefs different from your audience's? Your answers here will help determine the content of your argument and will alert you to extra research you may need to do to bolster your response to audience objections.

5. *What values, beliefs, or assumptions about the world do you and your audience share?* Despite differences of view on this issue, where can you find common links with your audience? How might you use these links to build bridges to your audience?

Suppose, for example, that you support universal mandatory testing for the HIV virus. It's important from the start that you understand and acknowledge the interests of those opposed to your position. Who are they, and what are their concerns? Gays and others in high-risk categories may fear discrimination from being publicly identified as HIV carriers. Moreover, gays may see mandatory AIDS testing as part of an ongoing attempt by homophobes to stigmatize the gay community. Liberals, meanwhile, will question the necessity of invading people's privacy and compromising their civil liberties in the name of public health.

What shared values might you use to build bridges to those opposed to mandatory testing? At a minimum, you share a desire to find a cure for AIDS and a fear of the horrors of an epidemic. Moreover, you also share a respect for the dignity and humanity of those afflicted with AIDS and do not see yourself as part of a backlash against gays.

Given all that, you begin to develop a strategy to reduce your audience's fears and to link your reasons to your audience's values. Your thinking might go something like this:

PROBLEM:	How can I create an argument rooted in shared values?
POSSIBLE SOLUTIONS:	I can try to reduce the audience's fear that mandatory AIDS testing implies a criticism of gays. I must assure that my plan ensures confidentiality. I must make clear that my first priority is stopping the spread of the disease and that this concern is shared by the gay community.
PROBLEM:	How can I reduce fear that mandatory HIV testing will violate civil liberties?

POSSIBLE SOLUTIONS: I must show that the enemy here is the HIV virus, not victims of the disease. Also, I might cite precedents for how we fight other infectious diseases. For example, many states require marriage license applicants to take a test for sexually transmitted diseases, and many communities have imposed quarantines to halt the spread of epidemics. I could also argue that the right of everyone to be free from this disease outweighs the right to privacy, especially when confidentiality is assured.

The preceding example shows how a writer's focus on audience can shape the actual invention of the argument.

FOR CLASS DISCUSSION

Working individually or in small groups, plan an audience-based argumentative strategy for one or more of the following cases. Follow the thinking process used by the writer of the mandatory HIV-testing argument: (1) State several problems that the writer must solve to reach the audience. (2) Develop possible solutions to those problems.

1. An argument for the right of software companies to continue making and selling violent video games: Aim the argument at parents who oppose their children's playing these games.

2. An argument to reverse grade inflation by limiting the number of A's and B's a professor can give in a course. Aim the argument at students who fear the results of getting lower grades.

3. An argument supporting a $1-per-gallon increase in gasoline taxes as an energy conservation measure: Aim your argument at business leaders who oppose the tax for fear it will raise the cost of consumer goods.

4. An argument supporting the legalization of cocaine: Aim your argument at readers of *Reader's Digest*, a conservative magazine that supports the current war on drugs.

Ethos And *Pathos* As Persuasive Appeals: An Overview

The previous section focused on audience-based reasons as a means of moving an audience. In terms of the rhetorical triangle introduced in Chapter 4, searching for audience-based reasons can be seen primarily as a function of *logos*—finding the best structure of reasons and evidence to sway an audience—although, as we shall see, it also affects the other points of the triangle. In what follows, we turn to the power of *ethos* (the appeal to credibility) and *pathos* (the appeal to an audience's sympathies) as further means of making your arguments more effective.

To see how *logos, ethos,* and *pathos* work together to create an impact on the reader, consider the different impacts of the following arguments:

1. People should adopt a vegetarian diet because only through vegetarianism can we prevent the cruelty to animals that results from factory farming.

2. I hope you enjoyed your fried chicken this evening. You know, of course, how much that chicken suffered just so you could have a tender and juicy meal. Commercial growers cram the chickens so tightly together into cages that their beaks must be cut off to keep them from pecking each others' eyes out. The only way to end the torture is to adopt a vegetarian diet.

3. People who eat meat are no better than sadists who torture other sentient creatures to enhance their own pleasure. Unless you enjoy sadistic tyranny over others, you have only one choice: Become a vegetarian.

4. People committed to justice might consider the extent to which our love of eating meat requires the agony of animals. A visit to a modern chicken factory—where chickens live their entire lives in tiny darkened coops without room to spread their wings—might raise doubts about our right to inflict such suffering on sentient creatures. Indeed, such a visit might persuade us that vegetarianism is a more just alternative.

Each argument has roughly the same logical core:

CLAIM:	People should adopt a vegetarian diet.
STATED REASON:	because only vegetarianism will end the suffering of animals subjected to factory farming
GROUNDS:	the evidence of suffering in commercial chicken farms, where chickens are crammed together and lash out at each other; evidence that only widespread adoption of vegetarianism will end factory farming
WARRANT:	If we have an alternative to making animals suffer, we should adopt it.

But the impact of each argument varies. The difference between Arguments 1 and 2, most of our students report, is the greater emotional power of 2. Whereas Argument 1 refers only to the abstraction "cruelty to animals," Argument 2 paints a vivid picture of chickens with their beaks cut off to prevent their pecking each other blind. Argument 2 makes a stronger appeal to *pathos* (not necessarily a stronger argument), stirring feelings by appealing simultaneously to the heart and to the head.

The difference between Arguments 1 and 3 concerns both *ethos* and *pathos*. Argument 3 appeals to the emotions through highly charged words like *torture, sadists,* and *tyranny.* But Argument 3 also draws attention to its writer, and most of our students report not liking that writer very much. His stance is self-righteous and insulting. In contrast, Argument 4's author establishes a more positive *ethos.* He establishes rapport with members of his audience by assuming they are committed to justice and by qualifying his argument with conditional terms such as *might* and *perhaps.* He also invites sympathy for his problem—an appeal to *pathos*— by offering a specific description of chickens crammed into tiny coops.

Which of these arguments is best? They all have appropriate uses. Arguments 1 and 4 seem aimed at receptive audiences reasonably open to exploration of the issue. Arguments 2 and 3 seem designed to shock complacent audiences or to rally a group of True Believers. Even Argument 3, which is too abusive to be effective in most instances, might work as a rallying speech at a convention of animal liberation activists.

Our point thus far is that *logos, ethos,* and *pathos* are different aspects of the same whole, different lenses for intensifying or softening the light beam you project onto the screen. Every choice you make as a writer affects in some way each of the three appeals. The rest of this chapter examines these choices in more detail.

HOW TO CREATE AN EFFECTIVE *ETHOS:* THE APPEAL TO CREDIBILITY

The ancient Greek and Roman rhetoricians recognized that an argument will be more persuasive if the audience trusts the speaker. Aristotle argued that such trust resides within the speech itself, not in the prior reputation of the speaker. In the speaker's manner and delivery, in tone, word choice, and arrangement of reasons, in the sympathy with which the speaker treats alternative views, he or she creates a trustworthy persona. Aristotle called the impact of the speaker's credibility the appeal from *ethos.* How does a writer create credibility? We will suggest three ways.

Be Knowledgeable about Your Issue

The first way to gain credibility is to *be* credible—that is, to argue from a strong base of knowledge, to have at hand the examples, personal experiences, statistics, and other empirical data needed to make a sound case. If you have done your homework, you will command the attention of most audiences.

Be Fair

Besides being knowledgeable about your issue, you need to demonstrate fairness and courtesy to alternative views. Because true argument can occur only where persons may reasonably disagree with one another, your *ethos* will be strengthened if you demonstrate that you understand and empathize with other points of view. There are times, of course, when you may appropriately scorn an opposing view. But these times are rare, and they mostly occur when you address audiences predisposed to your view. Demonstrating empathy to alternative views is generally the best strategy.

Build a Bridge to Your Audience

A third means of establishing credibility—building a bridge to your audience— has been treated at length in our earlier discussion of audience-based reasons. By grounding your argument in shared values and assumptions, you demonstrate your goodwill and enhance your image as a trustworthy person respectful of your audience's views. We mention audience-based reasons here to show how this aspect of *logos*—finding the reasons that are most rooted in the audience's values—also affects your *ethos* as a person respectful of your readers' views.

HOW TO CREATE *PATHOS:* THE APPEAL TO BELIEFS AND EMOTIONS

Although commonly defined as an "appeal to the emotions," *pathos* evokes effects that are subtler and more complex than the word *emotions* suggests. Because our understanding of something is a matter of feeling as well as perceiving, *pathos* can evoke nonlogical, but not necessarily nonrational, ways of knowing. When used effectively, pathetic appeals reveal the fullest human meaning of an issue, helping us walk in the writer's shoes. That is why arguments are often improved through the use of sensory details that allow us to see the reality of a problem or through stories that make specific cases and instances come alive. *Pathos* touches the heart and mind simultaneously.

Although it is difficult to classify all the ways that writers can create appeals from *pathos*, we will focus on five strategies: concrete language; specific examples and illustrations; narratives; visual images; and word connotations, metaphors, and analogies.

Use Concrete Language

Concrete language can increase the liveliness, interest level, and personality of one's prose and typically heightens *pathos* in an argument. Consider the differences between the first and second drafts of the following student argument:

First draft: People who prefer driving a car to taking a bus think that taking the bus will increase the stress of the daily commute. Just the opposite is true. Not being able to find a parking spot when in a hurry to work or school can cause a person stress. Taking the bus gives a person time to read or sleep, etc. It could be used as a mental break.

Second draft: Taking the bus can be more relaxing than driving a car. Having someone else behind the wheel gives people time to chat with friends or cram for a test. They can balance their checkbooks, do homework, doze off, read the daily newspaper, or get lost in a novel rather than foaming at the mouth looking for a parking space.

In the second draft, specific details enliven the prose by creating images that trigger positive feelings. Who wouldn't want some free time to doze off or to get lost in a novel?

Use Specific Examples and Illustrations

Specific examples and illustrations serve two purposes in an argument: They provide evidence that supports your reasons; simultaneously, they give your argument presence and emotional resonance. Note the flatness of the following draft arguing for the value of multicultural studies in a university core curriculum:

Early draft: Another advantage of a multicultural education is that it will help us see our own culture in a broader perspective. If all we know is our own heritage, we might not be inclined to see anything bad about this heritage because we won't know anything else. But if we study other heritages, we can see the costs and benefits of our own heritage.

Now note the increase in "presence" when the writer adds a specific example.

Revised draft: Another advantage of multicultural education is that it raises questions about traditional Western values. For example, owning private property (such as buying your own home) is part of the American dream and is a basic right guaranteed in our Constitution. However, in studying the beliefs of American Indians, students are confronted with a very different view of private property. When the U.S. Government sought to buy land in the Pacific Northwest from Chief Sealth, he replied:

> The president in Washington sends words that he wishes to buy our land. But how can you buy or sell the sky? The land? The idea is strange to us. If we do not own the freshness of the air and the sparkle of the water, how can you buy them? . . . We are part of the earth and it is part of us. [. . .] This we know: The earth does not belong to man, man belongs to the earth.

Our class was shocked by the contrast between traditional Western views of property and Chief Sealth's views. One of our best class discussions was initiated by this quotation from Chief Sealth. Had we not been exposed to a view from another culture, we would have never been led to question the "rightness" of Western values.

The writer begins his revision by evoking a traditional Western view of private property, which he then questions by shifting to Chief Sealth's vision of land as open, endless, and unobtainable as the sky. Through the use of a specific example, the writer brings to life his previously abstract point about the benefit of multicultural education.

Use Narratives

A particularly powerful way to evoke *pathos* is to tell a story that either leads into your claim or embodies it implicitly and that appeals to your readers' feelings and imagination. Brief narratives—whether real or hypothetical—are particularly effective as opening attention grabbers for an argument. To illustrate how an introductory narrative (either a story or a brief scene) can create pathetic appeals, consider the following first paragraph to an argument opposing jet skis:

> I dove off the dock into the lake, and as I approached the surface I could see the sun shining through the water. As my head popped out, I located my cousin a few feet away in a rowboat waiting to escort me as I, a twelve-year-old girl, attempted to swim across the mile-wide, pristine lake and back to our dock. I made it, and that glorious summer day is one of my most precious memories. Today, however, no one would dare attempt that swim. Jet skis have taken over this small lake where I spent many summers with my grandparents. Dozens of whining jet skis crisscross the lake, ruining it for swimming, fishing, canoeing, rowboating, and even water-skiing. More stringent state laws are needed to control jet-skiing because it interferes with other uses of lakes and is currently very dangerous.

This narrative makes a case for a particular point of view toward jet skis by winning our identification with the writer's experience. She invites us to relive that experience with her while she also taps into our own treasured memories of summer experiences that have been destroyed by change.

Opening narratives to evoke *pathos* can be powerfully effective, but they are also risky. If they are too private, too self-indulgent, too sentimental, or even too dramatic and forceful, they can backfire on you. If you have doubts about an opening narrative, read it to a sample audience before using it in your final draft.

◤ FOR CLASS DISCUSSION

Outside class rewrite the introduction to one of your previous papers (or a current draft) to include more appeals to *pathos*. Use any of the strategies discussed so far for giving your argument presence: concrete language, specific examples, or narratives. Bring both your original and your rewritten introduction to class. In pairs or in groups, discuss the comparative effectiveness of these introductions in trying to reach your intended audience.

Consider the Emotional Power of Visual Arguments

One of the most powerful ways to engage an audience emotionally is to use photos or other visual images. If you think of any news event that has captured wide media attention, you will probably recall memorable photos. Think of the famous photograph of three-year-old John F. Kennedy Jr. saluting his father's coffin. Or think of the image that most frequently accompanied stories of the U.S. women's soccer team's winning the world championship in 1999—not the great goal-keeping photo of African American Briana Scurry blocking the last penalty kick, but the photo of Brandi Chastain removing her jersey to reveal a black sports bra. Sometimes we are only partially aware of how the specific subject matter selected for a photo, its angle and cropping, the arrangement and posing of figures, and other details can encode an argument. Many analysts, for example, observed that the Brandi Chastain photograph linked women's sports with stereotypical views of women as sex objects rather than with athletic prowess.

Because of the power of visual images, professional writers often try to use photographs or drawings to enhance their arguments. Visual images can reinforce the message of an argument by grabbing viewers' attention, conveying the seriousness of an issue, and evoking strong emotions ranging from compassion to revulsion.

While many written arguments do not lend themselves to visual illustrations, we suggest that when you construct arguments you consider the potential of visual support. Imagine that your argument is to appear in a newspaper or magazine and space will be provided for one or two visuals. What photographs or drawings might help persuade your audience toward your perspective? When visual images work well, they are analogous to the verbal strategies of concrete language, specific illustrations, and narratives. The challenge in using visuals is to find material that is straightforward enough not to require elaborate explanations, that is timely and relevant, and that clearly adds impact to a specific part of your argument.

▼ FOR CLASS DISCUSSION

In the following exercise, we ask you to consider the effect of visual images on a recent event that pitted cultural values against the interests of environmentalists and animal rights activists, as well as raised numerous issues relating to world trade and international fisheries. This conflict centered on the desire of the Makah people to resume their traditional practice of hunting gray whales—a right guaranteed them by treaty. When a U.S. federal court granted the tribe permission to resume whaling (the Makah were allotted four whales), an extended conflict broke out between the tribe and antiwhaling protesters. Each side hired a public relations firm to help sway the general public toward its views and interests. On the day the Makah killed their first whale, the media filmed the event, creating photographs that had the potential of furthering the Makah's cause or creating a public relations disaster.

Working in small groups or as a whole class, respond to the following questions:

1. Figures 7.1 and 7.2 show two photographs taken on the day of the whale killing. Freewrite your response to these photos. How would you describe their emotional impact on the viewer? Then share your freewrites with classmates.

2. Here is a quotation from a specialist in public relations: "One of the first things you want to do in public relations is control the picture. Whichever side has the better picture very often controls the argument."* If you were a public relations consultant for the Makah, which of the two photos would you say best supports the tribe's view of whale hunting as noble action embracing the tribe's traditional values? Why?

FIGURE 7.1   Media photograph of a scene from a whale killing

---

*Eric Sorensen, "Tradition vs. a Full-Blown PR Problem: Now Come Reactions to a Very Public Death," *Seattle Times,* 18 May 1999: A9.

FIGURE 7.2   Another photograph of a scene from a whale killing

3. Which picture best supports the protesters' antiwhaling views? Why?

4. Find several different photos of a historical event or a recent news event, and explain how the photos have been used to present different perspectives on the event. What emotions do the photos appeal to?

Choose Words, Metaphors, and Analogies with Appropriate Connotations

A final way of appealing to *pathos* is to select words, metaphors, or analogies with connotations that match your aim. You might call a rapidly made decision by a city council "haughty and autocratic" or "bold and decisive," depending on whether you oppose or support the council. Similarly, writers can use favorable or unfavorable metaphors and analogies to evoke different imaginative or emotional responses. A tax bill might be viewed as a "potentially fatal poison pill" or as "unpleasant but necessary economic medicine."

The writer's control over word selection raises the problem of slant or bias. Some contemporary philosophers argue that bias-free, perfectly transparent language is impossible because all language is a lens. Thus, when we choose word A rather than word B, when we put this sentence in the passive voice rather than the active, when we select this detail and omit that detail, we create bias.

Let's illustrate. When you see an unshaven man sitting on a city sidewalk with his back up against a doorway, wearing old, shabby clothes, and drinking from a bottle hidden in a sack, what is the objective, "true" word for this person?

person on welfare?	welfare leech?	beggar?
panhandler?	bum?	hobo?
wino?	drunk?	alcoholic?
crazy guy?	homeless person?	transient?

None of these words can be called "true" or perfectly objective because each creates its own slant. Each word causes us to view the person through that word's lens. "Beggar," for example, brings to mind helpless poverty and the biblical call to give alms to the poor. It has a slightly more favorable connotation than "panhandler," which conjures up the image of someone pestering us for money. Calling the person "homeless" shifts the focus away from the person's behavior and onto a faulty economic system that fails to provide sufficient housing. "Wino," identifies a different reason for the person's condition—alcohol rather than economics.

Our point is that purely objective language may be impossible. But the absence of pure objectivity doesn't mean that all language is equally slanted or that truth can never be discerned. Readers can recognize degrees of bias in someone's language and distinguish between a reasonably trustworthy passage and a highly distortive one. By being on the lookout for slanted language—without claiming that any language can be totally objective—we can defend ourselves from distortive appeals to *pathos* while recognizing that responsible use of connotation can give powerful presence to an argument.

CONCLUSION

In this chapter, we have explored ways in which writers can strengthen the persuasiveness of their arguments by using audience-based reasons and by creating appeals to *ethos* and *pathos*. Arguments are more persuasive if they are rooted in underlying assumptions, beliefs, and values of the intended audience. Similarly, arguments are more persuasive if readers trust the credibility of the writer and if the argument appeals to readers' hearts and imaginations as well as their intellects. The chapter has suggested a variety of strategies for making appeals to *ethos* and *pathos*.

8

Accommodating Your Audience

Treating Differing Views

In the previous chapter we discussed ways of moving an audience. In this chapter we discuss a writer's options for accommodating differing views on an issue—whether to omit them, refute them, concede to them, or incorporate them through compromise and conciliation. In particular, we show you how your choices about structure, content, and tone may differ depending on whether your audience is sympathetic, neutral, or strongly resistant to your views. The strategies explained in this chapter will increase your flexibility as an arguer and enhance your chance of persuading a wide variety of audiences.

ONE-SIDED VERSUS MULTISIDED ARGUMENTS

Arguments are sometimes said to be one-sided or multisided. A *one-sided* argument presents only the writer's position on the issue without summarizing and responding to opposing viewpoints. A *multisided* argument presents the writer's position but also summarizes and responds to possible objections that an audience might raise. Which kind of argument is more persuasive to an audience?

According to some researchers, if people already agree with a writer's thesis, they usually find one-sided arguments more persuasive. A multisided argument appears wishy-washy, making the writer seem less decisive. But if people initially disagree with a writer's thesis, a multisided argument often seems more persuasive because it shows that the writer has listened to other views and thus seems more open-minded and fair. An especially interesting effect has been documented for neutral audiences. In the short run, one-sided arguments seem more persuasive to neutral audiences, but in the long run multisided arguments seem to have more staying power. Neutral audiences who have heard only one side of an issue tend to change their minds when they hear alternative arguments. By anticipating and in some cases refuting opposing views, the multisided argument diminishes the surprise and force of subsequent counterarguments and also exposes their weaknesses. In the rest of this chapter we will show you how your choice of writing one-sided or multisided arguments is a function of how you perceive your audience's resistance to your views.

DETERMINING YOUR AUDIENCE'S RESISTANCE TO YOUR VIEWS

When you write an argument, you must always consider your audience's point of view. One way to imagine your relationship to members of your audience is to place them on a scale of resistance ranging from "strongly supportive" of your position to "strongly opposed" (see Figure 8.1). At the "accord" end of this scale are like-minded people who basically agree with your position on the issue. At the "resistance" end are those who strongly disagree with you, perhaps unconditionally, because their values, beliefs, or assumptions sharply differ from your own. In between lies a range of opinions. Close to your position will be those leaning in your direction but with less conviction than you. Close to the resistance position will be those basically opposed to your view but willing to listen to your argument and perhaps willing to acknowledge some of its strengths. In the middle are those undecided people who are still sorting out their feelings, seeking additional information, and weighing the strengths and weaknesses of alternative views.

Seldom, however, will you encounter an issue in which the range of disagreement follows a simple line from accord to resistance. Resistant views often fall into different categories so that no single line of argument appeals to all those whose views are different from your own. You have to identify not only your audience's resistance to your ideas but also the causes of that resistance.

Consider, for example, an issue that divided the state of Washington when the Seattle Mariners baseball team demanded a new stadium. A ballot initiative asked citizens to raise taxes to build a new retractable-roof stadium for the

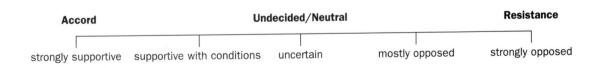

FIGURE 8.1 Scale of resistance

Mariners. Supporters of the initiative faced a complex array of resisting views (see Figure 8.2). Opponents of the initiative could be placed into four different categories. The first group simply had no interest in sports, cared nothing about baseball, and saw no benefit in building a huge sports facility in downtown Seattle. The second group loved baseball, perhaps followed the Mariners passionately, but was philosophically opposed to subsidizing rich players and owners with taxpayer money. Members of this group argued that the whole sports industry needed to be restructured so that stadiums were paid for out of sports revenues. The third group was opposed to tax hikes in general. This group's members focused on the principle of reducing the size of government and using tax revenues only for essential services. The fourth group supported baseball and supported the notion of public funding of a new stadium but opposed the kind of retractable-roof stadium specified in the initiative, preferring instead an old-fashioned, open-air stadium like Baltimore's Camden Yards or Cleveland's Jacobs Field.

Writers supporting the initiative found it impossible to address all these resisting audiences at once. A supporter of the initiative who wanted to aim an argument at sports haters could stress the spinoff benefits of a new ballpark (the new ball park would attract tourist revenue, renovate the deteriorating Pioneer Square neighborhood, create jobs, make sports lovers more likely to vote for public subsidies of the arts, and so forth). But these arguments were irrelevant to those who wanted an open-air stadium, who opposed tax hikes categorically, or who objected to public subsidy of millionaires.

The Mariners example illustrates that it is not always easy to adapt your argument to your audience's position on the scale of resistance. Yet identifying your audience is important because writers need a stable vision of their audience before they can determine an effective content, structure, and tone for an argument. Sometimes as a writer you will simply need to "invent" your audience—that is, to assume that a certain category of readers will be your primary audience. Making this decision gives you a stable base from which to create audience-based reasons and to craft an appropriate tone and structure. The next sections show

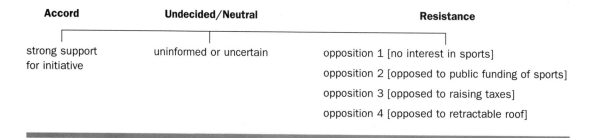

FIGURE 8.2   Scale of resistance, baseball stadium issue

how you can adjust your arguing strategy depending on whether you imagine your audience as supportive, neutral, or hostile.

APPEALING TO A SUPPORTIVE AUDIENCE: ONE-SIDED ARGUMENT

Although arguing to a supportive audience might seem like preaching to the choir, such arguments are common. Usually, the arguer's goal is to convert belief into action—to inspire a party member to contribute to a senator's campaign or a bored office worker to sign up for a change-your-life weekend seminar.

Typically, appeals to a supportive audience are structured as one-sided arguments that either ignore opposing views or reduce them to "enemy" stereotypes. Filled with motivational language, these arguments list the benefits that will ensue from your donations to the cause and the horrors just around the corner if the other side wins. One of the authors of this text received a fundraising letter from an environmental lobbying group declaring, "It's crunch time for the polluters and their pals on Capitol Hill." The "corporate polluters" and "anti-environment politicians," the letter continues, have "stepped up efforts to roll back our environmental protections—relying on large campaign contributions, slick PR firms and well-heeled lobbyists to get the job done before November's election." This letter makes the reader feel part of an in-group of good guys fighting big business "polluters." Nothing in the letter examines environmental issues from a business perspective or attempts to examine alternative views fairly. Since the intended audience already believes in the cause, nothing in the letter invites readers to consider the issues more complexly. Rather, the goal is to solidify support, increase the fervor of belief, and inspire action. Most appeal arguments make it easy to act, ending with an 800 phone number to call, a tear-out postcard to send in, or a congressperson's address to write to.

APPEALING TO A NEUTRAL OR UNDECIDED AUDIENCE: CLASSICAL ARGUMENT

The in-group appeals that motivate an already supportive audience can repel a neutral or undecided audience. Because undecided audiences are like jurors weighing all sides of an issue, they distrust one-sided arguments that caricature other views. Generally the best strategy for appealing to undecided audiences is the classical argument described in Chapter 3 (pp. 51–53). What characterizes the classical argument is the writer's willingness to summarize opposing views fairly and to respond to them openly—either by trying to refute them or by conceding to their strengths and then shifting to a different field of values. Let's look at these strategies in more depth.

Summarizing Opposing Views

The first step toward responding to opposing views in a classical argument is to summarize them fairly. Follow the *principle of charity,* which obliges you to avoid loaded, biased, or "straw man" summaries that oversimplify or distort opposing arguments, making them easy to knock over.

Consider the differences between an unfair and a fair summary of George Will's "Lies, Damned Lies and . . . " (pp. 23–25), which we examined in Chapter 2.

UNFAIR SUMMARY

In a recent *Newsweek* editorial, right-wing columnist George Will parrots the capitalist party line about the virtues and successes of the free enterprise system. He mocks women who complain about the gender pay gap, labeling them whiny feminists. Citing biased statistics gathered by two ultraconservative, antifeminist women authors, Will claims that women are not discriminated against in the workplace even though they make only 74 cents to a man's dollar and even though only a tiny percentage of top executives in Fortune 500 companies are women. He insults women by claiming that women's unequal pay is the result of their "cheerful" acceptance of their natural roles as mothers, which lead them to desire flexible jobs rather than well-paying ones. He blindly dismisses the need for government action. Normal women, he claims, should be able to see that women have the best of all possible worlds because our wonderful economy lets them combine family with jobs.

This summary both distorts and oversimplifies Will's position. By adopting a sarcastic tone ("our wonderful economy") and by using loaded phrases (such as "right-wing" and "parrots the capitalist party line"), the writer reveals a bias against Will that neutral readers will distrust. In failing to summarize Will's statistical explanations for both the current pay gap and the absence of women in top executive positions, the writer oversimplifies Will's argument, preventing the reader from understanding Will's reasoning. The writer thus sets up a straw man that is easier to knock over than is Will's original argument.

For an example of fair summaries of Will, see the versions we have written in Chapter 2 (p. 27). In those examples we follow the principle of charity by summarizing Will's views as justly and accurately as possible.

Refuting Opposing Views

Once you have summarized an opposing view, you can either refute it or concede to its strengths. In refuting an opposing view, you attempt to convince readers that its argument is logically flawed, inadequately supported, or based on erroneous assumptions or wrong values. In Toulmin's terms, you can refute (1) the writer's stated reason and grounds, (2) the writer's warrant and backing, or (3) both.

For example, suppose you want to refute the following argument: "We shouldn't elect Joe as chairperson because he is too bossy." Displayed in Toulmin terms, the argument looks like this:

CLAIM:	We shouldn't elect Joe as chairperson.
STATED REASON:	because he is too bossy
GROUNDS:	evidence that Joe is bossy
WARRANT:	Bossy people make bad chairpersons.

One way to refute this argument is to rebut the stated reason and grounds:

> I disagree with you that Joe is bossy. In fact, Joe is very unbossy. He's a good listener who is willing to compromise, and he involves others in decisions. The example you cite for his being bossy wasn't typical. It was a one-time circumstance that doesn't represent his normal behavior. [The writer could then provide examples of Joe's cooperative nature.]

Or you could concede that Joe is bossy but rebut the argument's warrant that bossiness is a bad trait:

> I agree that Joe is bossy, but in this circumstance bossiness is just the trait we need. This committee hasn't gotten anything done for six months, and time is running out. We need a decisive person who can come in, get the committee organized, assign tasks, and get the job done.

Let's now illustrate these strategies in a more complex situation. For an example, we'll look at the issue of whether recycling is an effective strategy for saving the environment. A controversial subissue of recycling is whether the United States is running out of space for sanitary landfills. Here is how one environmental writer argues that there are no places left to dump our garbage:

> Because the United States is running out of landfill space, Americans will simply not be able to put the 180 million tons of solid waste they generate each year into landfills, where 70 percent of it now goes. Since 1979, the United States has exhausted more than two-thirds of its landfills; projections indicate that another one-fifth will close over the next five years. Between 1983 and 1987, for example, New York closed 200 of its 500 landfills; this year Connecticut will exhaust its landfill capacity. If the problem seemed abstract to Americans, it became odiously real in the summer of 1989 as most of the nation watched the notorious garbage barge from Islip, New York, wander 6,000 miles, searching for a place to dump its rancid 3,100-ton load.*

---

*George C. Lodge and Jeffrey F. Rayport, "Knee-Deep and Rising: America's Recycling Crisis," *Harvard Business Review,* Sept.–Oct. 1991: 132.

This passage tries to persuade us that the United States is running out of land-fill space. Now watch how writer John Tierney attempts to refute this argument in an influential 1996 *New York Times Magazine* article entitled "Recycling Is Garbage":

[Proponents of recycling believe that] our garbage will bury us. The *Mobro's*[*] saga was presented as a grim harbinger of future landfill scarcity, but it actually represented a short-lived scare caused by new environmental regulations. As old municipal dumps were forced to close in the 1980's, towns had to send their garbage elsewhere and pay higher prices for scarce landfill space. But the higher prices predictably encouraged companies to open huge new landfills, in some re-gions creating a glut that set off price-cutting wars. Over the past few years, land-fills in the South and Middle West have been vying for garbage from the New York area, and it has become cheaper to ship garbage there than to bury it locally.

America has a good deal more landfill space available than it did 10 years ago. [. . .] A. Clark Wiseman, an economist at Gonzaga University in Spokane, Wash., has calculated that if Americans keep generating garbage at current rates for 1,000 years, and if all their garbage is put in a landfill 100 yards deep, by the year 3000 this national garbage heap will fill a square piece of land 35 miles on each side.

This doesn't seem a huge imposition in a country the size of America. The garbage would occupy only 5 percent of the area needed for the national array of solar panels proposed by environmentalists. The millennial landfill would fit on one-tenth of 1 percent of the range land now available for grazing in the conti-nental United States.[†]

In this case, Tierney uses counterevidence to rebut the reason and grounds of the original enthymeme: "Recycling is needed because the United States is run-ning out of landfill space." Tierney attacks this argument by disagreeing with the stated reason that the United States is running out of landfill space.

But writers are also likely to question the underlying assumptions (warrants) of an opposing view. For an example, consider another recycling controversy: From an economic perspective, is recycling cost-effective? In criticizing recycling, Tierney argues that recycling wastes money; he provides evidence that "every time a sanitation department crew picks up a load of bottles and cans from the curb, New York City loses money." The warrant of this argument is that "we should dispose of garbage in the most cost-effective way."

In rebutting Tierney's argument, proponents of recycling typically accepted Tierney's figures on recycling costs in New York City (that is, they agreed that in New York City recycling was more expensive than burying garbage). But in vari-

---

[*]*Mobro* is the name of the "notorious garbage barge" from Islip, New York, referred to at the end of the previous quotation.

[†]John Tierney, "Recycling Is Garbage," *New York Times Magazine,* 30 June 1996, 28.

ous ways they attacked his warrant. Typically, proponents of recycling said that even if the costs of recycling were higher than burying wastes in a landfill, recycling still benefited the environment by reducing the amount of virgin materials taken from nature. This argument says, in effect, that saving virgin resources takes precedence over economic costs.

These examples show how a refutation can focus on either the stated reasons and grounds of an argument or on the warrants and backing.

▼ FOR CLASS DISCUSSION

Imagine how each of the following arguments might be fleshed out with grounds and backing. Then attempt to refute each argument by suggesting ways to rebut the reason and grounds, the warrant and backing, or both.

1. Writing courses should be pass/fail because the pass/fail system would encourage more creativity.

2. The government should make cigarettes illegal because cigarettes cause cancer and heart disease.

3. Majoring in engineering is better than majoring in music because engineers make more money than musicians.

4. People should not eat meat because doing so causes needless pain and suffering to animals.

5. The endangered species law is too stringent because it seriously hampers the economy.

Strategies for Rebutting Evidence

Whether you are rebutting an argument's reasons and grounds or its warrant and backing, you will frequently need to question a writer's use of evidence. Here are some strategies that you can use.

Deny the Accuracy of the Data

What one writer considers a fact another may consider a case of wrong information. If you have reason to doubt a writer's facts, then call them into question.

Cite Counterexamples or Countertestimony

One of the most effective ways to counter an argument based on examples is to cite a counterexample. The effect of counterexamples is to deny the conclusiveness of the original data. Similarly, citing an authority whose testimony counters other expert testimony is a good way to begin refuting an argument based on testimony.

Cast Doubt on the Representativeness or Sufficiency of Examples

Examples are powerful only if the audience feels them to be representative and sufficient. Many environmentalists complained that John Tierney's attack on recycling was based too largely on data from New York City and that it didn't accurately take into account the more positive experiences of other cities and states. When data from outside New York City were examined, the cost-effectiveness and positive environmental impact of recycling seemed more apparent.

Cast Doubt on the Relevance or Recency of Examples, Statistics, or Testimony

The best evidence is up-to-date. In a rapidly changing universe, data that are even a few years out-of-date are often ineffective. For example, as the demand for recycled goods increases, the cost of recycling will be reduced. Out-of-date statistics will skew any argument about the cost of recycling. Another problem with data is their occasional lack of relevance. For example, in arguing that an adequate ozone layer is necessary for preventing skin cancer, it is not relevant to cite statistics on the alarming rise of lung cancer.

Call into Question the Credibility of an Authority

If an opposing argument is based on testimony, you can undermine its persuasiveness if you show that a person being cited lacks up-to-date or relevant expertise in the field. (This procedure is different from the *ad hominem* fallacy discussed in Appendix 1 because it attacks not the personal character of the authority but the authority's expertise on a specific matter.)

Question the Accuracy or Context of Quotations

Evidence based on testimony is frequently distorted by being either misquoted or taken out of context. Often scientists will qualify their findings heavily, but these qualifications will be omitted by the popular media. You can thus attack the use of a quotation by putting it in its original context or by restoring the qualifications accompanying the quotation in its original source.

Question the Way Statistical Data Were Produced or Interpreted

Chapter 6 provides fuller treatment of how to question statistics. In general, you can rebut statistical evidence by calling into account how the data were gathered, treated mathematically, or interpreted. It can make a big difference, for example, whether you cite raw numbers or percentages or whether you choose large or small increments for the axes of graphs.

Conceding to Opposing Views

In writing a classical argument, a writer must sometimes concede to an opposing argument rather than refute it. Sometimes you encounter portions of an argument that you simply can't refute. For example, suppose you support the legalization of hard drugs such as cocaine and heroin. Adversaries argue that legalizing hard drugs will increase the number of drug users and addicts. You might dispute the size of their numbers, but you reluctantly agree that they are right. Your strategy in this case is not to refute the opposing argument but to concede to it by admitting that legalization of hard drugs will promote heroin and cocaine addiction. Having made that concession, your task is then to show that the benefits of drug legalization still outweigh the costs you have just conceded.

As this example shows, the strategy of a concession argument is to switch from the field of values employed by the writer you disagree with to a different field of values more favorable to your position. You don't try to refute the writer's stated reason and grounds (by arguing that legalization will *not* lead to increased drug usage and addiction) or his warrant (by arguing that increased drug use and addiction is not a problem). Rather, you shift the argument to a new field of values by introducing a new warrant, one that you think your audience can share (that the benefits of legalization—eliminating the black market and ending the crime and violence associated with procurement of drugs—outweigh the costs of increased addiction). To the extent that opponents of legalization share your desire to stop drug-related crime, shifting to this new field of values is a good strategy. Although it may seem that you weaken your own position by conceding to an opposing argument, you may actually strengthen it by increasing your credibility and gaining your audience's goodwill. Moreover, conceding to one part of an opposing argument doesn't mean that you won't refute other parts of that argument.

APPEALING TO A RESISTANT AUDIENCE: DELAYED-THESIS OR ROGERIAN ARGUMENT

Classical argument is effective for neutral or undecided audiences, but it is often less effective for audiences strongly opposed to the writer's position. Because resisting audiences often hold values, assumptions, or beliefs widely different from the writer's, they are unswayed by classical argument, which attacks their worldview too directly. On many values-laden issues such as abortion, gun control, gay rights, and welfare reform the distance between a writer and a resisting audience can be so great that dialog hardly seems possible.

Because of these wide differences in basic beliefs and values, a writer's goal is seldom to convert resistant readers to the writer's position. The best that the writer can hope for is to reduce somewhat the level of resistance, perhaps by opening a channel of conversation, increasing the reader's willingness to listen, and preparing the way for future dialogue. If you can get a resistant audience to say, "Well, I still don't agree with you, but I now understand you better and respect your views more," you will have been highly successful.

Delayed-Thesis Argument

In many cases you can reach a resistant audience by using a *delayed-thesis* structure in which you wait until the end of your argument to reveal your thesis. Classical argument asks you to state your thesis in the introduction, support it with reasons and evidence, and then summarize and refute opposing views. Rhetorically, however, it is not always advantageous to tell your readers where you stand at the start of your argument or to separate yourself so definitively from alternative views. For resistant audiences, it may be better to keep the issue open, delaying the revelation of your own position until the end of the essay.

To illustrate the different effects of classical versus delayed-thesis arguments, we invite you to read a delayed-thesis argument by nationally syndicated columnist Ellen Goodman. The article appeared shortly after the nation was shocked by a brutal gang rape in New Bedford, Massachusetts, in which a woman was raped on a pool table by patrons of a local bar.*

Minneapolis Pornography Ordinance
Ellen Goodman

1   Just a couple of months before the pool-table gang rape in New Bedford, Mass., *Hustler* magazine printed a photo feature that reads like a blueprint for the actual crime. There were just two differences between *Hustler* and real life. In *Hustler,* the woman enjoyed it. In real life, the woman charged rape.

2   There is no evidence that the four men charged with this crime had actually read the magazine. Nor is there evidence that the spectators who yelled encouragement for two hours had held previous ringside seats at pornographic events. But there is a growing sense that the violent pornography being peddled in this country helps to create an atmosphere in which such events occur.

3   As recently as last month, a study done by two University of Wisconsin researchers suggested that even "normal" men, prescreened college students, were changed by their exposure to violent pornography. After just ten hours of viewing, reported researcher Edward Donnerstein, "the men were less likely to convict in a rape trial, less likely to see injury to a victim, more likely to see the victim as responsible." Pornography may not cause rape directly, he said, "but it maintains a lot of very callous attitudes. It justifies aggression. It even says you are doing a favor to the victim."

*The rape occurred in 1985 and was later made the subject of an Academy Award–winning movie, *The Accused,* starring Jodie Foster.

If we can prove that pornography is harmful, then shouldn't the victims have legal   4
rights? This, in any case, is the theory behind a city ordinance that recently passed the Minneapolis City Council. Vetoed by the mayor last week, it is likely to be back before the
Council for an overriding vote, likely to appear in other cities, other towns. What is unique
about the Minneapolis approach is that for the first time it attacks pornography, not because
of nudity or sexual explicitness, but because it degrades and harms women. It opposes
pornography on the basis of sex discrimination.

University of Minnesota Law Professor Catherine MacKinnon, who co-authored the   5
ordinance with feminist writer Andrea Dworkin, says that they chose this tactic because
they believe that pornography is central to "creating and maintaining the inequality of
the sexes. . . . Just being a woman means you are injured by pornography."

They defined pornography carefully as, "the sexually explicit subordination of   6
women, graphically depicted, whether in pictures or in words." To fit their legal definition it must also include one of nine conditions that show this subordination, like
presenting women who "experience sexual pleasure in being raped or . . . muti-
lated. . . ." Under this law, it would be possible for a pool-table rape victim to sue
Hustler. It would be possible for a woman to sue if she were forced to act in a pornographic movie. Indeed, since the law describes pornography as oppressive to all women,
it would be possible for any woman to sue those who traffic in the stuff for violating her
civil rights.

In many ways, the Minneapolis ordinance is an appealing attack on an appalling prob-   7
lem. The authors have tried to resolve a long and bubbling conflict among those who have
both a deep aversion to pornography and a deep loyalty to the value of free speech. "To
date," says Professor MacKinnon, "people have identified the pornographer's freedom with
everybody's freedom. But we're saying that the freedom of the pornographer is the subordination of women. It means one has to take a side."

But the sides are not quite as clear as Professor MacKinnon describes them. Nor is the   8
ordinance.

Even if we accept the argument that pornography is harmful to women—and I do—   9
then we must also recognize that anti-Semitic literature is harmful to Jews and racist literature is harmful to blacks. For that matter, Marxist literature may be harmful to government
policy. It isn't just women versus pornographers. If women win the right to sue publishers
and producers, then so could Jews, blacks, and a long list of people who may be able to
prove they have been harmed by books, movies, speeches or even records. The Manson
murders, you may recall, were reportedly inspired by the Beatles.

We might prefer a library or book store or lecture hall without *Mein Kampf* or the   10
Grand Whoever of the Ku Klux Klan. But a growing list of harmful expressions would inevitably strangle freedom of speech.

This ordinance was carefully written to avoid problems of banning and prior restraint,   11
but the right of any woman to claim damages from pornography is just too broad. It seems
destined to lead to censorship.

What the Minneapolis City Council has before it is a very attractive theory. What   12
MacKinnon and Dworkin have written is a very persuasive and useful definition of pornography. But they haven't yet resolved the conflict between the harm of pornography and the
value of free speech. In its present form, this is still a shaky piece of law.

Consider now how this argument's rhetorical effect would be different if Ellen Goodman had revealed her thesis in the introduction, using the classical argument form. Here is how this introduction might have looked:

GOODMAN'S INTRODUCTION REWRITTEN IN CLASSICAL FORM

Just a couple of months before the pool-table gang rape in New Bedford, Mass., *Hustler* magazine printed a photo feature that reads like a blueprint for the actual crime. There were just two differences between *Hustler* and real life. In *Hustler,* the woman enjoyed it. In real life, the woman charged rape. Of course, there is no evidence that the four men charged with this crime had actually read the magazine. Nor is there evidence that the spectators who yelled encouragement for two hours had held previous ringside seats at pornographic events.

But there is a growing sense that the violent pornography being peddled in this country helps to create an atmosphere in which such events occur. One city is taking a unique approach to attack this problem. An ordinance recently passed by the Minneapolis City Council outlaws pornography not because it contains nudity or sexually explicit acts, but because it degrades and harms women. Unfortunately, despite the proponents' good intentions, the Minneapolis ordinance is a bad law because it has potentially dangerous consequences.

Even though Goodman's position can be grasped more quickly in this classical form, our students generally find the original delayed-thesis version more effective. Why is this? Most people point to the greater sense of complexity and surprise in the delayed-thesis version, a sense that comes largely from the delayed discovery of the writer's position. The classical version immediately labels the ordinance a "bad law," but the original version withholds judgment, inviting the reader to examine the law more sympathetically and to identify with the position of those who drafted it. Rather than distancing herself from those who see pornography as a violation of women's rights, Goodman shares with her readers her own struggles to think through these issues, thereby persuading us of her genuine sympathy for the ordinance and for its feminist proponents. In the end, her delayed thesis renders her final rejection of the ordinance not only more surprising but more convincing.

Clearly, then, a writer's decision about when to reveal her thesis is critical. Revealing the thesis early makes the writer seem more hard-nosed, more sure of her position, more confident about how to divide the ground into friendly and hostile camps, more in control. Delaying the thesis, in contrast, complicates the issues, increases reader sympathy for more than one view, and heightens interest in the tension among alternative views and in the writer's struggle for clarity.

Rogerian Argument

An even more powerful strategy for addressing resistant audiences is a conciliatory strategy often called *Rogerian argument,* named after psychologist Carl

Rogers, who used this strategy to help people resolve differences.* Rogerian argument emphasizes "empathic listening," which Rogers defined as the ability to see an issue sympathetically from another person's perspective. He trained people to withhold judgment of another person's ideas until after they listened attentively to the other person, understood that person's reasoning, appreciated that person's values, respected that person's humanity—in short, walked in that person's shoes. Before disagreeing with another person, Rogers told his clients, you must be able to summarize that person's argument so accurately that he or she will say, "Yes, you understand my position."

What Carl Rogers understood is that traditional methods of argumentation are threatening. When you try to persuade people to change their minds on an issue, Rogers claimed, you are actually demanding a change in their worldview—to get other people, in a sense, to quit being their kinds of persons and start being your kind of person. Research psychologists have shown that individuals are often not swayed by a logical argument if it somehow threatens their own view of the world. Carl Rogers was therefore interested in finding ways to make arguments less threatening. In Rogerian argument the writer typically waits until the end of the essay to present his position, and that position is often a compromise between the writer's original views and those of the resisting audience. Because Rogerian argument stresses the psychological as well as logical dimensions of argument, and because it emphasizes reducing threat and building bridges rather than winning an argument, it is particularly effective for dealing with emotionally laden issues.

Under Rogerian strategy, the writer reduces the sense of threat in her argument by showing that *both writer and resistant audience share many basic values.* Instead of attacking the audience as wrongheaded, the Rogerian writer respects her audience's intelligence and humanity and demonstrates an understanding of the audience's position before presenting her own position. Finally, the Rogerian writer never asks the audience to capitulate entirely to the writer's side—just to shift somewhat toward the writer's views. By acknowledging that he or she has already shifted toward the audience's views, the writer makes it easier for the audience to accept compromise. All of this negotiation ideally leads to a compromise between—or better, a synthesis of—the opposing positions.

The key to successful Rogerian argument, besides the art of listening, is the ability to point out areas of agreement between the writer's and reader's positions. For example, if you support a woman's right to choose abortion and you are arguing with someone completely opposed to abortion, you're unlikely to convert your reader but you might reduce the level of resistance. You begin this process by summarizing your reader's position sympathetically, stressing your

---

*See Carl Rogers's essay "Communication: Its Blocking and Its Facilitation" in his book *On Becoming a Person* (Boston: Houghton, 1961), 329–37. For a fuller discussion of Rogerian argument, see Richard Young, Alton Becker, and Kenneth Pike, *Rhetoric: Discovery and Change* (New York: Harcourt, 1972).

shared values. You might say, for example, that you also value babies; that you also are appalled by people who treat abortion as a form of birth control; that you also worry that the easy acceptance of abortion diminishes the value society places on human life; and that you also agree that accepting abortion lightly can lead to lack of sexual responsibility. Building bridges like these between you and your readers makes it more likely that they will listen to you when you present your own position.

In its emphasis on establishing common ground, Rogerian argument has much in common with recent feminist theories of argument. Many feminists criticize classical argument as rooted in a male value system and tainted by metaphors of war and combat. Thus, classical arguments, with their emphasis on assertion and refutation, are typically praised for being "powerful," "forceful," or "disarming." The writer "defends" his position and "attacks" his "opponent's" position using facts and data as "ammunition" and reasons as "big guns" to "blow away" his opponent's claim. According to some feminists, viewing argument as war can lead to inauthenticity, posturing, and game playing. The traditional pro-con debate—defined in one desk dictionary as "a formal contest of argumentation in which two opposing teams defend and attack a given proposition"—treats argument as verbal jousting, more concerned to determine a winner than to clarify an issue.

One of our woman students, who excelled as a debater in high school and received straight A's in argument classes, recently explained in an essay her growing alienation from male rhetoric: "Although women students are just as likely to excel in 'male' writing . . . we are less likely to feel as if we were saying something authentic and true." Later the student elaborated on her distrust of "persuasion":

> What many writing teachers have told me is that "the most important writing/ speaking you will ever do will be to persuade someone." My experience as a person who has great difficulty naming and expressing emotions is that the most important communication in my life is far more likely to be simply telling someone how I feel. To say "I love you," or "I'm angry with you," will be far more valuable in most relationship contexts than to say "These are the three reasons why you shouldn't have done what you did. . . ."*

Writers who share this woman's distrust of classical argumentation often find Rogerian argument appealing because it stresses self-examination, clarification, and accommodation rather than refutation. Rogerian argument is more in tune with win-win negotiation than with win-lose debate.

To illustrate a conciliatory or Rogerian approach to an issue, here is how one student wrote a letter to her boss recommending a change in the kind of merchandise stocked in a small town music store.

---

*Our thanks to Catherine Brown for this paragraph from an unpublished paper written at Seattle University.

Letter to Beth Downey

Ms. Beth Downey, Owner/Manager
Downey's Music
Grayfish

Dear Ms. Downey:

I would just like to comment on the success of "Downey's Music" in Grayfish and say that,   1
as owner and manager, you have done a wonderful job. I'm sure that you have the most extensive classical music, music teaching books, piano and acoustic guitar inventory of any store in a 100-square-mile area. After working for you for three years, I have encountered music teachers and classical music lovers coming as far as 70 miles to buy their music from Downey's. All have had nothing but compliments for you and for the store. However, I would once again like to bring up the subject of introducing an inventory of electronic music equipment to the store. Since Grayfish is mainly a tourist town, many times a week I have people from touring bands, visiting Canadians, and also locals coming into the store looking for such things as electronic keyboards, electric guitars, and amplifiers. I know that you have qualms about this idea, but I believe that I have a suggestion that we could both agree on.

First, let me restate your reasons for objecting to such a move. You have already stated   2
that if a change will benefit the store, the initial investment is well worth the expense in the long run (e.g., when pianos were added to the inventory). Therefore, I assume that cost is not a factor at this time. However, you feel that the "kind of people" that electronics may draw could possibly offend our present clientele. You feel, as well as others, that the people who are drawn by electronics are often long haired, dirty, and give a bad impression. This would in effect change the store's image. Also, you are afraid that the noise caused by these instruments could turn classical music lovers away from the store. The sounds of electronic instruments are not always pleasing, and since most of our clientele are older, more refined persons, you feel that these sounds will force some to go to other stores. Mainly, however, you are worried about the result that the change in the store's image could have upon a community the size of Grayfish. Many people in this area, I realize, feel that electronic music means heavy rock music, while this in turn means alcohol and drugs.

Basically, I agree with you that Grayfish needs a "classical" music store and that the culture that your store brings to Grayfish greatly enhances the area. I also love classical   3
music and want to see it growing and alive. I also have some of the same fears about adding electronic music to the inventory. I enjoy the atmosphere of Downey's, and I have always enjoyed working there, so I don't want to see anything adverse happen to it, either. On the other hand, I feel that if a large electronic music section were added to the store with soundproof rooms, a "sit and try it" atmosphere, and a catalog inventory large enough to special order anything that a customer might want that is not in the store, it would help immensely in the success of the store. With the way that Downey's is built, on two levels, it would be very easy to accommodate the needs of both departments. Even now we are only using about half the floor space available, while the rest is empty storage area. By

building soundproof rooms on the lower level, we could easily double the in-use floor area, increase our tourist clientele, have the music business in *all* areas cornered for approximately 60 square miles, and also add practice rooms for our present customers to use when they are choosing music.

4   I know that you are wrestling with this idea of such a drastic changeover, so I would like to propose a nonthreatening, easy-to-reverse first step. My solution is to start slowly, on a trial basis, and see how it works. I suggest that we start with a few small electronic keyboards, a few electric guitars, and one or two amps. In this way, we could begin to collect the information and literature on other electronic equipment that may be added later on, see how the community responds to such a move, find out how our present clientele reacts, get a feel for the demand in this field, and yet still be a small hometown music store without a great investment in this electronic area. I still feel that a large addition would be more successful, but I also believe that this little test may help prove to you, or disprove to me, that electronic music instruments in this area are in high demand. I honestly feel that electronics could produce fantastic profits for the people who get in the business first. I would love it if these "people" could be the owners and workers at Downey's Music.

Sincerely,

Mary Doe

FOR CLASS DISCUSSION

1. In this letter, what values shared by the writer and her audience does the writer stress?

2. Imagine the letter rewritten as a classical argument. How would it be different?

CONCLUSION

This chapter has shown you the difference between one-sided and multisided arguments and explained why multisided arguments are likely to be more persuasive to neutral or resisting audiences. A multisided argument generally includes a fair summary of differing views, followed by refutation, concession, or Rogerian synthesis. The strategies you use for treating resistant views depend on the audience you are trying to reach and your purpose. We explained how audiences can be placed on a scale of resistance ranging from "strongly supportive" to "strongly resistant." In addressing supportive audiences, writers typically compose one-sided arguments with strong motivational appeals to action. Neutral or undecided audiences generally respond most favorably to classical arguments that set out strong reasons in support of the writer's position and yet openly address alternative views, which are first summarized and then either rebutted or conceded to. When the audience is strongly resistant, a delayed-thesis or Rogerian strategy is most effective at reducing resistance and helping move the audience slightly toward the writer's views.

WRITING ASSIGNMENT FOR CHAPTERS 7 AND 8

The assignment for Chapters 7 and 8 has two parts. Part One is an argumentative essay that you will write. Part Two is your own self-reflective analysis on how you chose to appeal to and accommodate your audience.

Part One: For this assignment, argue against a popular cultural practice or belief that you think is wrong, or argue for an action or belief that you think is right even though it will be highly unpopular. Your claim, in other words, must be controversial—going against the grain of popular actions, values, and beliefs—so that you can predict considerable resistance to your views. This essay invites you to stand up for something you believe in even though your view will be highly contested. Your goal is to persuade your audience toward your position.

In writing and revising your argument, draw on appropriate strategies from Chapters 7 and 8. From Chapter 7 consider the concept of audience-based reasons and strategies for increasing your appeals to *ethos* and *pathos*. From Chapter 8 consider strategies for appealing to audiences according to their level of resistance. Choose the most resistant audience that you think you can sway to your point of view. Whether you use a refutation strategy, a delayed-thesis strategy, a Rogerian strategy, or some combination of these approaches is up to you.

Part Two: Attach to your argument a self-reflective letter to your instructor and classmates explaining and justifying the choices you made for appealing to your audience and accommodating their views. In your letter address questions such as the following:

1. At the most "resistant" end of the spectrum, why are people opposed to your claim? How does your claim challenge their views and perhaps threaten their own value system?
2. Whom did you picture as the audience you were trying to sway? Where on the spectrum from "accord" to "resistance" did you address your argument? Why?
3. What strategies did you use for appealing to that audience?
4. What choices did you make in trying to accommodate differing views?
5. What challenges did this assignment present for you? How successful do you think you were in meeting those challenges?

part three

Arguments in Depth

Six Types of Claims

9

An Introduction to the Types of Claims

In Part One we discussed the reading and writing of arguments, linking argument to both persuasion and inquiry. In Part Two we examined the internal structure of arguments and showed how persuasive writers link their arguments to the beliefs and values of their audiences. We also showed how writers can vary their content, structure, and style to reach audiences offering varying degrees of resistance to the writers' views.

Now in Part Three we examine arguments in depth by explaining six types of claims and by showing how each type has its own characteristic patterns of development and support. Because almost all arguments use one or more of these types of claims as basic argumentative "moves" or building blocks, knowing how to develop each claim type will advance your skills in argument. The types of claims to be examined in Part Three are related to an ancient rhetorical concept called *stasis*, from a Greek term meaning "stand" as in "to take a *stand* on something." There are many competing theories of stasis, so no two rhetoricians discuss stasis in exactly the same way. But all the theories have valuable components in common.

In Part Three we present our own version of stasis theory or, to use more ordinary language, our own approach to argument based on the types of claims. The payoff for you will be twofold. First, understanding the types of claims will help you to focus an argument and generate ideas for it. Second, a study of claim types teaches you characteristic patterns of support for each type, thereby helping you organize and develop your arguments.

AN OVERVIEW OF THE TYPES OF CLAIMS

To appreciate what a study of claim types can do, imagine one of those heated but frustrating arguments—let's suppose it's about gun control—where the question at issue keeps shifting. Everyone talks at cross-purposes, voice levels rising. No speaker's point seems to relate clearly to the previous speaker's. Rational discussion turns into a shouting match. Sometimes you can get such a discussion back on track if one person says, "Hold it for a moment. What are we actually disagreeing about here? Are we arguing about all guns or just handguns? Do we agree that gun ownership prevents crimes or not? Do we think that getting a gun license would be like getting a driver's license? Let's figure out what we agree on and where we disagree, because we can't debate all these questions at once." Whether she recognizes it or not, this person is applying the concept of claim types to get the argument focused.

To understand how claim types work, let's return to the concept of stasis. A *stasis* is an issue or question that focuses a point of disagreement. You and your audience might agree on the answer to Question A and so have nothing to argue about. Likewise you might agree on the answer to Question B. But on Question C you disagree. Question C constitutes a stasis where you and your audience diverge. It is the place where disagreement begins, where as an arguer you take a stand against another view. Thus you and your audience might agree that handgun ownership is legal. You might agree further that widespread ownership of handguns reduces crime. But if you ask the question "Is widespread handgun ownership a good thing?" you and your audience might disagree. This last question constitutes a stasis, the point where you and your audience part company.

Rhetoricians have discovered that the kinds of questions that divide people have classifiable patterns. In this text we identify six broad types of claims—each type originating in a different kind of question. To emphasize the structural pattern of each type, we will first use the letters X and Y to represent slots so that you can focus on the structure rather than the content of the claim type. Then we'll move quickly to actual examples. Here is a brief overview of the six claim types.

Type 1: Simple Categorical Arguments (Is X a Y? [Where You and Your Audience Agree on the Meaning of Y])

A categorical argument occurs when persons disagree about the category (Y) that a given thing (X) belongs to. A categorical question is said to be simple if there is no dispute about the meaning of the Y term. Here are three examples of questions leading to simple categorical arguments:

Was Richard Nixon a workaholic?

Is surfing the Internet a new kind of addiction?

Was Senator Weasel's vote for increased military spending politically motivated?

In these examples, we assume that writer and audience agree on the meaning of "workaholic," "addiction," and "politically motivated." At issue is whether Nixon, surfing the Internet, and Senator Weasel's vote for military spending belong to these categories.

The strategy for conducting a simple categorical argument is to provide examples or other evidence to show that X does or does not belong to category Y. Yes, Nixon was a workaholic (provide examples). Yes, surfing the Internet is a new kind of addiction (provide examples, testimony from psychologists). No, Senator Weasel's support for new weapons funding was not politically motivated (provide evidence that Weasel has a long record of pro-military spending). Simple categorical arguments are discussed in the first part of Chapter 10.

Type 2: Definitional Arguments (Is X a Y? [Where the Definition of Y Is Contested])

A categorical argument becomes more complex if you and your audience disagree about the meaning of the Y term. In this second type of claim, you have to define the Y term and defend your definition against objections and alternative definitions. Suppose, for example, you want to argue that using animals for medical research constitutes cruelty to animals. You would have to define what you mean by "cruelty to animals" and show how using animals for medical research fits your definition. Almost all legal disputes require definitional arguing because courts must determine whether an action meets or does not meet the criteria for a crime or civil tort as defined by a law, statute, or series of previous court rulings. Here are three examples of questions leading to definitional arguments:

Is the occasional telling of off-color jokes in the workplace an instance of sexual harassment?

Is flag burning constitutionally protected free speech?

Is Pluto a planet or an asteroid?

The general strategy for conducting a definitional argument is to define the second term and then argue whether the first term meets or does not meet the definition. We call this strategy *criteria-match arguing* because to define the second term you must specify the criteria that something must meet to fit the category, and then you must argue that your first term does or does not match these criteria. Definitional arguments are treated in depth in Chapter 10.

Type 3: Cause/Consequence Arguments (Does X Cause Y? Is Y a Consequence of X?)

Another major argument type entails cause-and-effect reasoning. Such arguments often arise from disagreements about the cause of an event or a trend: "What caused the crash of American Airlines Flight 800?" or "What causes teenage males to become violent?" Just as frequently, causal arguments arise from speculations about the possible consequences of an action: "What will be the consequences of changing from a progressive to a flat income tax?" "Will gun control legislation reduce violence in the schools?"

The general strategy for conducting causal arguments is to describe the chain of events that lead from X to Y. If a causal chain cannot be directly established, you can argue indirectly, using inductive methods, statistical analyses, or analogies. Causal arguments are treated in detail in Chapter 11.

Type 4: Resemblance Arguments (Is X like Y?)

A fourth argument type involves disputes about appropriate analogies or precedents. Suppose you disapproved of investing in the stock market and wanted to argue that stock market investing is like gambling. In showing the similarities between investing and gambling, you would be making a resemblance argument. Here are three examples of questions that lead to resemblance arguing:

> Was Slobodan Milosovic's policy of "ethnic cleansing" in Kosovo like Hitler's "final solution" against the Jews?
>
> Is killing starlings in your attic like killing rats in your attic? (Are starlings like rats?)
>
> Does pornography disparage women the way neo-Nazi propaganda disparages people of color? (Is pornography like racist propaganda?)

The general strategy for resemblance arguments is to compare the first term to the second, pointing out similarities between them (if your goal is to make X like Y) or differences between them (if your goal is to make X unlike Y). Resemblance arguments are covered in Chapter 12.

Type 5: Evaluation Arguments (Is X Good or Bad? Is X a Good or Bad Y?)

Categorical, causal, and resemblance arguments (types 1–4) are often called reality or truth arguments. In such arguments, people question the way things are, were, or will be; they are disagreeing about the nature of reality. In contrast, evaluation and proposal arguments (types 5 and 6) deal with values, what people consider important, good, or worth doing. Although a person's values often begin as feelings founded on personal experience, they can nevertheless form the basis of reasonable argument in the public sphere if they are articulated and justified. When you articulate your values, explain their source (if necessary), and apply them consistently to specific cases, you make your values transpersonal and shareable, and you can use them to build coherent and reasonable arguments.

Evaluation arguments (type 5) ask questions about whether X is good or bad. Here are three examples of evaluation questions:

Is a European-style, single-payer health insurance system a good policy for the United States to enact?

Is acquiring job experience between college and graduate school a good career plan?

Is a sports utility vehicle a good urban vehicle?

The general strategy for evaluation arguments uses criteria-match arguing similar to that used for definitional arguments: You first establish your criteria for "good" in the specific case and then show how your first term does or does not meet the criteria. Evaluation arguments are covered in Chapter 13. A special category of evaluation arguments—dealing with ethical or moral issues (for example, "Is it morally justifiable to spank children?" or "Are cloning experiments ethical?")—is treated in Chapter 15.

Type 6: Proposal Arguments
(Should We Do X?)

Whereas argument types 1–5 all involve changing your audience's beliefs about something—whether about reality (types 1–4) or about the value of something (type 5)—proposal arguments call for action. Proposals ask your audience to do something, to act in some way. Typically, proposals use words like *should, ought,* or *must* followed by an action of some kind. The following questions would all lead to proposal arguments:

Should the United States shift from a progressive to a flat income tax?

Should teens who commit crimes receive the same sentences as adult criminals?

Should gay marriages be legalized?

The most typical strategy for making proposal arguments is to follow a problem-solution-justification structure: The opening section convinces the audience that a problem exists. The second section proposes a solution to solve the problem. The last section justifies the solution by demonstrating that the benefits of acting on the proposal outweigh the costs or that the inherent "rightness" of the solution (on moral grounds) compels action. Proposal arguments are covered in Chapter 14.

FOR CLASS DISCUSSION

Working as a whole class or in small groups, decide which claim type is represented by each of the following questions. Sometimes the argument categories overlap or blend together. For example, the question "Is airline travel safe" might be considered either a simple categorical question or an evaluation question.

1. Should violent video games be made illegal?

2. How effective is aspirin in reducing the risk for heart attacks and stroke?

3. Why is anorexia nervosa primarily a disease of white, middle-class females?

4. Is depression in the elderly common in Asian cultures?

5. Will military intervention in Country X be like U.S. intervention in Vietnam or like U.S. intervention in Iraq?

6. Should professional baseball impose a salary cap on its superstar players?

7. Is this Web site racist?

8. Is tobacco a drug?

9. Are Nike's Asian shoe factories sweatshops?

10. What causes American girls to lose self-esteem when they reach puberty?

WHAT IS THE VALUE OF STUDYING CLAIM TYPES?

Having provided an overview of the types of claims, we conclude this chapter by showing you two substantial benefits you will derive from knowing about each type: help in focusing and generating ideas for an argument and help in organizing an argument.

Help in Focusing an Argument and Generating Ideas

Knowing the different types of claims can help you focus an argument and generate ideas for it. Understanding claim types helps you focus by asking you to determine what's at stake between you and your audience. Where do you and your audience agree and disagree? What are the questions at issue? It helps you generate ideas by guiding you to pose questions that suggest lines of development.

To illustrate, let's take a hypothetical case—one Isaac Charles Little (affectionately known as I. C. Little), who desires to chuck his contact lenses and undergo the new lasik procedure to cure his nearsightedness. ("Lasik" is the common name for laser in-situ keratomileusis, a recent advance in surgical treatments for myopia. Sometimes known as "flap and zap" surgery, it involves using a laser to cut a layer of the corneal tissue thinner than a human hair and then flattening the cornea. It's usually not covered by insurance and is quite expensive.) I.C. has two different arguments he'd like to make: (1) He'd like to talk his parents into helping him pay for the procedure. (2) He'd like to convince insurance companies that the lasik procedure should be covered by standard medical insurance policies.

In the discussions that follow, note how the six types of claims can help I.C. identify points of disagreement for each audience and simultaneously suggest lines of argument for persuading each. Note too how the questions at issue vary for each audience.

First imagine what might be at stake in I.C.'s discussions with his parents:

Claim-Type Analysis: Parents as Audience

- *Simple categorical argument:* I.C.'s parents will be concerned about the safety and effectiveness of this procedure. Is lasik safe? Is it effective? (These are the first questions at issue. I.C.'s mom has heard a horror story about an earlier surgical procedure for myopia, so I.C. knows he will have to persuade her that lasik is safe and effective.)

- *Definitional argument:* With parents as audience, I.C. will have to define what lasik surgery is so they won't have misconceptions about what is involved. However, he can't think of any arguments that would ensue over this definition, so he proceeds to the next claim type.

- *Causal argument:* Both parents will question I.C.'s underlying motivation for seeking this surgery. "What causes you to want this lasik procedure?" they will ask. (I.C.'s dad, who has worn eyeglasses all his adult life, will not be swayed by cosmetic desires. "If you don't like contacts," he will say, "just wear glasses.") Here I.C. needs to argue that permanently correcting his nearsightedness will improve his quality of life. I.C. decides to emphasize his desire for an active, outdoor life, and especially his passion for water sports including swimming and scuba diving, where his need for contacts or glasses is a serious handicap. Also, I.C. says that if he doesn't have to wear contacts he can get a summer job as a lifeguard.

- *Resemblance argument:* I.C. can't think of any resemblance questions at issue.

- *Evaluation argument:* When the pluses and minuses are weighed, is lasik a good thing? Would the results of the surgery be beneficial enough to justify the cost and the risks? In terms of costs, I.C. might argue that even though the procedure is initially expensive (from $1,000 to $4,000), over the years he will save money by not needing contacts or glasses. The pleasure of seeing well in the water and not being bothered by contacts or glasses while hiking and camping constitutes a major psychological benefit. (He decides to leave out the cosmetic benefits—I.C. thinks he'll look cooler without glasses—because his dad thinks wearing glasses is fine.)

- *Proposal argument:* Should I.C. (or a person in general) get this operation for treatment of myopia? (All the previous points of disagreement are subissues related to this overarching proposal issue.)

What this example should help you see is that the values arguments in the last two claim types (evaluation and proposal) depend on the writer's resolving related reality/truth questions in one or more of the first four types (simple categorical, definitional, cause, resemblance). In this particular case, before convincing his parents that they should help him pay for the lasik procedure (I.C.'s proposal claim), I.C. would need to convince them that the procedure is safe and effective (simple categorical arguments), that having the surgery would significantly improve the quality of I.C.'s life (causal argument), and that the benefits outweigh the costs (evaluation argument). Almost all arguments combine subarguments in this way so that lower-order claims provide supporting materials for addressing higher-order claims.

The previous illustration focused on parents as audience. If we now switch audiences, we can use our theory of claim types to identify different questions at issue. Let's suppose I.C. wants to persuade insurance companies to cover the lasik procedure. He imagines insurance company decision makers as his primary audience, along with the general public and state legislators who may be able to influence them.

Claim-Type Analysis: Insurance Decision Makers as Audience

- *Simple categorical argument:* No disagreements come immediately to mind. (This audience shares I.C.'s belief that lasik is safe and effective.)
- *Definitional argument:* Should lasik be considered "cosmetic surgery" (as insurance companies contend) or "medically justifiable surgery" (as I.C. contends)? This definitional question constitutes a major stasis. I.C. wants to convince his audience that lasik belongs in the category "medically justifiable surgery" rather than "cosmetic surgery." He will need to define "medically justifiable surgery" in such a way that lasik can be included.
- *Causal argument:* What will be the consequences to insurance companies and to the general public of making insurance companies pay for lasik? For this audience, consequence issues are crucial. Will insurance companies be deluged with claims? What will happen to insurance rates? Will optometrists and eyeglass manufacturers go out of business?
- *Resemblance argument:* Does lasik more resemble a facelift (not covered by insurance) or plastic surgery to repair a cleft palate (covered by insurance)?
- *Evaluation argument:* Would it be good for society as a whole if insurance companies had to pay for lasik?
- *Proposal argument:* Should insurance companies be required to cover lasik?

As this analysis shows, the questions at issue change when you consider a different audience. Now the chief question at issue is definition: Is lasik cosmetic surgery or medically justifiable surgery? I.C. needs to spend no time arguing that the surgery is safe and effective (major concerns for his parents); instead he must establish criteria for "medically justifiable surgery" and then argue that lasik meets these criteria. Again note how the higher-order issues of value depend on resolving one or more lower-order issues of truth/reality.

So what can a study of claim types teach you about focusing an argument and generating ideas? First it teaches you to analyze what's at stake between you and your audience by determining major points of disagreement. Second, it shows you that you can make any of the claim types your argument's major focus. Rather than tackle a values issue, you might tackle only a reality/truth issue. You could, for example, focus an entire argument on the simple categorical question "Is lasik safe?" (an argument requiring you to research the medical literature). Likewise you could write a causal argument focusing on what might happen to optometrists and eyeglass manufacturers if the insurance industry decided to cover lasik. Often arguers jump too quickly to issues of value without first resolving issues of reality/truth. Finally, a study of claim types helps you pose questions that generate ideas and suggest lines of reasoning. Later in Part Three we will show you a particularly powerful way of using lower-order questions about reality/truth to generate supporting ideas for a proposal argument (see Chapter 14, pp. 220–23).

FOR CLASS DISCUSSION

Select an issue familiar to most members of the class—perhaps a current campus issue, an issue prominent in the local or national news, or an issue that the class has recently discussed—and analyze it using our sequence of claim types. Consider how a writer or speaker might address two different audiences on this issue. Hypothesizing the writer/speaker's perspective and claim, make a list of points of agreement and disagreement for both audiences, using as a pattern our claim type analyses for lasik.

Help in Organizing and Developing an Argument

The second main benefit of studying claim types will become clearer as you read the chapters in Part Three. Because each type of claim has its own characteristic pattern of development, learning these patterns will help you organize and develop your arguments. Studying claim types shows you how different arguments are typically structured, teaching you generic moves needed in many different kinds of argumentative situations. If, for example, you make a proposal claim, a study of claim types will show you the generic moves typically needed in proposal arguments. If one of your supporting reasons is a definitional claim or an evaluation claim, study of claim types will show you how to do the criteria-match arguing typical of such claims. Likewise such a study shows you how to develop each of the other claim types to help you construct arguments that tap into your audience's values and that include strong support to overcome your audience's resistance. In the following chapters in Part Three, we discuss each claim type in depth.

10 Categorical and Definitional Arguments

X Is (Is Not) a Y

EXAMPLE CASE

The impeachment trial of President Bill Clinton, following his affair with Monica Lewinsky, involved a number of definitional issues: Did Clinton's behavior with Lewinsky and his evasions of the truth while testifying to a grand jury in the Paula Jones lawsuit constitute "Treason, Bribery, or other high Crimes and Misdemeanors"—the constitutional phrase that describes an impeachable offense? More narrowly, did Clinton's testimony in the Paula Jones lawsuit, when he denied having sexual relations with Monica Lewinsky, constitute "perjury"? More narrowly still, did Clinton's behavior with Monica Lewinsky meet the legal definition of *sexual relations*? At each of these levels of debate, lawyers and pundits put forth competing definitions of these disputed terms and argued that Clinton's actions did or did not meet the definitions.

AN OVERVIEW OF CATEGORICAL ARGUMENTS

Categorical arguments are among the most common argument types you will encounter. They can occur whenever you claim that any given X belongs in category Y. Did NATO bombing of Serbia during the Kosovo crisis belong in the category "a just war"? Does skateboarding belong in the category "a true sport"? Does my swerving across the center lane while trying to slap a bee on my windshield belong in the category "reckless driving"?

We place items in categories all the time, and the categories we choose can have subtle but powerful rhetorical effects, creating implicit mini-arguments. Consider, for example, the competing categories proposed for whales in an international whaling controversy accelerated in the late 1990s by the Makah Indians' pursuit of their U.S. treaty rights to hunt whales. What category does a whale belong to? Some arguers placed whales in the category "sacred animals" that should never be killed because of their intelligence, beauty, grace, and power. Others grouped whales with tuna, crabs, cattle, and chickens in the category "renewable food resource." Others worried whether the specific kinds of whales being hunted were "an endangered species"—a concept that argues for the preservation of whale stocks but not necessarily for a ban on controlled hunting of individual whales once population numbers rise sufficiently. Each of these whaling arguments places whales within a different category that implicitly urges the reader to adopt that category's perspective on whaling.

Categorical claims shift from implicit to explicit arguments whenever the arguer supplies reasons and evidence to persuade us that X does or does not belong in category Y. In the rest of this chapter we discuss two kinds of categorical arguments: (1) simple categorical arguments in which writer and an audience agree on the meaning of the Y term and (2) definitional arguments in which the meaning of the Y term itself is controversial.

SIMPLE CATEGORICAL ARGUMENTS

A categorical argument can be said to be "simple" if there is no disagreement about the meaning of the Y term. For example, suppose you are discussing with fellow committee members whom to select as committee chairperson. You want to make the case that "David won't make a good committee chair because he is too bossy." Your supporting reason ("David is too bossy") is a simple categorical claim. You assume that everyone agrees what "bossy" means; the point of contention is whether David is or is not bossy. To support your claim, you would supply examples of David's bossiness; to refute it, someone else might supply counterexamples of David's cooperative and kind nature. As this example suggests, the basic procedural rule for developing a simple categorical claim is to supply examples and other data that show how X is or is not a member of category Y.

Difference between Facts and Simple Categorical Claims

Simple categorical claims are interpretive statements about reality. They claim that something does or does not exist or that something does or does not possess the qualities of a certain category. Often simple categorical claims look like facts, so it is important to distinguish between a fact and a simple categorical claim.

A *fact* is a statement that can be verified in some way, either by empirical observation or by reference to a reliable source (say, an encyclopedia) trusted by you and your audience. Here are some facts: Water freezes at 32 degrees. Boise is in

Idaho, not Montana. The bald eagle is no longer on the EPA's endangered species list. These are all facts because they can be verified; no supporting arguments are needed or called for.

In contrast, a *simple categorical claim* is a contestable interpretation of facts. Consider the difference between these two sentences:

Fact: The bald eagle is no longer on the EPA's endangered species list.

Simple categorical claim: The bald eagle is no longer an endangered species.

We can verify the factual statement by looking at the list of endangered species published by the Environmental Protection Agency. We can see the date on which the bald eagle was placed on the list and the date it was removed. The second statement is a claim. Imagine all the debates and arguments that EPA scientists had as they pored over statistical data about eagle population numbers and over field reports from observers of eagles before they decided to remove the bald eagle from the list.

FOR CLASS DISCUSSION

Working individually or in small groups, determine which of the following statements are facts and which are categorical claims. If you think a statement could be a "fact" for some audiences and a "claim" for others, explain your reasoning.

1. State sales taxes are not deductible on your federal income tax form.
2. State sales taxes are annoying to both buyers and sellers.
3. State sales taxes are a hardship on low income families.
4. *The Phantom Menace* is a George Lucas film.
5. *The Phantom Menace* is a racist movie.

Variations in the Wording of Simple Categorical Claims

Simple categorical claims typically take the grammatical structure "X is a Y." Grammarians describe this structure as a subject followed by a linking verb (such as "to be" or "to seem") followed by a predicate noun or adjective.

David is bossy.

State sales taxes are annoying.

The Phantom Menace is a racist movie.

But other grammatical constructions can be used to make the same categorical claims.

> David frequently bosses people around. (He belongs to the category "people who are bossy.")
>
> Sales taxes really annoy people. (Sales taxes belong to the category "things that are annoying.")
>
> Racism abounds in *The Phantom Menace*. (*The Phantom Menace* belongs to the category of things in which racism abounds.)

Almost any kind of interpretive statement about reality (other than causal statements, which are covered in Chapter 11) is a categorical claim of some kind. Whether they are worded directly as "X is Y" statements or disguised in different grammatical structures, they assert that item X belongs in category Y or possesses the features of category Y.

Supporting Simple Categorical Claims: Supply Examples

The basic strategy for supporting a simple categorical claim is to give examples or other data showing how X belongs in category Y. If you want to argue that Sam is a party animal, provide examples of his partying behavior. If you want to argue that *The Phantom Menace* is racist, give examples of its racist features. Because simple categorical arguments are common building blocks for longer, more complex arguments, they often take no more than one or two paragraphs inside a longer piece. But a simple categorical claim can also be the thesis for a whole argument. We provide such an example on pages 163–64, where columnist John Leo cites numerous examples from the *Star Wars* movie *Episode I: The Phantom Menace* to argue that this film "is packed with awful [racial] stereotypes."

Refuting Simple Categorical Claims

If you wish to challenge or question someone else's simple categorical claim, you have three common strategies at your disposal:

- *Deny the accuracy or truth of the examples and data.* "You say that David is bossy. But you are remembering incorrectly. That wasn't David who did those bossy things; that was Paul."
- *Provide counterexamples that place X in a different category.* "Well, maybe David acted bossy on a few occasions. But more often he is kind and highly cooperative. For example . . . ."
- *Raise definitional questions about the Y term.* "Well, that depends on what you mean by 'bossy.' What you call bossiness, I call decisiveness."

The last of these strategies shows how easily a simple categorical claim can slip into a definitional dispute. In the rest of this chapter we turn our attention to definitional arguments.

▼ FOR CLASS DISCUSSION

Working as a whole class or in small groups, prepare brief arguments in support of each of the following categorical claims. Then discuss ways in which you might call these claims into question.

1. Americans today are obsessed with their appearance.

2. Professional athletes are overpaid.

3. The video games most enjoyed by children are extremely violent.

AN OVERVIEW OF DEFINITIONAL ARGUMENTS

As we turn now to definitional arguments, it is important to distinguish between cases where definitions are *needed* and cases where definitions are *disputed*. Many arguments require a definition of key terms. If you are arguing, for example, that after-school jobs are harmful to teenagers because they promote materialism, you will probably need to define *materialism* somewhere in your argument. Writers regularly define key words for their readers by providing synonyms, by citing a dictionary definition, by stipulating a definition, or by some other means.

In the rest of this chapter, we focus on arguments in which the meaning of a key term is disputed. Consider, for example, the environmental controversy over the definition of *wetland*. Section 404 of the federal Clean Water Act provides for federal protection of wetlands but leaves the task of defining *wetland* to administrative agencies and the courts. Currently about 5 percent of the land surface of the contiguous forty-eight states is potentially affected by the wetlands provision, and 75 percent of this land is privately owned. Efforts to define *wetland* have created a battleground between pro-environment and pro-development (or pro–private property rights) groups. Farmers, homeowners, and developers often want a narrow definition so that more property is available for commercial or private use. Environmentalists favor a broad definition in order to protect different habitat types and maintain the environmental safeguards that wetlands provide (control of water pollution, spawning grounds for aquatic species, floodwater containment, and so forth).

The problem is that defining *wetland* is tricky. For example, one federal regulation defines a wetland as any area that has a saturated ground surface for twenty-one consecutive days during the year. But how would you apply this law to a pine flatwood ecosystem that was wet for ten days this year but thirty days last year? And how should the courts react to lawsuits claiming that the regulation itself is either too broad or too narrow? It is easy to see why the wetlands controversy provides hefty incomes for lawyers and congressional lobbyists.

THE CRITERIA-MATCH STRUCTURE OF DEFINITIONAL ARGUMENTS

As the wetlands example suggests, definitional arguments usually have a two-part structure—a definition part that tries to establish the meaning of the Y term (What do we mean by *wetland*?) and a match part that argues whether a given X meets that definition (Does this 30-acre parcel of land meet the criteria for wetlands?) We use the term *criteria-match* to describe this structure, which occurs regularly not only in definitional arguments but also in evaluation arguments of the type "X is (is not) a good Y" (see Chapter 13). The "criteria" part of the structure defines the Y term by setting forth the criteria that must be met for something to be considered a Y. The "match" part examines whether the X term meets these criteria.

Let's consider another example. Suppose you work for a consumer information group that wishes to encourage patronage of socially responsible companies while boycotting irresponsible ones. Your group's first task is to define *socially responsible company*. After much discussion and research, your group establishes three criteria that a company must meet to be considered socially responsible:

> *Your definition:* A company is socially responsible if it (1) avoids polluting the environment, (2) sells goods or services that contribute to the well-being of the community, and (3) treats its workers justly.

The criteria section of your argument would explain and illustrate these criteria. The match part of the argument would then try to persuade readers that a specific company does or does not meet the criteria. A typical thesis statement might be as follows:

> *Your thesis statement:* Although the Hercules Shoe Company is nonpolluting and provides a socially useful product, it is *not* a socially responsible company because it treats workers unjustly.

Here is how the core of the argument could be displayed in Toulmin terms (note how the criteria established in your definition serve as warrants for your argument):

INITIAL ENTHYMEME:	The Hercules Shoe Company is not a socially responsible company because it treats workers unjustly.
CLAIM:	The Hercules Shoe Company is *not* a socially responsible company.

STATED REASON:	because it treats workers unjustly
GROUNDS:	evidence that the company manufactures its shoes in East Asian sweatshops; evidence of the inhumane conditions in these shops; evidence of hardships imposed on displaced American workers
WARRANT:	Socially responsible companies treat workers justly.
BACKING:	arguments showing that just treatment of workers is right in principle and also benefits society; arguments that capitalism helps society as a whole only if workers achieve a reasonable standard of living, have time for leisure, and are not exploited
POSSIBLE CONDITIONS OF REBUTTAL	Opponents of this thesis might argue that justice needs to be considered from an emerging nation's standpoint: The wages paid workers are low by American standards but are above average by East Asian standards. Displacement of American workers is part of the necessary adjustment of adapting to a global economy and does not mean that a company is unjust.

As this Toulmin schema illustrates, the writer's argument needs to contain a criteria section (warrant and backing) showing that just treatment of workers is a criterion for social responsibility and a match section (stated reason and grounds) showing that the Hercules Shoe Company does not treat its workers justly. The conditions of rebuttal help the writer imagine alternative views and see places where opposing views need to be acknowledged and rebutted.

▼ FOR CLASS DISCUSSION

Consider the following definitional claims. Working as individuals or in small groups, identify the criteria issue and the match issue for each of the following claims.

EXAMPLE: A Honda assembled in Ohio is (is not) an American-made car.

CRITERIA PART: What criteria have to be met before a car can be called "American made"?

MATCH PART: Does a Honda assembled in Ohio meet these criteria?

1. Computer programming is (is not) a creative profession.

2. Writing graffiti on subways is (is not) vandalism.

3. American Sign Language is (is not) a "foreign language" for purposes of a college graduation requirement.

4. Beauty contests are (are not) sexist events.

5. Bungee jumping from a crane is (is not) a "carnival amusement ride" subject to state safety inspections.

CONCEPTUAL PROBLEMS OF DEFINITION

Before moving on to discuss ways of defining the Y term in a definitional argument, we should explore briefly some of the conceptual difficulties of definition. Language, for all its wonderful powers, is an arbitrary system that requires agreement among its users before it can work. And it's not always easy to get that agreement. In fact, the task of defining something can be devilishly complex.

Why Can't We Just Look in the Dictionary?

What's so hard about defining? you might ask. Why not just look in a dictionary? To get a sense of the complexity of defining something, consider again the word *wetland*. A dictionary can tell us the ordinary meaning (the way a word is commonly used), but it can't resolve a debate about competing definitions when different parties have interests in defining the word in different ways. For example, *Webster's Seventh New Collegiate Dictionary* defines *wetland* as "land containing much soil moisture"—a definition that is hardly helpful in determining whether the federal government can prevent the development of a beach resort on some landowner's private property. Moreover, dictionary definitions rarely tell us such things as *to what degree* a given condition must be met before something qualifies for class membership. How wet does land have to be before it is *legally* a wetland? How long does this wetness have to last? When is a wetland a mere swamp that ought to be drained rather than protected?

Definitions and the Rule of Justice: At What Point Does X Stop Being a Y?

For some people, all this concern about definition may seem misplaced. How often, after all, have you heard people accuse each other of getting bogged down in "mere semantics"? But how you define a given word can have significant implications for people who must either use the word or have the word used on them. Take, for example, what some philosophers refer to as the *rule of justice*. According to this rule, "beings in the same essential category should be treated in the same way." Should an insurance company, for example, treat anorexia nervosa as a physical illness like diabetes (in which case treatment is paid for by the insurance company) or as a mental illness like paranoia (in which case insurance payments are minimal)? Or, to take another example, if a company gives "new baby" leave to a mother, should it also give "new baby" leave to a father? In other words, is this kind of leave "new mother" leave or is it "new parent" leave? And what if a couple adopts an infant? Should "new mother" or "new parent" leave be available to adoptive parents also? These questions are all definitional issues involving arguments about what class of beings an individual belongs to and about what actions to take to comply with the rule of justice, which demands that all members of that class be treated equally.

The rule of justice becomes even harder to apply when we consider X's that grow, evolve, or otherwise change through time. When Young Person back in Chapter 1 argued that she could set her own curfew because she was mature, she raised the question "What are the attributes or criteria of a 'mature' person?" In this case, a categorical distinction between two separate kinds of things ("mature" versus "not mature") evolves into a distinction of degree ("mature enough"). So perhaps we should ask not whether Young Person is mature but whether she is "mature enough." At what point does a child become an adult? (When does a fetus become a human person? When does a social drinker become an alcoholic?)

Although we may be able arbitrarily to choose a particular point and declare, through stipulation, that "mature" means eighteen years old or that "human person" includes a fetus at conception, or at three months, or at birth, in the everyday world the distinction between child and adult, between egg and person, between social drinking and alcoholism seems an evolution, not a sudden and definitive step. Nevertheless, our language requires an abrupt shift between classes. In short, applying the rule of justice often requires us to adopt a digital approach to reality (switches are either on or off, either a fetus is a human person or it is not), whereas our sense of life is more analogical (there are numerous gradations between on and off; there are countless shades of gray between black and white).

As we can see by the preceding examples, the promise of language to fix what psychologist William James called "the buzz and confusion of the world" into an orderly set of categories turns out to be elusive. In most definitional debates, an argument, not a quick trip to the dictionary, is required to settle the matter.

KINDS OF DEFINITIONS

In this section we discuss two methods of definition commonly used in definitional arguments: Aristotelian and operational.

Aristotelian Definition

Aristotelian definitions, regularly used in dictionaries, define a term by placing it within the next larger class or category and then showing the specific attributes that distinguish the term from other terms within the same category. For example, a *pencil* is a "writing implement" (next larger category) that differs from other writing implements in that it makes marks with lead or graphite rather than ink. You could elaborate this definition by saying, "Usually the lead or graphite is a long, thin column embedded in a slightly thicker column of wood with an eraser on one end and a sharpened point, exposing the graphite, on the other." You could even distinguish a wooden pencil from a mechanical pencil, thereby indicating again that the crucial identifying attribute is the graphite, not the wooden column.

As you can see, an Aristotelian definition of a term identifies specific attributes or criteria that enable you to distinguish it from other members of the next larger class. We created an Aristotelian definition in our example about socially responsible companies. A *socially responsible company,* we said, is any company (next larger class) that meets three criteria: (1) It doesn't pollute the environment, (2) it creates goods/services that promote the well-being of the community, and (3) it treats its workers justly.

Operational Definition

In some rhetorical situations, particularly those arising in the physical and social sciences, writers need *operational definitions*—precise definitions that can be measured empirically and are not subject to problems of context and disputed criteria. Consider, for example, an argument involving the concept "aggression": "Do violent television programs increase the incidence of aggression in children?" To do research on this issue, a scientist needs a precise, measurable definition of *aggression.* Typically, a scientist might measure "aggression" by counting the number of blows or kicks a child gives to an inflatable bozo doll over a fifteen-minute period when other play options are available. The scientist might then define "aggressive behavior" as six or more blows to the bozo doll.

In our wetlands example, a federal authority created an operational definition of *wetland*: A wetland is a parcel of land that has a saturated ground surface for twenty-one consecutive days during the year. Such definitions are useful because they are precisely measurable, but they are also limited because they omit criteria that may be unmeasurable but important. Many scientists, for example, object to definitions of *wetland* based on consecutive days of wetness. What is more relevant, they argue, is not the duration of wetness in any parcel of land, but the kind of plants and animals that depend on the wetland as a habitat. As another example, we might ask whether it is adequate to define a "superior student" as someone with a 3.5 GPA or higher or a "successful sex education program" as one that results in a 25 percent reduction in teenage pregnancies. What important aspects of a superior student or a successful sex education program are not considered in these operational definitions?

STRATEGIES FOR DEFINING THE CONTESTED TERM IN A DEFINITIONAL ARGUMENT

In constructing criteria to define your contested term, you can take two basic approaches—what rhetoricians call reportive and stipulative definitions. A *reportive definition* cites how others have used the term. A *stipulative definition* cites how you define the term. You can take a reportive approach by turning to standard or specialized dictionaries, judicial opinions, or expert testimony to establish a definition based on the authority of others. A lawyer defining *wetland* as land with twenty-one consecutive days of saturated ground surface would be using a reportive definition with a federal regulation as her source. The other approach requires you to use your own critical thinking to stipulate a definition, thereby defining the contested term yourself. Our definition of *socially responsible company*, specifying three criteria, is a stipulative definition. This section explains these approaches in more detail.

Reportive Approach: Research How Others Have Used the Term

When you take a reportive approach, you research how others have used the term, searching for authoritative definitions acceptable to your audience yet favorable to your case. Student writer Kathy Sullivan uses this approach in her argument that photographs displayed at the Oncore Bar are not obscene (see pp. 165–66). To define *obscenity*, she turns to *Black's Law Dictionary* and Pember's *Mass Media Laws*. (Specialized dictionaries are a standard part of the reference section of any library—see your reference librarian for assistance.) Other sources of specialized definitions are state and federal appellate court decisions, legislative and administrative statutes, and scholarly articles examining a given definitional conflict. Lawyers use this research strategy exhaustively when preparing court briefs. They begin by looking at the actual text of laws as passed by legislatures or written by administrative authorities. Then they look at all the court cases in which the laws have been tested, and they examine the ways courts have refined legal definitions and applied them to specific cases. Using these refined and elaborated definitions, lawyers then apply them to their own case at hand.

When research fails to uncover a definition favorable to the arguer's case, the arguer can sometimes adopt an *original intentions strategy*. For example, if a scientist is dissatisfied with definitions of *wetland* based on consecutive days of saturated ground surface, she might proceed as follows: "The original intention of the Congress in passing the Clean Water Act was to preserve the environment." What members of Congress intended, she could then claim, was to prevent development of those wetland areas that provide crucial habitat for wildlife or that inhibit water pollution. She could then propose an alternative definition (either a stipulative one that she develops herself or a reportive one that she uncovers in research) based on criteria other than consecutive days of ground saturation. (Of course, original intentions arguments can often be refuted by a "times have changed" strategy or by a "we can't know what they originally intended; we can only know what they wrote" strategy.)

Another way to make a reportive definition is to employ a strategy based on etymology, the *earlier meaning strategy*. Using an etymological dictionary or the *Oxford English Dictionary* (which traces the historical evolution of a word's meaning), an arguer can often unveil insights favorable to the writer's case. For example, if you wanted to argue that portrayal of violence in films is obscene, you could point to the etymology of the word *obscene*, which literally means "offstage." The word derives from classical Greek tragedy, in which violent acts occurred offstage and were only reported by a messenger. This strategy allows you to show how the word originally applied to violence rather than to sexual explicitness.

Stipulative Approach: Create Your Own Definition Based on Positive, Contrastive, and Borderline Cases*

Often you need to create your own definition of the contested term. An effective strategy for developing your own definition is to brainstorm examples of positive, contrastive, and borderline cases. Suppose, for example, you want to argue the claim that "computer programming is (is not) a creative activity." Your first goal is to establish criteria for creativity. You could begin by thinking of examples of obvious creative behaviors, then of contrastive behaviors that seem similar to the previous behaviors but yet are clearly not creative, and then finally of borderline behaviors that may or may not be creative. Your list might look like this:

EXAMPLES OF CREATIVE BEHAVIORS

Beethoven composes a violin concerto.

An architect designs a house.

Edison invents the light bulb.

---

*The defining strategies and collaborative exercises in this section are based on the work of George Hillocks and his research associates at the University of Chicago. See George Hillocks Jr., Elizabeth A. Kahn, and Larry R. Johannessen, "Teaching Defining Strategies as a Mode of Inquiry: Some Effects on Student Writing," *Research in the Teaching of English* 17 (Oct. 1983): 275–84. See also Larry R. Johannessen, Elizabeth A. Kahn, and Carolyn Calhoun Walter, *Designing and Sequencing Prewriting Activities* (Urbana: NCTE, 1982).

An engineer designs a machine that will make widgets in a new way.

A poet writes a poem. (Later revised to "A poet writes a poem that poetry experts say is beautiful"—see following discussion.)

CONTRASTIVE EXAMPLES OF NONCREATIVE BEHAVIORS

A conductor transposes Beethoven's concerto into a different key.

A carpenter builds a house from the architect's plan.

I change a lightbulb in my house.

A factory worker uses the new machine to stamp out widgets.

A graduate student writes sentimental "lovey-dovey" verses for greeting cards.

EXAMPLES OF BORDERLINE CASES

A woman gives birth to a child.

An accountant figures out your income tax.

A musician arranges a rock song for a marching band.

A monkey paints an oil painting by smearing paint on canvas; a group of art critics, not knowing a monkey was the artist, call the painting beautiful.

Next you can begin developing your criteria by determining what features "clearly creative" examples have in common and what features "clearly noncreative" examples lack. Then refine your criteria by deciding on what grounds you might include or eliminate your borderline cases from the category "creative." For example, you might begin with the following criterion:

DEFINITION: FIRST TRY

> For an act to be creative, it must result in an end product that is significantly different from other products.

But then, by looking at some of the examples in your creative and noncreative columns, you decide that just producing a different end product isn't enough. A bad poem might be different from other poems, but you don't want to call a bad poet creative. So you refine your criteria.

DEFINITION: SECOND TRY

> For an act to be creative, it must result in an end product that is significantly different from other products and is yet useful or beautiful.

This definition would allow you to include all the acts in your creative column but eliminate the acts in the noncreative column.

Your next step is to refine your criteria by deciding whether to include or reject items in your borderline list. You decide to reject the childbirth case by arguing that creativity must be a mental or intellectual activity, not a natural process.

You reject the monkey as painter example on similar grounds, arguing that although the end product may be both original and beautiful, it is not creative because it is not a product of the monkey's intellect.

When you consider the example of the musician who arranges a rock song for a marching band, you encounter disagreement. One member of your group says that arranging music is not creative. Like a carpenter who makes a few alterations in the blueprint of a house, this person says, the musician isn't designing a new product but rather is adapting an already existing one. A musician in the group reacts angrily, arguing that musicians—in their arrangements of music and in their renditions of musical pieces—"interpret" music. She contends that different renditions of music are actually significantly different pieces that are experienced differently by audiences, and therefore both arranging music and playing a piece in a different musical style are creative acts. The group hesitantly acknowledges that arranging a rock song in marching band style is different from the example of a carpenter who adds a door between the kitchen and the dining room in a new house. The group concedes to the music major and keeps the example of arranging a musical piece in a different musical style. Your group's final definition, then, looks like this:

DEFINITION: THIRD TRY

> For an act to be creative, it must be produced by intellectual design, and it must result in an end product that is significantly different from other products and is yet useful or beautiful.

Having established these criteria, you are ready to apply them to your controversial case of computer programming. Based on your criteria, you decide to argue that computer programming exists on a continuum ranging from "noncreative activity" to "highly creative activity." At the "noncreative" end of the continuum, computer programmers following algorithmic procedures churn out lines of code. This work requires intelligence, knowledge, problem-solving skills, and a high level of craftsmanship, but not creative thought. Such programmers apply established procedures to new situations; although the applications are new, the programs themselves are not significantly different or innovative. At the other end of the continuum, computer programmers are highly creative. The original Macintosh computer, with its icon-based operating system (later imitated by Microsoft in its Windows© programs), has been heralded as one of the twentieth century's most creative inventions. Programmers who develop ideas for new products, who solve old problems in new ways, or who do research in artificial intelligence, computer simulation, or other interdisciplinary fields requiring synthetic thought are all meeting the criteria of significant newness, usefulness (or beauty), and intellectual design required by our stipulated definition of *creativity*.

This strategy using positive examples, contrastive examples, and borderline cases produces a systematic procedure for developing a definitional argument. Moreover, it provides the examples you will need to explain and illustrate your criteria.

▼ FOR CLASS DISCUSSION

1. Suppose you wanted to define the concept "courage." Working in groups, try to decide whether each of the following cases is an example of courage:
   a. A neighbor rushes into a burning house to rescue a child from certain death and emerges, coughing and choking, with the child in his arms. Is the neighbor courageous?
   b. A firefighter rushes into a burning house to rescue a child from certain death and emerges with the child in her arms. The firefighter is wearing protective clothing and a gas mask. When a newspaper reporter calls her courageous, she says, "Hey, this is my job." Is the firefighter courageous?
   c. A teenager rushes into a burning house to recover a memento given to him by his girlfriend, the first love of his life. Is the teenager courageous?
   d. A parent rushes into a burning house to save a trapped child. The fire marshal tells the parent to wait because there is no chance the child can be reached from the first floor. The fire marshal wants to try cutting a hole in the roof to reach the child. The parent rushes into the house anyway and is burned to death. Was the parent courageous?

2. As you make your decisions on each of these cases, create and refine the criteria you use.

3. Make up your own series of controversial cases, like those above for "courage," for one or more of the following concepts:
   a. cruelty to animals
   b. child abuse
   c. true athlete
   d. sexual harassment
   e. free speech protected by the First Amendment

Then, using the strategy of positive, contrastive, and borderline cases, construct a definition of your chosen term.

CONDUCTING THE MATCH PART OF A DEFINITIONAL ARGUMENT

In conducting a match argument, you need to show that your contested case does or does not meet the criteria you established in your definition, supplying evidence and examples showing why the case meets or does not meet the criteria. In essence, you support the match part of your argument in much the same way you would support a simple categorical claim.

For example, if you were developing the argument that the Hercules Shoe Company is not socially responsible because it treats its workers unjustly, your match section would provide evidence of this injustice. You might supply data about the percentage of shoes produced in East Asia, about the low wages paid these workers, and about the working conditions in these factories. You might also describe the suffering of displaced American workers when Hercules closed its American factories and moved operations to Asia, where the labor was nonunion and cheap. The match section should also summarize and respond to opposing views.

ORGANIZING A DEFINITIONAL ARGUMENT

As you compose a first draft of your essay, you may find it helpful to know a prototypical structure for definitional arguments. Here are several possible plans.

Plan 1 (Criteria and Match in Separate Sections)

- Introduce the issue by showing disagreements about the definition of a key term or about the application of a key term to a problematic case.
- State your claim.
- Present your definition of the key term.

  State and develop Criterion 1.

  State and develop Criterion 2.

  Continue with the rest of your criteria.

- Summarize and respond to possible objections to your definition.
- Restate your claim about the contested case (it does or does not meet your definition).

  Apply Criterion 1 to your case.

  Apply Criterion 2 to your case.

  Continue the match argument.

- Summarize and respond to possible objections to your match argument.
- Conclude your argument.

Plan 2 (Criteria and Match Interwoven)

- Introduce the issue by showing disagreements about the definition of a key term or about the application of a key term to a problematic case.
- Present your claim.

  State Criterion 1 and argue that the contested case meets or does not meet the criterion.

State Criterion 2 and argue that the contested case meets or does not meet the criterion.

Continue with criteria-match sections for additional criteria.

- Summarize opposing views.
- Refute or concede to opposing views.
- Conclude your argument.

QUESTIONING AND CRITIQUING A DEFINITIONAL ARGUMENT

In refuting a definitional argument, you need to appreciate its criteria-match structure. Your refutation can question the argument's criteria, the argument's match, or both.

Questioning the Criteria

Might a skeptic claim that your criteria are not the right ones? This is the most common way to attack a definitional argument. Skeptics might say that one or more of your argument's criteria are irrelevant or too narrow or too broad. Or they might argue for different criteria or point out crucial missing criteria.

Might a skeptic point out possible bad consequences of accepting your argument's criteria? Here a skeptic could raise doubts about your definition by showing how it would lead to unintended bad consequences.

Might a skeptic cite extraordinary circumstances that weaken your argument's criteria? Skeptics might argue that your criteria are perfectly acceptable in ordinary circumstances but are rendered unacceptable by extraordinary circumstances.

Might a skeptic point out a bias or slant in your definition? Writers create definitions favorable to their case. By making this slant visible, a skeptic may be able to weaken the persuasiveness of your definition.

Questioning the Match

A match argument usually uses examples and other evidence to show that the contested case meets or does not meet the criteria in the definition. The standard methods of refuting evidence thus apply (see pp. 123–24). Thus skeptics might ask one or more of the following questions:

Are your examples out-of-date or too narrow and unrepresentative?

Are your examples inaccurate?

Are your examples too extreme?

Are there existing counterexamples that alter the case?

By using the questions to test your own argument, you can reshape and develop your argument to make it thought provoking and persuasive for your audience.

READINGS

In the following op-ed piece, syndicated columnist John Leo makes the simple categorical claim that the *Star Wars* movie *Episode I: The Phantom Menace* perpetuates racist stereotypes. The movie's appearance in May 1999 was a media event generating much discussion in the newspapers.

Stereotypes No Phantom in New Star Wars *Movie*

John Leo

Everyone's a victim these days, so America's touchiness industry is dedicated to seeing group slights everywhere. But sometimes even touchy people are right. Complaints about the new *Star Wars* movie, for instance, are correct. *Episode I: The Phantom Menace* is packed with awful stereotypes.   1

Consider the evil Neimodians. They are stock Oriental villains out of black-and-white B movies of the 1930s and 1940s, complete with Hollywood Asian accents, sinister speech patterns, and a space-age version of stock Fu Manchu clothing.   2

Watto, the fat, greedy junk dealer with wings, is a conventional, crooked Middle Eastern merchant. This is a generic and anti-Semitic image, Jewish if you want him to be, or Arab if you don't.   3

Law Professor Patricia Williams says Watto looks strikingly like an anti-Jewish caricature published in Vienna at the turn of the century—round-bellied, big-nosed, with spindly arms, wings sprouting from his shoulders, and a scroll that says "anything for money."   4

Perhaps Watto isn't supposed to be Jewish. Some people thought he sounded Italian. But by presenting the character as an unprincipled, hook-nosed merchant (and a slave-owner, to boot), the movie is at least playing around with traditional anti-Semitic imagery. It shouldn't.   5

The loudest criticism has been directed at Jar Jar Binks, the annoying, computer-generated amphibian who looks like a cross between a frog and a camel and acts, as one critic put it, like a cross between Butterfly McQueen and Stepin Fetchit. His voice, the work of a black actor, is a sort of slurred, pidgin Caribbean English, much of it impossible to understand.   6

"Me berry, berry scay-yud," says Jar Jar, in one of his modestly successful attempts at English. For some reason, he keeps saying "yousa" and "meesa," instead of "you" and "me." He is the first character in the four *Star Wars* movies to mess up Galactic Basic (the English language) on a regular basis.   7

8   Trouble with English is one of the key traits of a racist caricature, from all the 19th-century characters named Snowball down to the sophisticated wit of Amos 'n' Andy. Whether endearing or pathetic, this trouble with language is supposed to demonstrate the intellectual inferiority of blacks.

9   Childlike confusion is another familiar way of stereotyping blacks, and Jar Jar shows that trait too. He steps in alien-creature doo-doo, gets his tongue caught in a racing engine and panics during the big battle scene. He is, in fact, a standard-issue black caricature.

10   A stereotype on this level is more than insult. It is a teaching instrument and a powerful, non-verbal argument saying that racial equality is a hopeless cause. If blacks talk and act like this movie says they do, how can they possibly expect equal treatment?

11   What is going on in this movie? George Lucas, director of the *Star Wars* movies, says media talk about stereotypes is creating "a controversy out of nothing."

12   But many visual cues support the charge that stereotypes are indeed built into the film. Jar Jar has head flaps drawn to look like dreadlocks. The ruler of his tribe, Boss Nass, wears what looks to be an African robe and African headdress. (Nass, fat and slobbering, seems to come right out of an old movie about Zulu.)

13   A Neimodian senator named Lott (Trent Lott?), representing the evil viceroy Nute Gunray (Newt Gingrich?), wears a version of a Catholic bishop's miter and a Catholic priest's stole over a dark robe. This can't be an accident. It duplicates, almost exactly, the appearance of a real bishop. It's a small reference, but an unmistakable one. So Catholics, along with Asians and Republicans, are at least vaguely associated with Neimodian treachery.

14   Lucas is a visually sophisticated and careful moviemaker. In a TV interview, he said that he researched imagery of Satan in every known culture before deciding on how evil warrior Darth Maul should look in the film (tattooed, with horns). A *Star Wars* book that came out with the movie, *The Visual Dictionary,* describes in detail almost every image used in the film. So it's hard to believe that all the stereotyped imagery just happened.

15   One of the keys to Lucas' success is that his movies are made up of brilliantly re-imagined themes and scenes from earlier films (World War II aerial dogfights, cowboys and Indians, swashbuckling sword fights, a *Ben Hur* chariot race, etc.). After three very inventive *Star Wars* movies, the not-so-inventive fourth seems to have fallen back on some tired Hollywood ethnic themes and characters he mostly avoided in the first three.

16   So *The Phantom Menace* offers us revived versions of some famous stereotypes. Jar Jar Binks as the dithery Butterfly McQueen; Watto, a devious, child-owning wheeler-dealer, as the new Fagin; the two reptilian Neimodian leaders as the inscrutably evil Fu Manchu and Dr. No. What's next—an interplanetary version of the Frito Bandito?

17   The *Star Wars* films deserve better than this. Let's put all these characters to sleep and start over in the next movie.

Our second reading, by student Kathy Sullivan, was written for the definition assignment on page 166. The definitional issue that she addresses—"Are the Menasee photographs obscene?"—became a local controversy in the state of Washington when the state liquor control board threatened to revoke the liquor license of a Seattle gay bar, the Oncore, unless it removed a series of photographs that the board deemed obscene.

Oncore, Obscenity, and the Liquor Control Board

Kathy Sullivan (student)

In early May, Geoff Menasee, a Seattle artist, exhibited a series of photographs with the theme of "safe sex" on the walls of an inner-city, predominantly homosexual restaurant and lounge called the Oncore. Before hanging the photographs, Menasee had to consult with the Washington State Liquor Control Board because, under the current state law, art work containing material that may be considered indecent has to be approved by the board before it can be exhibited. Of the almost thirty photographs, six were rejected by the board because they partially exposed "private parts" of the male anatomy. Menasee went ahead and displayed the entire series of photographs, placing Band-Aids over the "indecent" areas, but the customers continually removed the Band-Aids.

The liquor control board's ruling on this issue has caused controversy in the Seattle community. The *Seattle Times* has provided news coverage, and a "Town Meeting" segment was filmed at the restaurant. The central question is this: Should an establishment that caters to a predominantly homosexual clientele be enjoined from displaying pictures promoting "safe sex" on the grounds that the photographs are obscene?

Before I can answer this question, I must first determine whether the art work should truly be classified as obscene. To make that determination, I will use the definition of *obscenity* in *Black's Law Dictionary:*

> Material is "obscene" if to the average person, applying contemporary community standards, the dominant theme of material taken as a whole appeals to prurient interest, if it is utterly without redeeming social importance, if it goes substantially beyond customary limits of candor in description or representation, if it is characterized by patent offensiveness, and if it is hard core pornography.

An additional criterion is provided by Pember's *Mass Media Laws:* "A work is obscene if it has a tendency to deprave and corrupt those whose minds are open to such immoral influences (children for example) and into whose hands it might happen to fall" (394). The art work in question should not be prohibited from display at predominantly homosexual establishments like the Oncore because it does not meet the above criteria for obscenity.

First of all, to the average person applying contemporary community standards, the predominant theme of Menasee's photographs is not an appeal to prurient interests. The first element in this criterion is "average person." According to Rocky Breckner, manager of the Oncore, 90 percent of the clientele at the Oncore is made up of young white homosexual males. This group therefore constitutes the "average person" viewing the exhibit. "Contemporary community standards" would ordinarily be the standards of the Seattle community. However, this art work is aimed at a particular group of people—the homosexual community. Therefore, the "community standards" involved here are those of the gay community rather than the city at large. Since the Oncore is not an art museum or gallery, which attracts a broad spectrum of people, it is appropriate to restrict the scope of "community standards" to that group who voluntarily patronize the Oncore.

6   Second, the predominant theme of the photographs is not "prurient interest" nor do the photographs go "substantially beyond public limits of candor." There are no explicit sexual acts found in the photographs; instead, their theme is the prevention of AIDS through the practice of safe sex. Homosexual displays of affection could be viewed as "prurient interest" by the larger community, but same-sex relationships are the norm for the group at whom the exhibit is aimed. If the exhibit were displayed at McDonald's or even the Red Robin it might go "substantially beyond customary limits of candor," but it is unlikely that the clientele of the Oncore would find the art work offensive. The manager stated that he received very few complaints about the exhibit and its contents.

7   Nor is the material pornographic. The liquor control board prohibited the six photographs based on their visible display of body parts such as pubic hair and naked buttocks, not on the basis of sexual acts or homosexual orientation. The board admitted that the photographs depicted no explicit sexual acts. Hence, it can be concluded that they did not consider the suggestion of same-sex affection to be hard-core pornography. Their sole objection was that body parts were visible. But visible genitalia in art work are not necessarily pornographic. Since other art work, such as Michelangelo's sculptures, explicitly depicts both male and female genitalia, it is arguable that pubic hair and buttocks are not patently offensive.

8   It must be conceded that the art work has the potential of being viewed by children, which would violate Pember's criterion. But once again the incidence of minors frequenting this establishment is very small.

9   But the most important reason for saying these photographs are not obscene is that they serve an important social purpose. One of Black's criteria is that obscene material is "utterly without redeeming social importance." But these photographs have the explicit purpose of promoting safe sex as a defense against AIDS. Recent statistics reported in the *Seattle Times* show that AIDS is now the leading cause of death of men under forty in the Seattle area. Any methods that can promote the message of safe sex in today's society have strong redeeming social significance.

10   Those who believe that all art containing "indecent" material should be banned or covered from public view would most likely believe that Menasee's work is obscene. They would disagree that the environment and the clientele should be the major determining factors when using criteria to evaluate art. However, in the case of this exhibit I feel that the audience and the environment of the display are factors of overriding importance. Therefore, the exhibit should have been allowed to be displayed because it is not obscene.

WRITING ASSIGNMENT FOR CHAPTER 10

Write an argument that develops a definitional claim of the form "X is (is not) a Y," where Y is a controversial term with a disputed definition. Typically your argument will have a criteria section in which you develop an extended definition of your Y term and a match section in which you argue that your X does or does not meet the criteria for Y.

11 Causal Arguments

X Causes (Does Not Cause) Y

EXAMPLE CASE

In the spring of 1999 two male students of Columbine High School in Littleton, Colorado, opened fire on their classmates. Twelve students and a teacher were killed; twenty-three were wounded. For months following the killings, social scientists and media commentators analyzed the massacre, trying to determine what caused it and what solutions might be enacted to reduce teen violence. Among the causes proposed were the following: violent movies, violent video games, violent TV, the music of Marilyn Manson, easy access to guns, breakdown of the traditional family, absence of parental involvement in teen lives, erosion of school discipline, inadequate school counseling, Internet neo-Nazi chat rooms, Internet lessons on how to make bombs, and the irresponsible prescribing of antidepressants to teenagers (one of the assailants was on Prozac). For each proposed cause, the arguer suggested a different approach for reducing teen violence.

AN OVERVIEW OF CAUSAL ARGUMENTS

We encounter causal issues all the time. What caused the Columbine High School massacre? What would be the consequences of legalizing cocaine and heroin? What caused the traditional image of female beauty in Fiji (robust plumpness) to give way to the current American image (emaciated thinness)?

Sometimes an argument can be devoted entirely to a causal issue. Just as frequently, causal arguments support proposal arguments in which the writer argues that we should (should not) do X because doing X will lead to good (bad) consequences. Convincing readers how X will lead to these consequences—a causal argument—thus bears on the success of many proposal arguments.

Because causal arguments require close analysis of phenomena, effective causal arguing is closely linked to critical thinking. Studies of critical thinking show that good problem-solvers systematically explore the causes of a problem before proposing a solution. Equally important, before making a decision, good problem-solvers predict and weigh the consequences of alternative solutions to a problem, trying to determine a solution that produces the greatest benefits with the least cost. Adding to the complexity of causal arguing is the way a given event can have multiple causes and multiple consequences. In an effort to save salmon, for example, environmentalists have proposed the elimination of several dams on the Snake River above Lewiston, Idaho. Will the removal of these dams save the salmon? Nobody knows for sure, but three universally agreed-on consequences of removing the dams will be the loss of several thousand jobs in the Lewiston area, the loss of some hydroelectric power, and the shift in wheat transportation from river barges to overland trucks and trains. So the initial focus on consequences to salmon soon widens to include consequences to jobs, to power generation, and to agricultural transportation.

THE NATURE OF CAUSAL ARGUING

Typically, causal arguments try to show how one event brings about another. On the surface, causal arguments may seem a fairly straightforward matter—more concrete, to be sure, than the larger moral issues in which they are often embedded. But consider for a moment the classic illustration of causality—one billiard ball striking another on a pool table. Surely we are safe in saying that the movement of the second ball was "caused" by a transfer of energy from the first ball at the moment of contact. Well, yes and no. British philosopher David Hume (among others) argued long ago that we don't really perceive "causality"; what we perceive is one ball moving and then another ball moving. We infer the notion of causality, which is a human construct, not a property of billiard balls.

When humans become the focus of a causal argument, the very definition of causality is immediately vexed. When we say, for example, that a given factor X "caused" a person to do Y, we might mean that X "forced her to do Y," thereby negating her free will (for example, the presence of a brain tumor caused my erratic behavior, which caused me to lose my job). But we might simply mean that factor X "motivated" her to do Y, in such a way that doing Y is still an expression of freedom (for example, my love of the ocean caused me to give up my job as a Wal-Mart greeter and become a California surf bum).

When we argue about causality in human beings, we must guard against confusing these two senses of "cause" or assuming that human behavior can be predicted or controlled in the same way that nonhuman behavior can. A rock dropped from a roof will always fall to the ground at 32 feet per second squared; and a rat zapped for making left turns in a maze will always quit making left turns. But if we raise interest rates, will consumers save more? If so, how much? This is the sort of question we debate endlessly.

Fortunately, most causal arguments can avoid the worst of these scientific and philosophic quagmires. As human beings, we share a number of assumptions about what causes events in the observable world, and we can depend on the goodwill of our audiences to grant us most of these assumptions. Most of us, for example, would be satisfied with the following explanation for why a car went into a skid: "In a panic the driver locked the brakes of his car, causing the car to go into a skid."

panic → slamming brake pedal → locking brakes → skid

We probably do not need to defend this simple causal chain because the audience will grant the causal connections between events A, B, C, and D. The sequence seems reasonable according to our shared assumptions about psychological causality (panic leads to slamming brake pedal) and physical causality (locked brakes lead to skid).

But if you are an attorney defending a client whose skidding car caused considerable damage to an upscale boutique, you might see all sorts of additional causal factors. ("Because the stop sign at that corner was obscured by an untrimmed willow tree, my client innocently entered what he assumed was an open intersection only to find a speeding beer truck bearing down on him. When my client took immediate decelerating corrective action, the improperly maintained, oil-slicked roadway sent his car into its near-fatal skid and into the boutique's bow windows— windows that extrude into the walkway 11 full inches beyond the limit allowed by city code.") Okay, now what's the cause of the crash and who's at fault?

As the previous example shows, explaining causality entails creating a plausible chain of events linking a cause to its effect. Let's take another example—this time a real rather than hypothetical one. Consider an argument put forward by syndicated columnist John Leo as an explanation for the Columbine High School massacre.* Leo attributes part of the cause to the desensitizing effects of violent video games. After suggesting that the Littleton killings were partly choreographed on video game models, Leo suggests the following causal chain:

Many youngsters are left alone for long periods of time → they play violent video games obsessively → their feelings of resentment and powerlessness "pour into the killing games" → the video games break down a natural aversion to killing, analogous to psychological techniques employed by the military → realistic touches in modern video games blur the "boundary between fantasy and reality"

---

*John Leo, "Kill-for-Kicks Video Games Desensitizing Our Children," *Seattle Times,* 27 Apr. 1999: B4.

→ youngsters begin identifying not with conventional heroes but with sociopaths who get their kicks from blowing away ordinary people ("pedestrians, marching bands, an elderly woman with a walker") → having enjoyed random violence in the video games, vulnerable youngsters act out the same adrenaline rush in real life.

DESCRIBING A CAUSAL ARGUMENT IN TOULMIN TERMS

Because causal arguments can involve lengthy or complex causal chains, they are often harder to summarize in *because* clauses than are other kinds of arguments. Likewise, they are not as likely to yield quick analysis through Toulmin's schema. Nevertheless, a causal argument can usually be stated as a claim with *because* clauses. Typically, a *because* clause for a causal argument pinpoints one or two key elements in the causal chain rather than trying to summarize every link. Leo's argument could be summarized in the following claim with *because* clause:

Violent video games may have been a contributing cause to the Littleton massacre because playing these games can make random, sociopathic violence seem pleasurable.

Once stated as an enthymeme, the argument can be analyzed with Toulmin's schema. (It is easiest to apply Toulmin's schema to causal arguments if you think of the grounds as the observable phenomena at any point in the causal chain and the warrants as the shareable assumptions about causality that join links together.)

CLAIM:	Violent video games may have been a contributing cause to the Littleton massacre.
STATED REASON:	because playing these games can make random, sociopathic violence seem pleasurable
GROUNDS:	evidence that the killers, like many young people, played violent video games; evidence that the games are violent; evidence that the games involve random, sociopathic violence (not heroic cops against aliens or gangsters, but a killer blowing away ordinary people—marching bands, little old ladies, etc.); evidence that young people derive pleasure from these games
WARRANT:	If youngsters derive pleasure from random, sociopathic killing in video games, they can transfer this pleasure to real life, thus leading to the Littleton massacre.

BACKING:	testimony from psychologists; evidence that violent video games desensitize persons to violence; analogy to military training where video game strategies are used to "make killing a reflex action"; evidence that the distinction between fantasy and reality becomes especially blurred for unstable children
CONDITIONS OF REBUTTAL:	*Questioning the reason and grounds:* Perhaps the killers didn't play video games. Perhaps the video games are no more violent than traditional kids' games (such as cops and robbers). Perhaps the video games do not feature sociopathic killing.
	Questioning the warrant and backing: Perhaps kids are fully capable of distinguishing fantasy from reality. Perhaps the games are just fun with no transference to real life. Perhaps these video games are substantially different from military training strategies.
QUALIFIER:	(Claim is already qualified by *may* and *contributing cause*.)

☑ FOR CLASS DISCUSSION

1. Working individually or in small groups, create a causal chain to show how the item on the left could help lead to the item on the right.

   a. invention of the automobile   redesign of cities

   b. invention of the automobile   changes in sexual mores

   c. invention of the telephone   loss of sense of community in neighborhoods

   e. development of the "pill"   rise in the divorce rate

   f. development of a way to prevent rejections in transplant operations   liberalization of euthanasia laws

2. For each of your causal chains, compose a claim with an attached *because* clause summarizing one or two key links in the causal chain. For example, "The invention of the automobile helped cause the redesign of cities because automobiles made it possible for people to live farther away from their places of work."

THREE METHODS FOR ARGUING THAT ONE EVENT CAUSES ANOTHER

One of the first things you need to do when preparing a causal argument is to note what sort of causal relationship you're dealing with. Are you concerned with the causes of a specific event or phenomenon such as NATO's decision to bomb Serbia or the crash of John F. Kennedy Jr.'s private airplane? Or are you planning to write about the cause of some recurring phenomenon such as eating disorders or the economic forces behind global warming? Or are you writing about a puzzling trend such as the decline of salmon runs on the Columbia River or the rising popularity of extreme sports?

With recurring phenomena or with trends, you have the luxury of being able to study multiple cases over long periods of time and establishing correlations between suspected causal factors and effects. In some cases you can even intervene in the process and test for yourself whether diminishing a suspected causal factor results in a lessening of the effect or whether increasing the causal factor results in a corresponding increase in the effect. Additionally, you can spend time exploring how the mechanics of causation might work.

But with a one-time occurrence your focus is on the details of the event and specific causal chains that may have contributed to the event. Sometimes evidence has disappeared or changed its nature. You often end up in the position more of a detective than of a scientific researcher, and your conclusion will have to be more tentative as a result.

Having briefly stated these words of caution, let's turn now to the various ways you can argue that one event causes another.

First Method: Explain the Causal Mechanism Directly

The most convincing kind of causal argument identifies every link in the causal chain, showing how X causes A, which causes B, which in turn causes C, which finally causes Y. In some cases, all you have to do is fill in the missing links. In other cases—when your assumptions about causality may seem questionable to your audience—you have to argue for the causal connection with more vigor.

A careful spelling out of each step in the causal chain is the technique used by science writer Robert S. Devine in the following passage from his article "The Trouble with Dams." Although the benefits of dams are widely understood cheap, pollution-free electricity; flood control; irrigation; barge transportation), the negative effects are less commonly known and under-stood. In this article, Devine tries to persuade readers that dams have serious negative consequences. In the following passage, he explains how dams reduce salmon flows by slowing the migration of smolts (newly hatched young salmon) to the sea.

CAUSAL ARGUMENT DESCRIBING A CAUSAL CHAIN

Such transformations lie at the heart of the ongoing environmental harm done by dams. Rivers are rivers because they flow, and the nature of their flows defines much of their character. When dams alter flows, they alter the essence of rivers.

Consider the erstwhile river behind Lower Granite [a dam on Idaho's Snake River]. Although I was there in the springtime, when I looked at the water it was moving too slowly to merit the word "flow"—and Lower Granite Lake isn't even one of the region's enormous storage reservoirs, which bring currents to a virtual halt. In the past, spring snowmelt sent powerful currents down the Snake during April and May. Nowadays hydropower operators of the Columbia and Snake systems store the runoff behind the dams and release it during the winter, when demand—and the price—for electricity rises. Over the ages, however, many populations of salmon have adapted to the spring surge. The smolts used the strong flows to migrate, drifting downstream with the current. During the journey smolts' bodies undergo physiological changes that require them to reach salt water quickly. Before dams backed up the Snake, smolts coming down from Idaho got to the sea in six to twenty days; now it takes from sixty to ninety days, and few of the young salmon reach salt water in time. The emasculated current is the single largest reason that the number of wild adult salmon migrating up the Snake each year has crashed from predevelopment runs of 100,000–200,000 to what was projected to be 150–175 this year.*

This tightly constructed passage connects various causal chains to explain the decline of salmon runs:

> Smolts use river flow to reach the sea → dams restrict flow of river → a trip that before development took 6–20 days now takes 60–90 days → migrating smolts undergo physiological changes that demand quick access to salt water → delayed migration time kills the smolts.

Describing each link in the causal chain—and making each link seem as plausible as possible—is the most persuasive means of convincing readers that X causes Y.

Second Method: Use Various Inductive Methods to Establish a High Probability of a Causal Link

If we can't explain a causal link directly, we often employ a reasoning strategy called *induction*. Through induction we infer a general conclusion based on a limited number of specific cases. For example, if on several occasions you got a

---

*Robert S. Devine, "The Trouble with Dams," *Atlantic* Aug. 1995: 64–75. The example quotation is from page 70.

headache after drinking red wine but not after drinking white wine, you would be likely to conclude inductively that red wine causes you to get headaches. However, because there are almost always numerous variables involved, because there are exceptions to most principles arrived at inductively, and because we can't be certain that the future will always be like the past, inductive reasoning gives only probable truths, not certain ones.

When your brain thinks inductively, it sorts through data looking for patterns of similarity and difference. But the inductive process does not explain the causal mechanism itself. Thus, through induction you know that red wine gives you a headache, but you don't know how the wine actually works on your nervous system—the causal chain itself.

In this section we explain three kinds of inductive reasoning: informal induction, scientific experimentation, and correlation.

Informal Induction

Informal induction is our term for the habitual kind of inductive reasoning people do all the time. Toddlers think inductively when they learn the connection between flipping a wall switch and watching the ceiling light come on. They hold all variables constant except the position of the switch and infer inductively a causal connection between the switch and the light.

According to the nineteenth-century philosopher John Stuart Mill, typical ways in which the mind infers causality include looking for a common element that can explain a repeated circumstance. For example, psychologists attempting to understand the causes of anorexia have discovered that many anorexics (but not all) come from perfectionistic, highly work-oriented homes that emphasize duty and responsibility. This common element is thus a suspected causal factor leading to anorexia. Another of Mill's methods involves looking for a single difference. When infant death rates in the state of Washington shot up in July and August 1986, one event stood out making these two months different: increased radioactive fallout from the Chernobyl nuclear meltdown in the Ukraine. This single difference thus led some researchers to suspect radiation as a possible cause of infant deaths. Informal induction typically proceeds from this kind of "common element" or "single difference" reasoning.

Largely because of its power, informal induction can often lead you to wrong conclusions. You should be aware of two common fallacies of inductive reasoning that can tempt you into erroneous assumptions about causality. (Both fallacies are treated more fully in Appendix 1.)

The *post hoc, ergo propter hoc* fallacy ("after this, therefore because of this") mistakes precedence for cause. Just because event A regularly precedes event B does not mean that event A causes event B. The same reasoning that tells us that flipping a switch causes the light to go on can make us believe that low levels of radioactive fallout from the Chernobyl nuclear disaster caused a sudden rise in infant death rates in the state of Washington. The nuclear disaster clearly preceded the rise in death rates. But did it clearly *cause* it? Our point is that precedence alone is no proof of causality and that we are guilty of this fallacy whenever we are swayed to believe that X causes Y primarily because X precedes Y. We can guard against this fallacy by seeking plausible link-by-link connections showing how X causes Y.

The *hasty generalization* fallacy occurs when you make a generalization based on too few cases or too little consideration of alternative explanations: You flip the switch, but the light bulb doesn't go on. You conclude—too hastily—that the power has gone off. (Perhaps the light bulb has burned out or the switch is broken.) How many trials does it take before you can make a justified generalization rather than a hasty generalization? It is difficult to say. Both the *post hoc* fallacy and the hasty generalization fallacy remind us that induction requires a leap from individual cases to a general principle and that it is always possible to leap too soon.

Scientific Experimentation

One way to avoid inductive fallacies is to examine causal hypotheses as carefully as possible. When we deal with a recurring phenomenon such as cancer, we can create scientific experiments that give us inductive evidence of causality with a fairly high degree of certainty. If, for example, we were concerned that a particular food source such as spinach might contain cancer-causing chemicals, we could test our hypothesis experimentally. We could take two groups of rats and control their environment carefully so that the only difference between them (in theory, anyway) was that one group ate large quantities of spinach and the other group ate none. Spinach eating, then, is the one variable between the two groups that we are testing. After a specified period of time, we would check to see what percentage of rats in each group developed cancer. If twice as many spinach-eating rats contracted cancer, we could probably conclude that our hypothesis had held up.

Correlation

Still another method of induction is *correlation,* which expresses a statistical relationship between X and Y. A correlation between X and Y means that when X occurs, Y is likely to occur also, and vice versa. To put it another way, correlation establishes a possibility that an observed link between X and Y is a causal link rather than mere coincidence. The existence of a correlation, however, does not tell us whether X causes Y, whether Y causes X, or whether both are caused by some third phenomenon.

For example, there is a fairly strong correlation between near-sightedness and intelligence. (In a given sample of nearsighted people and people with normal eyesight, a higher percentage of the nearsighted people will be highly intelligent. Similarly, in a sample of high-intelligence people and people with normal intelligence, a higher percentage of the high-intelligence group will be nearsighted.) But the direction of causality isn't clear. It could be that high intelligence causes people to read more, thus ruining their eyes (high intelligence causes near-sightedness).

Or it could be that near-sightedness causes people to read more, thus raising their intelligence (near-sightedness causes high intelligence). Or it could be that some unknown phenomenon inside the brain causes both near-sightedness and high intelligence.

In recent years, correlation studies have been made stunningly sophisticated through the power of computerized analyses. For example, we could attempt to do the spinach-cancer study without resorting to a scientific experiment. If we identified a given group that ate lots of spinach (for example, vegetarians) and another group that ate little if any spinach (Inuits) and then checked to see if their rates of cancer correlated to their rates of spinach consumption, we would have the beginnings of a correlation study. But it would have no scientific validity until we factored out all the other variables between vegetarians and Inuits that might skew the findings—variables such as lifestyle, climate, genetic inheritance, and differences in diet other than spinach. Factoring out such vari-ables is one of the complex feats that modern statistical analyses attempt to accomplish. But the fact remains that the most sophisticated correlation studies still cannot tell us the direction of causality or even for certain that there is causality.

Conclusion about Inductive Methods

Induction, then, can tell us within varying degrees of certainty whether X causes Y. It does not, however, explain the causal mechanism itself. Typically, the *because* clause structure of an inductive argument would take one of the following three shapes: (1) "Although we cannot explain the causal mechanism directly, we believe that X and Y are very probably causally linked because we have repeatedly observed their conjunction"; (2) " . . . because we have demonstrated the linkage through controlled scientific experiments"; or (3) " . . . because we have shown that they are statistically correlated and have provided a plausible hypothesis concerning the causal direction."

FOR CLASS DISCUSSION

Working individually or in small groups, develop plausible causal chains that might explain the correlations between the following pairs of phenomena:

a. A person who registers low stress level on electrochemical stress meter   Does daily meditation

b. A person who regularly consumes frozen dinners   Is likely to vote for improved rapid transit

c. A high achiever   Is first-born child

d. A member of the National Rifle Association   Favors tough treatment of criminals

Third Method: Argue by Analogy or Precedent

Another common method of causal arguing is through analogy or precedent. (See also Chapter 12, which deals in more depth with the strengths and weaknesses of this kind of arguing.) When you argue through resemblance, you try to find a case that is similar to the one you are arguing about but is better known and less controversial to the reader. If the reader agrees with your view of causality in the similar case, you then try to transfer this understanding to the case at issue. In the following example, the writer tries to explain the link between environmental and biological factors in the creation of teen violence. In this analogy, the biological predisposition for violent behavior is compared to some children's biological predisposition for asthma. Cultural and media violence is then compared to air pollution.

CAUSAL ARGUMENT BY ANALOGY

To deny the role of these influences [bad parenting, easy access to guns, violence in the media] is like denying that air pollution triggers childhood asthma. Yes, to develop asthma a child needs a specific, biological vulnerability. But as long as some children have this respiratory vulnerability—and some always will—then allowing pollution to fill our air will make some children wheeze, and cough, and die. And as long as some children have a neurological vulnerability [to violent behavior]—and some always will—then turning a blind eye to bad parenting, bullying, and the gun culture will make other children seethe, and withdraw, and kill.*

Causal arguments by analogy and precedent are logically weaker than arguments based on causal chains or scientific induction. Although they can be powerfully persuasive, you should be aware of their limits. If any two things are alike in some ways (analogous), they are different in others (disanalogous), and these differences shouldn't be ignored. Consider the following example:

A huckster markets a book called *30 Days to a More Powerful Brain.* The book contains logical puzzles and other brain-teasing exercises that he calls "weight training for the mind."

This argument depends on the warrant that the brain is like a muscle. Because the audience accepts the causal belief that weight training strengthens muscles, the marketers hope to transfer that same belief to the field of mental activity (mind exercises strengthen the brain). However, cognitive psychologists have shown that the brain does *not* work like a muscle, so the analogy is false. Although the argument seems powerful, you should realize that the warrant that says X is like Y is almost always vulnerable.

---

*Sharon Begley, "Why the Young Kill," *Newsweek,* 3 May 1999, 35.

All resemblance arguments, therefore, are in some sense "false analogies." But some analogies are so misleading that logicians have labeled them fallacious—the fallacy of *false analogy*. The false analogy fallacy covers those truly blatant cases where the differences between X and Y are too great for the analogy to hold. An example might be the following: "Putting red marks all over students' papers causes great emotional distress just as putting knife marks over their palms would cause great physical distress." It is impossible to draw a precise line, however, between an analogy that has true clarifying and persuasive power and one that is fallacious. Whether the analogy works in a particular situation depends on the audience's shared assumptions with the arguer.

GLOSSARY OF TERMS ENCOUNTERED IN CAUSAL ARGUMENTS

Because causal arguments are often easier to conduct if writer and reader share a few specialized terms, we offer the following glossary for your convenience.

Fallacy of Oversimplified Cause: One of the greatest temptations when establishing causal relationships is to fall into the habit of looking for *the* cause of something. Most phenomena, especially the ones we argue about, have multiple causes. For example, scientists know that a number of different causes must work together to create a complex disease such as cancer. But though we know all this, we still long to make the world less complex by looking for *the* cause of cancer, thus attributing a single cause to puzzling effects.

Universal/Existential Quantifiers: Closely related to the fallacy of the single clause is the tendency to confuse what logicians call the universal quantifier (*all*) with the existential quantifier (*some*). The mixing up of universal and existential quantifiers can falsify an argument. For example, to argue that *all* the blame for recent school shootings comes from the shooters' playing violent video games is to claim that playing violent video games is the sole cause—a universal statement. An argument will be stronger and more accurate if the arguer makes an existential statement: *Some* of the blame for this violent behavior can be attributed to playing violent video games. Arguers sometimes deliberately mix up these quantifiers to misrepresent and dismiss opposing views. For example, someone might argue that because the violent video games are not totally and exclusively responsible for the students' violent behavior, they are not an influential factor at all. In this instance, arguers are attempting to dismiss potential causes by framing them as universal statements that can be rejected because they are too extreme and indefensible. Because something is not a sole or total cause does not mean that it could not be a partial cause.

Immediate/Remote Causes: Every causal chain links backward indefinitely into the past. An immediate cause is the closest in time to the event being examined. When John F. Kennedy Jr.'s plane crashed into Atlantic Ocean south of Martha's Vineyard in July 1999, experts speculated that the *immediate cause* was Kennedy's becoming disoriented in the night haze, losing visual control of the plane, and sending the plane into a fatal dive. A slightly less immediate cause was his decision to make an over-water flight at night without being licensed for instrument flying. The cause of that decision was the need to get to Hyannis Port quickly to attend a wedding. Farther back in time were all the factors that made Kennedy the kind of risk taker who took chances with his own life. For example, several months earlier he had broken an ankle in a hang-gliding accident. Many commentators said that the numerous tragedies that befell the Kennedy family helped shape his risk-taking personality. Such causes going back into the past are considered *remote causes.* It is sometimes difficult to determine the relative significance of remote causes, which are not obviously linked to an event and often have to be dug out or inferred. It's difficult to know, for example, just how seriously to take Hillary Clinton's explanation for her husband's extramarital affairs with Monica Lewinsky and other women. Clinton's womanizing tendencies, she claimed, were caused by "a terrible conflict between his mother and grandmother" when Clinton was four years old. During this period, she said, he "was scarred by abuse."*

Precipitating/Contributing Causes: These terms are similar to *immediate* and *remote* causes but don't designate a temporal linking going into the past. Rather, they refer to a main cause emerging out of a background of subsidiary causes. The *contributing causes* are a set of conditions that give rise to the *precipitating cause,* which triggers the effect. If, for example, a husband and wife decide to separate, the precipitating cause may be a stormy fight over money, which itself is a symptom of their inability to communicate with each other any longer. All the factors that contribute to that inability to communicate—preoccupation with their respective careers, anxieties about money, in-law problems—may be considered contributing causes. Note that the contributing causes and precipitating cause all coexist simultaneously in time—none is temporally more remote than another. But the marriage might have continued had the contributing causes not finally resulted in frequent angry fighting, which doomed the marriage.

Constraints: Sometimes an effect occurs not because X happened but because another factor—a *constraint*—was removed. At other times a possible effect does not occur because a given constraint prevents it from happening. A constraint is a kind of negative cause that limits choices and possibilities. As soon as the constraint is removed, a given effect may occur. For example, in the marriage we have been discussing, the presence of children in the home might have been a constraint against divorce; as soon as the children graduate from high school and leave home, the marriage may dissolve.

---

*"First Lady's Remarks Take White House by Surprise," *Seattle Times,* 2 Aug. 1999, A1.

Necessary/Sufficient Causes: A *necessary* cause is one that has to be present for a given effect to occur. For example, fertility drugs are necessary to cause the conception of septuplets. Every couple who has septuplets must have used fertility drugs. In contrast, a *sufficient* cause is one that always produces or guarantees a given effect. Smoking more than a pack of cigarettes per day is sufficient to raise the cost of one's life insurance policy. This statement means that if you are a smoker, life insurance companies will always place you in a higher risk bracket and charge you more for life insurance. In some cases, a single cause can be both necessary and sufficient. For example, lack of ascorbic acid is both a necessary and a sufficient cause of scurvy. (Think of all those old sailors who didn't eat fruit for months.) It is a necessary cause because you can't get scurvy any other way except through absence of ascorbic acid; it is a sufficient cause because the absence of ascorbic acid always causes scurvy.

FOR CLASS DISCUSSION

The terms in the preceding glossary can be effective brainstorming tools for thinking of possible causes of an event. For the following events, try to think of as many causes as possible by brainstorming possible *immediate causes, remote causes, precipitating causes, contributing causes,* and *constraints.*

1. Working individually, make a list of different kinds of causes/constraints for one of the following:
   a. your decision to attend your present college
   b. an important event in your life or your family (a divorce, a major move, etc.)
   c. a personal opinion you hold that is not widely shared

2. Working as a group, make a list of different kinds of causes/constraints for one of the following:
   a. why women's fashion and beauty magazines are the most frequently purchased magazines in college bookstores
   b. why the majority of teenagers don't listen to classical music
   c. why the number of babies born out of wedlock has increased dramatically in the last thirty years

ORGANIZING A CAUSAL ARGUMENT

At the outset, it is useful to know some of the standard ways to organize a causal argument. Later, you may decide on a different organizational pattern, but these standard ways will help you get started.

Plan 1 (When Your Purpose Is to Describe and Explain All the Links in a Causal Chain)

- Introduce phenomenon to be explained and show why it is problematical.
- Present your thesis in summary form.
- Describe and explain each link in the causal chain.

Plan 2

When your purpose is to explore the relative contribution of several causes to a phenomenon or to explore multiple consequences of a phenomenon:

- Introduce the phenomenon to be explained and suggest how or why it is controversial.
- Devote one section to each possible cause/consequence and decide whether it is necessary, sufficient, contributory, remote, and so forth. (Arrange sections so that the causes most familiar to the audience come first and the most surprising ones come last.)

Plan 3

When your purpose is to argue for a cause or consequence that is surprising or unexpected to your audience:

- Introduce a phenomenon to be explained and show why it is controversial.
- One by one, examine and reject the causes or consequences your audience would normally assume or expect.
- Introduce your unexpected or surprising cause or consequence and argue for it.

Plans 2 and 3 are similar in that they examine numerous possible causes or consequences. Plan 2, however, tries to establish the relative importance of each cause or consequence, whereas plan 3 aims at rejecting the causes or consequences normally assumed by the audience and argues for an unexpected surprising cause or consequence.

Plan 4

When your purpose is to change your audience's mind about a cause or consequence:

- Introduce the issue and show why it is controversial.
- Summarize your opponent's causal argument and then refute it.
- Present your own causal argument.

Plan 4 is a standard structure for all kinds of arguments. This is the structure you would use if you were the attorney for the person whose car skidded into the boutique (p. 169). The opposing attorney would blame your client's reckless driving. You would lay blame on a poorly signed intersection, a speeding beer truck, and violation of building codes.

QUESTIONING AND CRITIQUING A CAUSAL ARGUMENT

Because of the strenuous conditions that must be met before causality can be proven, causal arguments are vulnerable at many points. The following strategies will generally be helpful.

If you described every link in a causal chain, would skeptics point out weaknesses in any of the links?   Describing a causal chain can be a complex business. A skeptic can raise doubts about an entire argument simply by questioning one of the links. Your best defense is to make a diagram of the linkages and role-play a skeptic trying to refute each link in turn. Whenever you find possible arguments against your position, see how you can strengthen your own argument at that point.

If your argument is based on a scientific experiment, could skeptics question the validity of the experiment?   The scientific method attempts to demonstrate causality experimentally. If the experiment isn't well designed, however, the demonstration is less likely to be acceptable to skeptical audiences. Here are ways to question and critique a scientific argument:

- *Question the findings.*   Skeptics may have reason to believe that the data collected were not accurate or representative. They might provide alternative data or simply point out flaws in the way the data were collected.

- *Question the interpretation of the data.*   Many research studies are divided into a "findings" and a "discussion" section. In the discussion section the researcher analyzes and interprets the data. A skeptic might provide an alternative interpretation of the data or otherwise argue that the data don't support what the original writer claims.

- *Question the design of the experiment.*   A detailed explanation of research design is beyond the scope of this text, but we can give a brief example of how a typical experiment did go wrong. When home computers were first developed in the 1980s, a group of graduate students conducted an experiment to test the effect of word processors on students' writing in junior high school. They reported that students who used the word processors for revising all their essays did significantly better on a final essay than a control group of students who didn't use word processors. It turned out, however, that there were at least two major design flaws in the experiment. First, the researchers allowed students to volunteer for the experimental group. Perhaps these students were already better writers than the control group from the start. (Can you think of a causal explanation of why the better students might volunteer to use the computers?) Second, when the teachers graded essays from both the computer group and the control group, the essays were not retyped uniformly. Thus the computer group's essays were typed with "computer perfection," whereas the control group's essays were handwritten or typed on ordinary typewriters. Perhaps the readers were affected by the pleasing appearance of the computer-typed essays. More significantly, perhaps the graders were biased in favor of the computer project and unconsciously scored the computer-typed papers higher.

If you have used correlation data, could skeptics argue that the correlation is much weaker than you claim or that you haven't sufficiently demonstrated causality? As we discussed earlier, correlation data tell us only that two or more phenomena are likely to occur together. They don't tell us that one caused the other. Thus, correlation arguments are usually accompanied by hypotheses about causal connections between the phenomena. Correlation arguments can often be refuted as follows:

■ Find problems in the statistical methods used to determine the correlation.

■ Weaken the correlation by pointing out exceptions.

■ Provide an alternative hypothesis about causality.

If you have used an analogy argument, could skeptics point out disanalogies? Although among the most persuasive of argumentative strategies, analogy arguments are also among the easiest to refute. The standard procedure is to counter your argument that X is like Y by pointing out all the ways that X is *not* like Y. Once again, by role playing an opposing view, you may be able to strengthen your own analogy argument.

Could a skeptic cast doubt on your argument by reordering your priority of causes? Up to this point we've focused on refuting the claim that X causes Y. However, another approach is to concede that X helps cause Y but argue that X is only one of several contributing causes and not the most significant one.

READING

The following essay, by student writer Daeha Ko, appeared as an op-ed piece in the *University of Washington Daily* on May 9, 1999, several weeks after the Columbine High School massacre in Littleton, Colorado. Ko's motivation for writing is his anger at media attempts to explain the massacre—none of which focused on the cliquish social structure of high school itself.

_____

The Monster That Is High School
Daeha Ko (Student)

1   In the past weeks, intensive media coverage has surrounded the shooting incident in Littleton, Colorado, where 12 students and a teacher died, along with 23 wounded. Yet people forget the real victims of the Littleton massacre are Dylan Klebold and Eric Harris.

2   What they did was against the law, but let's face it—the incident was waiting to happen. And there's nothing surprising about it.

3   The social priorities of high school are to blame. In truth, high school is a place where jocks, cheerleaders and anyone associated with them can do whatever they want and get away with it. Their exploits are celebrated in pep rallies, printed in school papers and shown off in trophy cases. The popular cliques have the most clout, and are—in a sense—local celebrities. If they ever run into disciplinary problems with the school or police, they get let off the hook under the guise that they are just kids.

4   Public schools claim to support all students, but in reality choose to invest their priorities in activities associated with popular cliques. Schools are willing to go to any means necessary to support the sports teams, for example. They care less about students who don't belong to popular cliques, leaving them almost nothing. School becomes less about getting a good education, instead priding itself on the celebration of elite cliques.

5   The popular cliques are nice to their own but spit out extremely cruel insults to those who don't fit in. As noted in *Time,* jocks admitted they like to pick on unpopular kids "because it's just fun to do." Their insulting words create deep emotional wounds, while school authorities ignore the cruelty of the corrupt high-school social system.

6   Schools refuse to accept any accountability and point to parents instead. While it is the job of parents to condition their kids, it is impossible for them to supervise their kids 24 hours a day.

7   As an outcast, I was harassed on an everyday basis by jocks, and received no help from school authorities. It got so bad that I attempted suicide.

8   Yes, I did (and still do) wear all black, play Doom and listen to raucous heavy metal, punk and Goth music. I was into the occult and had extensive knowledge on guns and how to build bombs.

9   I got into several fights, including one where I kicked the shit out of a basketball player. The only reason why I didn't shoot him and his jock cronies is because I lacked access to guns. I would've blown every single one of them away and not cared.

To defend myself, I carried around a 7-inch blade. If anyone continued to mess with   10
me, I sent them anonymous notes with a big swastika drawn on them. I responded to harassment with "Yeah, heil Hitler," while saluting.

They got the hint. Eventually, I found some friends who were also outcasts. We banded   11
together and didn't judge each other by the way we looked or what we liked. But I still held
contempt for jocks whom I believed should be shot and fed to the sharks.

Even in their deaths, Klebold and Harris are still treated like outcasts. How dare *Time*   12
call them "The Monsters Next Door." News analysis poured over the "abnormal" world of
"Goth" culture, Marilyn Manson, violent computer games and gun control. It also targeted
other outcast students as trenchcoat-goth, submerged, socially challenged kids who fail to
fit the "correct" image of American teens.

The popular cliques have their likeness reinforced through the images of trashy teen   13
media as seen on MTV, *90210* and *Dawson's Creek.* It's heard in the bubble-gum pop of
Britney Spears and Backstreet Boys, along with their imitators. Magazines like *YM* and
Seventeen feature pretty-looking girls, offering advice on the latest trends in dress, makeup
and dating.

Media coverage was saturated with memorials and funeral services of the deceased.   14
Friends and family remembered them as "good kids." Not all those killed knew or made
fun of Klebold or Harris. Obviously there were members of the popular cliques who made
fun of them and escaped harm. But innocent people had to die in order to bring injustices
to light that exist in our society.

It's tragic, but perhaps that's the price that had to be paid. Perhaps they are shocked   15
by the fact that some "nerds" have actually defeated them for once because teasing isn't
fun and games anymore.

With the last of the coffins being laid to rest, people are looking for retribution,   16
someone to prosecute. Why? The two kids are dead—there is no sense in pursuing
this problem any further. But lawyers are trying to go after those who they believe influenced Harris and Klebold: namely their parents, gun dealers, and the Trenchcoat Mafia.
Police heavily questioned Harris' girlfriend about the guns she gave them and arrested one
person.

The families of the deceased, lawyers and the police need to get a clue and leave the   17
two kids' families and friends alone. They are dealing with just as much grief and do not
need to be punished for someone else's choices. Filing lawsuits will drag on for years, bur-
dening everyone and achieving little.

It's not like you can bring your loved ones back to life after you've won your case.   18

What we need is bigger emphasis on academic discipline and more financing toward   19
academic programs. Counselors and psychiatrists need to be hired to attend to student
needs. People need practical skills, not the pep-rally fluff of popular cliques.

The people of Littleton need to be at peace with the fate of their town and heal wounds   20
instead of prying them open with lawsuits.

WRITING ASSIGNMENT FOR CHAPTER 11

Choose an issue involving the causes or consequences of a trend, event, or other phenomenon. Write an argument that persuades an audience to accept your explanation of the causes or consequences of your chosen phenomenon. Within your essay you should examine alternative hypotheses or opposing views and explain your reasons for rejecting them. You can imagine your issue either as a puzzle or as a disagreement. If a puzzle, your task will be to create a convincing case to an audience that doesn't already have in mind an answer to your causal question. If a disagreement, your task will be more overtly persuasive because your goal will be to change your audience's views.

12 Resemblance Arguments

X Is (Is Not) like Y

EXAMPLE CASE

When NATO began bombing Serbia during the Kosovo crisis, the Clinton administration, along with the United States media, likened Yugoslavian president Slobodan Milosovic to Adolf Hitler and compared the "ethnic cleansing" of Kosovo to the Nazi's "final solution" against the Jews. When justifying the bombing, Clinton frequently evoked the Holocaust and the lessons of World War II. "Never again," he said. Meanwhile, the Serbian community in the United States (and many Balkan scholars) criticized the Holocaust analogy. The Serbian community likened the Kosovo crisis not to the Nazi annihilation of the Jews but to a civil war in which Serbs were protecting their homeland against Albanian terrorists.

AN OVERVIEW OF RESEMBLANCE ARGUMENTS

Resemblance arguments support a claim by comparing one thing to another with the intention of transferring the audience's understanding of (or feelings about) the second thing back to the first. Sometimes an entire argument can be devoted to a resemblance claim. More commonly, resemblance arguments are brief pieces of larger arguments devoted to a different argument type.

Consider, for example, how writer Richard M. Weaver attempted to refute a Vietnam War–era argument for reducing the voting age from twenty-one to eighteen: "If you are old enough to fight for your country in a war, you are old enough to vote." Weaver claimed that this analogy is true

> only if you believe that fighting and voting are the same kind of thing which I, for one, do not. Fighting requires strength, muscular coordination and, in a modern army, instant and automatic response to orders. Voting requires knowledge of men, history, reasoning power; it is essentially a deliberative activity. Army mules and police dogs are used to fight; nobody is interested in giving them the right to vote.*

The strategy of resemblance arguments is to take the audience's understanding of the point made in the comparison (it would be ludicrous to give police dogs and army mules the right to vote) and transfer it to the issue being debated (therefore we shouldn't base voting rights on the ability to fight in battles). Resemblance arguments are seldom strictly logical; they possess instead a kind of imaginative or metaphorical persuasiveness.

The power of resemblance arguments comes from their ability to clarify an audience's conception of contested issues while conveying strong emotions. Resemblance arguments typically take the form "X is (is not) like Y." Resemblance arguments work best when the audience has a clear (and sometimes emotionally charged) understanding of the Y term. The writer then hopes to transfer this understanding, along with accompanying emotions, to the X term. The danger of resemblance arguments, as we shall see, is that the differences between the X and Y terms are often so significant that the resemblance argument collapses under close examination.

Like most other argument types, resemblance arguments can be analyzed with Toulmin's schema. Weaver's argument against giving eighteen-year-olds the right to vote can be displayed in Toulmin terms as follows:

ENTHYMEME:	Being old enough to fight does not mean being old enough to vote because making this equation would be like granting voting rights to police dogs and army mules.
CLAIM:	Being old enough to fight does not mean being old enough to vote.
STATED REASON:	because making this equation would be like granting voting rights to police dogs and army mules
GROUNDS:	all the ways that eighteen-year-old soldiers are like police dogs and army mules in their ability to fight in war (strength, coordina-

---

*Richard M. Weaver, "A Responsible Rhetoric," *Intercollegiate Review,* Winter 1976–77: 86–87.

	tion, instant and automatic response to or-ders) and in their inability to be good voters
WARRANT:	Voting and fighting involve totally different skills and abilities.
BACKING:	Fighting requires strength, obedience, etc.; voting requires reasoning, knowledge, etc.
CONDITIONS OF REBUTTAL:	*Questioning the stated reason and grounds:* Eighteen-year-old soldiers differ signifi-cantly from police dogs and army mules. Many eighteen-year-olds do have the rea-soning ability and historical knowledge to be good voters.
	Questioning the warrant and backing: Most people will agree with the warrant that fighting and voting require different abili-ties. However, this warrant seems to assume that twenty-one-year-olds are more quali-fied to vote than eighteen-year-olds. This assumption is questionable.
QUALIFIER:	(Weaver does not qualify his claim.)

Displaying Weaver's argument in Toulmin terms suggests the power and peril of resemblance arguments. Because everyone agrees that it would be ludicrous to give voting rights to police dogs and army mules, our hearty affirmation of that principle transfers to Weaver's main claim that it is bad policy to base voting rights on fighting ability. But the analogy also invites skeptics to think of *disanalogies:* all the ways in which eighteen-year-old soldiers are *not like* police dogs and army mules. Dogs and mules, unlike humans, are categorically excluded from being voters. Humans, however, are granted voting rights at some arbitrary age set by law. The fact that dogs and mules should not vote is logically irrelevant to the issue of whether the voting age should be eighteen or twenty-one.

With this background, we now proceed to the two types of resemblance ar-guments: analogy and precedent.

ARGUMENTS BY ANALOGY

The use of *analogies* can constitute the most imaginative form of argument. If you don't like your new boss, you can say that she's like a marine drill sergeant, a distraught captain of a sinking ship, or a mother hen. Each of these analogies suggests a different management style, clarifying the nature of your dislike through a comparison that grips your audience emotionally.

Of course, this power to make things clear comes at a price. Analogies often clarify one aspect of a relationship at the expense of other aspects. For example, in nineteenth-century America many commentators were fond of justifying certain negative effects of capitalism (such as the squalor of the poor) by comparing social and economic processes to Darwinian evolution—the survival of the fittest. In particular, they fastened on one aspect of evolution, competition, and spoke darkly of life as a cutthroat struggle for survival. Clearly the analogy clarified one aspect of human interaction: People and institutions do indeed compete for limited resources, markets, and territory; and the consequences of failure are often dire (the weak get eaten by the strong). But competition is only one aspect of evolution—albeit a particularly dramatic one. The ability to dominate an environment is less important to the long-term survival of a species than is the ability to adapt to that environment. Thus, the mighty dinosaur disappeared, but the lowly cockroach continues to flourish because of its uncanny ability to adjust to circumstance.

The use of the evolutionary analogies to account for the competitive nature of human existence fit the worldview (and served the interests) of those who were most fond of invoking them, in particular the so-called robber barons and conservative Social Darwinists. But in overlooking other dimensions of evolution, especially the importance of adaptation and cooperation to survival, the analogy created a great deal of mischief.

So analogies have the power to get an audience's attention like virtually no other persuasive strategy. But seldom are they sufficient in themselves to provide full understanding. At some point with every analogy you need to ask yourself, "How far can I legitimately go with this? At what point are the similarities between the two things I am comparing going to be overwhelmed by their dissimilarities?" Analogies are useful attention-getting devices; used carefully and cautiously, they can be extended to shape an audience's understanding of a complex situation. But they can conceal and distort as well as clarify. With this caveat, let's look at the uses of both undeveloped and extended analogies.

Using Undeveloped Analogies

Typically, writers use short, undeveloped analogies to drive home a point (and evoke an accompanying emotion) and then quickly abandon the analogy before the reader's awareness of disanalogies begins to set in. Thus conservative columnist James Kilpatrick, in arguing that it is not unconstitutional to require drug testing of federal employees, compares giving a urine specimen when applying for a federal job to going through an airport metal detector when flying:

> The Constitution does not prohibit all searches and seizures. It makes the people secure in their persons only from "unreasonable" searches and seizures. . . . A parallel situation may be observed at every airport in the land. Individuals may have a right to fly, but they have no right to fly without having their persons and bag-

gage inspected for weapons. By the same token, the federal worker who refuses a urine specimen [has no right to a federal job].*

Kilpatrick wants to transfer his audience's general approval of weapons searches as a condition for airplane travel to drug testing as a condition for federal employment. But he doesn't want his audience to linger too long on the analogy. (Is a urine specimen for employment really analogous to a weapons search before an airplane trip?)

Using Extended Analogies

Sometimes writers elaborate an analogy so that it takes on a major role in the argument. As an example of a claim based on an extended analogy, consider the following excerpt from a professor's argument opposing a proposal to require a writing proficiency exam for graduation. In the following portion of his argument, the professor compares development of writing skills to the development of physical fitness.

> A writing proficiency exam gives the wrong symbolic messages about writing. It suggests that writing is simply a skill, rather than an active way of thinking and learning. It suggests that once a student demonstrates proficiency then he or she doesn't need to do any more writing.
>
> Imagine two universities concerned with the physical fitness of their students. One university requires a junior-level physical fitness exam in which students must run a mile in less than 10 minutes, a fitness level it considers minimally competent. Students at this university see the physical fitness exam as a one-time hurdle. As many as 70 percent of them can pass the exam with no practice; another 10–20 percent need a few months' training; and a few hopeless couch potatoes must go through exhaustive remediation. After passing the exam, any student can settle back into a routine of TV and potato chips having been certified as "physically fit."
>
> The second university, however, believing in true physical fitness for its students, is not interested in minimal competency. Consequently, it creates programs in which its students exercise 30 minutes every day for the entire four years of the undergraduate curriculum. There is little doubt which university will have the most physically fit students. At the second university, fitness becomes a way of life with everyone developing his or her full potential. Similarly, if we want to improve our students' writing abilities, we should require writing in every course throughout the curriculum.

---

*James J. Kilpatrick, "A Conservative View." ©Universal Press Syndicate. Reprinted with permission. All rights reserved.

If you choose to write an extended analogy such as this, you will focus on the points of comparison that serve your purposes. The writer's purpose in the preceding case is to support the achievement of mastery rather than minimalist standards as the goal of the university's writing program. Whatever other disanalogous elements are involved (for example, writing requires the use of intellect, which may or may not be strengthened by repetition), the comparison reveals vividly that a commitment to mastery involves more than a minimalist test. The analogy serves primarily to underscore this one crucial point. In reviewing the different groups of students as they "prepare" for the fitness exam, the author makes clear just how irrelevant such an exam is to the whole question of mastery. Typically, then, in developing your analogy, you are not developing all possible points of comparison so much as you are bringing out those similarities consistent with the point you are trying to make.

FOR CLASS DISCUSSION

The following is a two-part exercise to help you clarify for yourself how analogies function in the context of arguments. Part 1 is to be done outside class; part 2 is to be done in class.

PART 1   Think of an analogy that accurately expresses your feeling toward each of the following topics. Then write your analogy in the following one-sentence format:

X is like Y: A, B, C . . . (where X is the main topic being discussed; Y is the analogy; and A, B, and C are the points of comparison).

EXAMPLES:

Cramming for an exam to get better grades is like pumping iron for ten hours straight to prepare for a weightlifting contest: exhausting and counterproductive. A right-to-lifer bombing an abortion clinic is like a vegetarian bombing a cattle barn: futile and contradictory.

a. Spanking a child to teach obedience is like . . . .
b. Building low-cost housing for poor people is like . . . .
c. The use of steroids by college athletes is like . . . .
d. The effect of American fast food on our health is like . . . .
e. The personal gain realized by people who have committed questionable or even illegal acts and then made money by selling book and movie rights is like . . . .

In each case, begin by asking yourself how you feel about the subject. If you have negative feelings about a topic, then begin by calling up negative pictures that express those feelings (or if you have positive feelings, call up positive comparisons). As they emerge, test each one to see if it will work as an analogy. An effective analogy will convey both the feeling you have toward your topic and your understanding of the topic. For instance, the writer in the "cramming for an exam" example obviously believes that pumping iron for ten hours before a weightlifting match is stupid. This feeling of stupidity is then transferred to the original topic— cramming for an exam. But the analogy also clarifies understanding. The writer imagines the mind as a muscle (which gets exhausted after too much exercise and which is better developed through some exercise every day rather than a lot all at once) rather than as a large container (into which lots of stuff can be "crammed").

PART 2   Bring your analogies to class and compare them to those of your classmates. Select the best analogies for each of the topics and be ready to say why you think they are good.

ARGUMENTS BY PRECEDENT

Precedent arguments are like analogy arguments in that they make comparisons between an X and a Y. In precedent arguments, however, the Y term is usually a past event where some sort of decision was reached, often a moral, legal, or political decision. An argument by precedent tries to show that a similar decision should or should not be reached for the present issue X because the situation of X is or is not like the situation of Y.

A good example of a precedent argument is the following excerpt from a speech by President Lyndon Johnson in the early years of the Vietnam War:

> Nor would surrender in Vietnam bring peace because we learned from Hitler at Munich that success only feeds the appetite of aggression. The battle would be renewed in one country and then another country, bringing with it perhaps even larger and crueler conflict, as we have learned from the lessons of history.*

Here the audience knows what happened at Munich: France and Britain tried to appease Hitler by yielding to his demand for a large part of Czechoslovakia, but Hitler's armies continued their aggression anyway, using Czechoslovakia as a staging area to invade Poland. By arguing that surrender in Vietnam would lead to the same consequences, Johnson brings to his argument about Vietnam the whole weight of his audience's unhappy knowledge of World War II.

---

*From *Public Papers of the Presidents of the United States*, vol. 2, *Lyndon B. Johnson* (Washington: GPO, 1965), 794.

Administration white papers developed Johnson's precedent argument by pointing toward the similarity of Hitler's promises with those of the Viet Cong: If you give us this, we will ask for no more. But Hitler didn't keep his promise. Why should the Viet Cong?

Johnson's Munich precedent persuaded many Americans during the early years of the war and helps explain U.S. involvement in Southeast Asia. Yet many scholars attacked Johnson's reasoning. Let's use Toulmin's schema to analyze the Munich argument.

ENTHYMEME:	The United States should not withdraw its troops from Vietnam because conceding to the Viet Cong will have the same disastrous consequences as did conceding to Hitler in Munich.
CLAIM:	The United States should not withdraw its troops from Vietnam.
STATED REASON:	because conceding to the Viet Cong will have the same disastrous consequences as did conceding to Hitler in Munich
GROUNDS:	evidence of the disastrous consequences of conceding to Hitler at Munich: Hitler's continued aggression; his using Czechoslovakia as a staging area to invade Poland
WARRANT:	What happened in Europe will happen in Southeast Asia.
BACKING:	evidence of similarities between 1939 Europe and 1965 Southeast Asia (for example, similarities in political philosophy, goals, and military strength of the enemy; similarities in the nature of the conflict between the disputants)
CONDITIONS OF REBUTTAL:	acknowledged differences between 1939 Europe and 1965 Southeast Asia that might make the outcomes different

Using Toulmin's schema, we see that the persuasiveness of the comparison depends on the audience's acceptance of the warrant, which posits close similarity between 1939 Europe and 1965 Southeast Asia. But many critics of the Vietnam War attacked this warrant. Thus, during the Vietnam era, historian Howard Zinn attacked Johnson's argument by claiming three crucial differences between

Europe in 1939 and Southeast Asia in 1965: First, the Czechs were being attacked from without by an external aggressor (Germany), whereas Vietnam was being attacked from within by rebels as part of a civil war. Second, Czechoslovakia was a prosperous, effective democracy, whereas the official Vietnam government was corrupt and unpopular. Third, Hitler wanted Czechoslovakia as a base for attacking Poland, whereas the Viet Cong and North Vietnamese aimed at reunification of their country as an end in itself.*

The Munich example shows again how arguments of resemblance depend on emphasizing the similarities between X and Y and playing down the dissimilarities. One could try to refute the counterargument made by Zinn by arguing first that the Saigon government was more stable than Zinn thinks and second that the Viet Cong and North Vietnamese were driven by goals larger than reunification of Vietnam—namely, communist domination of Asia. Such an argument would once again highlight the similarities between Vietnam and prewar Europe.

FOR CLASS DISCUSSION

1. Consider the following claims of precedent and evaluate how effective you think each precedent might be in establishing the claim.
   a. Gays should be allowed to serve openly in the U.S. military because they are allowed to serve openly in the militaries of most other Western countries.
   b. Gun control will reduce violent crime in the United States because many countries that have strong gun control laws (such as Japan and England) have low rates of violent crime.

2. Advocates for "right to die" legislation legalizing active euthanasia under certain conditions often point to the Netherlands as a country where acceptance of euthanasia works effectively. Assume for the moment that your state has a ballot initiative legalizing euthanasia. Assume further that you are being hired as a lobbyist for (or against) the measure and have been assigned to do research on euthanasia in the Netherlands. Working in small groups, make a list of research questions you would want to ask. Your long-range rhetorical goal is to use your research to support (or attack) the ballot initiative by making a precedence argument focusing on the Netherlands.

---

*Based on the summary of Zinn's argument in J. Michael Sproule, *Argument: Language and Its Influence* (New York: McGraw, 1980), 149–50.

ORGANIZING A RESEMBLANCE ARGUMENT

The most typical way to develop a resemblance argument is as follows:

- Introduce the issue and state your claim.
- Develop your analogy or precedent.
- Draw the explicit parallels you want to highlight between your claim and the analogy or precedent.
- Anticipate and respond to objections (optional depending on space and context).

Of course, this structure can be varied in many ways, depending on your issue and rhetorical context. Sometimes writers open an argument with the analogy, which serves as an attention grabber.

QUESTIONING AND CRITIQUING A RESEMBLANCE ARGUMENT

Once you have written a draft of your resemblance argument, you can test its effectiveness by role playing a skeptical audience. What follows are some typical questions audiences will raise about arguments of resemblance.

Will a skeptic say I am trying to prove too much with my analogy or precedent? The most common mistake people make with resemblance arguments is to ask them to prove more than they're capable of proving. Too often, an analogy is treated as if it were a syllogism or algebraic ratio wherein necessary truths are deduced (*a* is to *b* as *c* is to *d*) rather than as a useful, but basically playful, figure that suggests uncertain but significant insight. The best way to guard against this charge is to qualify your argument and to find other means of persuasion to supplement an analogy or precedent argument.

For a good example of an analogy that tries to do too much, consider President Ronald Reagan's attempt to prevent the United States from imposing economic sanctions on South Africa. Reagan wanted to argue that harming South Africa's economy would do as much damage to blacks as to whites. In making this argument, he compared South Africa to a zebra and concluded that one couldn't hurt the white portions of the zebra without also hurting the black.

Now, the zebra analogy might work quite well to point up the interrelatedness of whites and blacks in South Africa. But it has no force whatsoever in supporting Reagan's assertion that economic sanctions would hurt blacks as well as whites. To refute this analogy, one need only point out the disanalogies between the zebra stripes and racial groups. (There are, for example, no differences in income, education, and employment between black and white stripes on a zebra.)

Will a skeptic point out disanalogies in my resemblance argument?   Although it is easy to show that a country is not like a zebra, finding disanalogies is sometimes quite tricky. As an example, we have shown you how Howard Zinn identified disanalogies between Europe in 1939 and Southeast Asia in 1965 (see pages 194–95).

READINGS

Our first reading is a student argument written in response to the assignment on page 199. Notice how this student uses an analogy to analyze and protest an experience that has troubled her.

Don't Fake Sirens!

T. D. Hylton (Student)

As I drove down I-5 slightly over the 65-mph speed limit, I heard the scream of a siren. Naturally my adrenaline started to flow as I transferred attention from the road ahead to searching for the source of the howling siren. Then I realized my mistake: I had not heard a real emergency vehicle; I had heard a radio commercial. Distracted by the sound of the siren, I had put my fellow drivers at risk. The use of sirens in commercials has potentially dangerous consequences. We should not wait for a fatal car accident to ban such commercials.   1

Compare this type of commercial to a prank call. Pretend that your sister called you up, told you that a loved one had just died unexpectedly, and that she would get back to you about details as soon as she heard. Your attention would no longer be focused on what you had been doing before the phone call. Then, after getting all worked up, pretend your sister called you back and said it was all a joke. During the time you were distracted something bad might have happened: You might have left the stove on high or failed to meet an important deadline at work.   2

While this case is more extreme than a radio commercial siren, hearing a siren while driving does release in us a flood of fears and anxieties. I suspect my reaction is typical: I start to think I did something wrong. Am I speeding? I instinctively look at my speedometer and begin braking. Then I start scanning the road, searching my rearview mirror for flashing lights, and even pulling into the right lane. Flustered and distracted, I become momentarily a less safe driver. Then I realize that the commercial has played a joke on me.   3

Just as we would get mad at our sister for a stupid prank, we should get mad at the commercial writers for fooling us with a siren. It is currently a crime to impersonate a police officer; it ought to be a crime to fake an emergency vehicle. Let's ban these distracting commercials.   4

Our second reading was published as a guest editorial in the *Seattle Times*. It responds to proposals for stronger gun control laws following the Columbine High School massacre in Littleton, Colorado.

Creeping Loopholism Threatens Our Rights

Michael D. Lubrecht

1   Imagine for a moment that ethanol is recognized as a primary root of crime and social dysfunction in America. Not alcoholism, not drunken driving, not teen drinking, but ethanol, grain alcohol, booze.

2   To address the serious issues arising from the presence of ethanol in society, Congress passes "reasonable" legislation to ban malt liquor, reduce six-packs of beer to four-packs, and prohibit the import of fine French Bordeaux. When these "reasonable" efforts don't stop the problems, the search expands to find "loopholes" in the previous legislation and plug them. We limit the alcohol content in microbrews, require labeling changes on wine coolers, and ban the particularly evil double-malt Scotches. That doesn't work either.

3   The process goes on until there is no legal way left to purchase alcohol. The end result is functionally equivalent to Prohibition, and guess what—it didn't work. Alcohol abuse was rampant, crime soared and a new black market was created.

4   At least the misguided congressmen who engineered the original Prohibition had the courage to stand up and lay their principles on the line. Our current crop of gun-control proponents know that guns in the hands of law-abiding citizens do not increase criminal activity; in many demonstrated ways, they actually reduce crime. The current examples of gun prohibition in countries like Australia show astounding increases in violent crime when guns are removed from the citizenry.

5   But still, these proponents keep chipping away incrementally at, not criminal behavior, but the guns themselves—guns with bayonet lugs, guns that are inexpensive, guns that are painted black, guns that hold too many bullets, guns from other countries, guns that look too evil.

6   Before the Youth Violence Bill—with its "loophole filling" background checks, gunsmith licensing, and other misdirected contents—was even voted Yea or Nay, Rep. Rod Blagojevich (D–Ill.) introduced a new bill to restrict access to rifles in .50 caliber. These rifles, of course, are designed only for killing people.

7   Now, I could write a treatise advancing a plausible hunting, sporting or self-defense justification for individual ownership of each and every weapon on the gun-banners' list, despite the fact that we "know" they are all really just death-dealing instruments of destruction. But I won't, for the simple fact is that the gun-control lobby's ultimate goal is the total prohibition of firearms. No matter what "reasonable" law is compromised on, there is another waiting in the wings, to add to the stack of restrictions.

8   It is time to stop defending the functionality, "sporting use" or other arbitrarily selected evil qualities of particular classes of firearms, stand fast, and say, "No More!"

Congress? If guns are the root of all evil, then let's see the House resolution to ban   9
'em all, right here, right now. If you really think restricting law-abiding citizens' access to
particular types of guns will reduce crime in America, then banning them all should halt
crime entirely. If you believe that restricting firearms possession by citizens who are too
young or too poor will make the streets safer, then getting rid of all the guns will restore
our streets to perfect safety. If restricting magazine capacity to 10 rounds will reduce homi-
cides by some arbitrary number, then reducing their capacity to zero should result in a null
homicide rate.

History will not agree with you, but let's try your social experiment. Summon up some   10
backbone and ban them already. Show the character to reveal your agenda in one courageous piece of legislation and be done with it.

Or, come to your senses, address the real issues, leave guns and gun owners alone and   11
stop this endless, senseless, pointless trend of creeping loopholism.

WRITING ASSIGNMENT FOR CHAPTER 12

Write a letter to the editor of your campus or local newspaper or a slightly
longer guest editorial in which you try to influence public opinion on some issue
through the use of a persuasive analogy or precedent. T. D. Hylton's argument (see
p. 197) against using sirens in radio commercials is a student piece written in
response to this assignment.

13 Evaluation Arguments

X Is (Is Not) a Good Y

EXAMPLE CASE

A young engineer has advanced to the level of a design group leader. She is now being considered for promotion to a management position. Her present supervisor is asked to write a report evaluating her as a prospective manager. He is asked to pay particular attention to four criteria: technical competence, leadership, interpersonal skills, and communication skills.

In our roles as citizens and professionals we are continually expected to make difficult evaluations, to defend them, and even to persuade others to accept them. Often we will defend our judgments orally—in committees making hiring and promotion decisions, in management groups deciding which of several marketing plans to adopt, or at parent advisory meetings evaluating the success of school policies. Sometimes, too, we will be expected to put our arguments in writing.

Practice in thinking systematically about the process of evaluation is valuable experience. In this chapter we focus on *evaluation* arguments of the type "X is (is not) a good Y" or "X is good (bad)" and the strategy needed for conducting such arguments.* In Chapter 15, we will return to evaluation arguments to examine in more detail some special problems raised by ethical issues.

---

*In addition to the contrasting words *good/bad,* a number of other evaluative terms involve the same kinds of thinking: *effective/ineffective, successful/unsuccessful, workable/unworkable,* and so forth. Throughout this chapter, terms such as these can be substituted for *good/bad.*

CRITERIA-MATCH STRUCTURE
OF EVALUATION ARGUMENTS

An "X is (is not) a good Y" argument follows the same criteria-match structure that we examined in definitional arguments (see Chapter 10). A typical claim for such an argument has the following form:

X is (is not) a good Y because it meets (fails to meet) criteria A, B, and C.

The main structural difference between an evaluation argument and a definitional argument involves the Y term. In a definitional argument, one argues whether a particular Y term is the correct class in which to place X. (Does this swampy area qualify as a *wetland*?) In an evaluation argument, we know the Y term—that is, what class to put X into (Dr. Choplogic is a *teacher*)—but we don't know whether X is a good or bad instance of that class. (Is Dr. Choplogic a *good* teacher?) As in definitional arguments, warrants specify the criteria to be used for the evaluation, whereas the stated reasons and grounds assert that X meets these criteria.

Let's look at an example that, for the sake of illustration, asserts just one criterion for "good" or "bad." (Most arguments will develop several criteria.)

ENTHYMEME:	Computer-aided instruction (CAI) is an effective teaching method because it encourages self-paced learning. (The complete argument would develop other reasons also.)
CLAIM:	Computer-aided instruction is an effective teaching method.
STATED REASON:	Computer-aided instruction encourages self-paced learning.
GROUNDS:	evidence that CAI encourages self-paced learning; examples of different learners working at different paces
WARRANT (CRITERION):	Self-paced learning is an effective teaching method.
BACKING:	explanations of why self-paced learning is effective; research studies or testimonials showing effectiveness of self-pacing
CONDITIONS OF REBUTTAL:	*Questioning stated reason and grounds:* Perhaps students don't really pace themselves in CAI.
	Questioning the warrant and backing: Perhaps self-paced learning isn't any more effective than other methods. Perhaps the disadvantages of other features of CAI outweigh the value of self-pacing.

As this Toulmin schema shows, the writer needs to show that self-paced learning is an effective teaching method (the warrant or criterion) and that computer-aided instruction meets this criterion (the stated reason and grounds—the match argument).

GENERAL STRATEGY FOR EVALUATION ARGUMENTS

The general strategy for evaluation arguments is to establish criteria and then to argue that X meets or does not meet the criteria. In writing your argument, you have to decide whether your audience is likely to accept your criteria. If you want to argue, for example, that pit bulls do not make good pets because they are potentially vicious, you can assume that most readers will share your assumption that viciousness is bad. Likewise, if you want to praise the new tax bill because it cuts out tax cheating, you can probably assume readers agree that tax cheating is bad.

Often, however, selecting and defending your criteria are the most difficult parts of a criteria-match argument. For example, people who own pit bulls because they *want* a vicious dog for protection may not agree that viciousness is bad. In this case, you would need to argue that another kind of dog, such as a German shepherd or a doberman, would make a better choice than a pit bull or that the bad consequences of a vicious dog outweigh the benefits. Several kinds of difficulties in establishing criteria are worth discussing in more detail.

The Problem of Standards: What's Commonplace or What's Ideal?

To get a sense of this problem, consider again Young Person's archetypal argument with Parent about her curfew (see Chapter 1). She originally argued that staying out until 2 A.M. is fair "because all the other kids' parents let their kids stay out late," to which Parent might respond: "Well, *ideally*, all the other parents should not let their kids stay out that late." Young Person based her criterion for fairness on what is *commonplace;* her standards arose from common practices of a social group. Parent, however, argued from what is *ideal*, using criteria based on some external standard that transcends social groups.

We experience this dilemma in various forms throughout our lives. It is the conflict between absolutes and cultural relativism, between written law and customary practice. There is hardly an area of human experience that escapes the dilemma: Is it fair to get a ticket for going 70 mph on a 65-mph freeway when most of the drivers go 70 mph or higher? Is it better for high schools to pass out free contraceptives to students because the students are having sex anyway (what's *commonplace*), or is it better not to pass them out in order to support abstinence (what's *ideal*)? When you select criteria for an evaluation argument, you may well have to choose one side or the other of this dilemma, arguing for what is ideal or for what is usual. Neither position should be seen as necessarily better than the other; commonplace practice may be corrupt just as surely as ideal behavior may be impossible.

The Problem of Mitigating Circumstances

When confronting the dilemma raised by the "commonplace" versus the "ideal," we sometimes have to take into account circumstances as well as behavior. In particular, we have the notion of *mitigating* circumstances, or circumstances that are extraordinary or unusual enough to cause us to change our standard measure of judgment. Ordinarily it is wrong to be late for work or to miss an exam. But what if your car had a flat tire?

When you argue for mitigating circumstances as a reason for modifying judgment in a particular case, you are arguing against the conditions of both common behavior and ideal behavior as the proper criterion for judgment. Thus, when you make such an argument, you will likely assume an especially heavy burden of proof. People assume the rightness of usual standards of judgment unless there are compelling arguments for abnormal circumstances.

The Problem of Choosing
between Two Goods or Two Bads

Not all arguments of value, of course, clearly deal with bad and good, but with choosing between two bads or two goods. Often we are caught between a rock and a hard place. Should we cut pay or cut people? Put our parents in a nursing home or let them stay at home where they have become a danger to themselves? In such cases one has to weigh conflicting criteria, knowing that the choices are too much alike—either both bad or both good.

The Problem of Seductive Empirical Measures

The need to make distinctions among relative goods or relative bads has led many persons to seek quantifiable criteria that can be weighed mathematically. Thus we use grade point averages to select scholarship winners, MCAT scores to decide who gets into medical school, and student evaluation scores to decide which professor gets the University Teaching Award.

In some cases, such empirical measures can be quite acceptable. But they can be dangerous if they don't adequately measure the value of the people or things they purportedly evaluate. (Some people would argue that they *never* adequately measure anything significant.) To illustrate the problem further, consider the problems of relying on grade point average as a criterion for employment. Many employers rely heavily on grades when hiring college graduates. But according to every major study of the relationship between grades and work achievement, grades are about as reliable as palm reading when it comes to predicting life success. Why do employers continue to rely so heavily on grades? Clearly because it is so easy to classify job applicants according to a single empirical measure that appears to rank order everyone along the same scale.

The problem with empirical measures, then, is that they seduce us into believing that complex judgments can be made mathematically, thus rescuing us from the messiness of alternative points of view and conflicting criteria. Empirical measures seem extremely persuasive next to written arguments that try to qualify and hedge and raise questions. We suggest, however, that a fair evaluation of any X might require such hedging.

The Problem of Cost

A final problem that can crop up in evaluations is cost. In comparing an X to others of its kind, we may find that on all the criteria we can develop, X comes out on top. X is the best of all possible Y's. But if X costs too much, we have to rethink our evaluation.*

If we're looking to hire a new department head at Median State University, and the greatest scholar in the field, a magnificent teacher, a regular dynamo of diplomacy, says she'll come—for a hundred Gs a year—we'll probably have to withdraw our offer. Whether the costs are expressed in dollars or personal discomfort or moral repugnance or some other terms, our final evaluation of X must take cost into account, however elusive that cost might be.

HOW TO DETERMINE CRITERIA FOR YOUR ARGUMENT

Now that we have explored some of the difficulties you may encounter in establishing and defending criteria for your evaluation of X, let's turn to the practical problem of trying to determine criteria themselves. How do you go about finding the criteria you'll need for distinguishing a good teacher from a poor teacher, a good movie from a bad movie, a successful manager from an unsuccessful manager, a healthy diet from an unhealthy diet, and so forth?

Step 1: Determine the Category in Which the Object Being Evaluated Belongs

In determining the quality or value of any given X, you must first figure out what your standard of comparison is. If, for example, you asked one of your professors to write you a letter of recommendation for a summer job, what class of

---

*We can avoid this problem somewhat by placing items into different classes on the basis of cost. For example, a Mercedes may come out far ahead of a Hyundai, but the more relevant evaluative question to ask is "How does a Mercedes compare to a Cadillac?"

things should the professor put you into? Is he or she supposed to evaluate you as a student? a leader? a worker? a storyteller? a party animal? or what? This is an important question because the criteria for excellence in one class (student) may be very different from criteria for excellence in another class (party animal).

To write a useful letter, your professor should consider you first as a member of the general class "summer job holder" and base her evaluation of you on criteria relevant to that class. To write a truly effective letter, however, your professor needs to consider your qualifications in the context of the smallest applicable class of candidates: not "summer job holder," but "law office intern" or "highway department flagperson" or "golf course groundsperson." Clearly, each of these subclasses has very different criteria for excellence that your professor needs to address.

We thus recommend placing X into the smallest relevant class because of the apples-and-oranges law: To avoid giving a mistaken rating to a perfectly good apple, you need to make sure you are judging an apple under the class "apple" and not under the next larger class "fruit" or a neighboring class "orange." And to be even more precise, you may wish to evaluate your apple in the class "eating apple" as opposed to "pie apple" because the latter class is supposed to be tarter and the former class juicier and sweeter.

Obviously, there are limits to this law. For example, the smallest possible class of apples would contain only one member—the one being evaluated. At that point, your apple is both the best and the worst member of its class, and, hence, evaluation of it is meaningless. Also, we sometimes can't avoid apples-and-oranges comparisons because they are thrust on us by circumstances, tradition, or some other factor. Thus, the Academy Award judges selecting "best movie" aren't allowed to distinguish between "great big box office hits" and "serious little films that make socially significant points."

Step 2: Determine the Purpose or Function of This Class

Once you have located X in its appropriate class, you should next determine what the purpose or function of this class is. Let's suppose that the summer job you are applying for is tour guide at the city zoo. The function of a tour guide is to make people feel welcome, to give them interesting information about the zoo, to make their visit pleasant, and so forth. Consequently, you wouldn't want your professor's evaluation to praise your term paper on Napoleon Bonaparte or your successful synthesis of some compound in your chemistry lab. Rather, the professor should highlight your dependability, your neat appearance, your good speaking skills, and your ability to work with groups. In contrast, if you were applying for graduate school, then your term paper on Bonaparte or your chem lab wizardry would be relevant. In other words, the professor has to evaluate you according to the class "tour guide," not "graduate student," and the criteria for each class derive from the purpose or function of the class.

Let's take another example. Suppose that you are the chair of a committee charged with evaluating the job performance of Lillian Jones, director of the admissions office at Clambake College. Ms. Jones has been a controversial manager because several members of her staff have filed complaints about her management style. In making your evaluation, your first step is to place Ms. Jones into an appropriate class, in this case, the general class "manager," and then the more specific class "manager of an admissions office at a small, private college." You then need to identify the purpose or function of these classes. You might say that the function of the general class "manager" is to "oversee actual operations of an organization so that the organization meets its goals as harmoniously and efficiently as possible," whereas the function of the specific class "manager of an admissions office at a small, private college" is "the successful recruitment of the best students possible."

Step 3: Determine Criteria Based on the Purposes or Function of the Class to Which X Belongs

Once you've worked out the purposes of the class, you are ready to work out the criteria by which you judge all members of the class. Criteria for judgment will be based on those features of Y that help it achieve the purposes of its class. For example, once you determine the purpose and function of the position filled by Lillian Jones, you can develop a list of criteria for managerial success:

1. Criteria related to "efficient operation"
   - articulates priorities and goals for the organization
   - is aggressive in achieving goals
   - motivates fellow employees
   - is well organized, efficient, and punctual
   - is articulate and communicates well
2. Criteria related to "harmonious operation"
   - creates job satisfaction for subordinates
   - is well groomed, sets good example of professionalism
   - is honest, diplomatic in dealing with subordinates
   - is flexible in responding to problems and special concerns of staff members
3. Criteria related to meeting specific goals of a college admissions office
   - creates a comprehensive recruiting program
   - demonstrates that recruiting program works

Step 4: Give Relative Weightings
to the Criteria

Even though you have established criteria, you must still decide which of the criteria are most important. In the case of Lillian Jones, is it more important that she bring in lots of students to Clambake College or that she create a harmonious, happy office? These sorts of questions are at the heart of many evaluative controversies. Thus, a justification for your weighting of criteria may well be an important part of your argument.

DETERMINING WHETHER X
MEETS THE CRITERIA

Once you've established your criteria, you've got to figure out how well X meets them. You proceed by gathering evidence and examples. The success of the recruiting program at Clambake College can probably be measured empirically, so you gather statistics about applications to the college, SAT scores of applicants, number of acceptances, academic profiles of entering freshmen, and so forth. You might then compare those statistics to those compiled by Ms. Jones's predecessor or to those of her competitors at other, comparable institutions.

You can also look at what the recruiting program actually does—the number of recruiters, the number of high school visitations, quality of admissions brochures, and other publications. You can also look at Ms. Jones in action, searching for specific incidents or examples that illustrate her management style. For example, you can't measure a trait such as diplomacy empirically, but you can find specific instances where the presence or absence of this trait was demonstrated. You could turn to examples where Ms. Jones may or may not have prevented a potentially divisive situation from occurring or where she offered or failed to offer encouragement at psychologically the right moment to keep someone from getting demoralized. As with criteria-match arguments in definition, one must provide examples of how the X in question meets each of the criteria that have been set up.

Your final evaluation of Ms. Jones, then, might include an overview of her strengths and weaknesses along the various criteria you have established. You might say that Ms. Jones has done an excellent job with recruitment (an assertion you can support with data on student enrollments over the last five years) but was relatively poor at keeping the office staff happy (as evidenced by employee complaints, high turnover, and your own observations of her rather abrasive management style). Nevertheless, your final recommendation might be to retain Ms. Jones for another three-year contract because you believe that an excellent recruiting record is the most important criterion for her position at Clambake. You might justify this heavy weighting of recruiting on the grounds that the institution's survival depends on its ability to attract adequate numbers of good students.

FOR CLASS DISCUSSION

The following small-group exercise can be accomplished in one or two class hours. It gives you a good model of the process you will need to go through in order to write your own evaluation essay. Working in small groups, suppose that you are going to evaluate a controversial member of one of the following classes:

a. your institution's library, computer labs, classrooms or another facility
b. a political figure
c. an athlete
d. a school newspaper or school policy
e. a play, film, or Web site
f. a recent Supreme Court decision
g. a rock singer or group or MTV video
h. a dorm or living group
i. a restaurant or college hangout
j. an X of your choice

1. Choose a controversial member within one of these classes as the specific person, thing, or event you are going to evaluate (Professor Choplogic, the Wild Dog Bar, Eminem, and so forth).

2. Narrow down the general class by determining the smallest relevant class to which your X belongs (from "athlete" to "basketball guard"; from "college hangout" to "college hangout for people who want to hold late-night bull sessions").

3. Make a list of the purposes or functions of that class, and then list the criteria that a good member of that class would have to have in order to accomplish the purposes.

4. If necessary, rank order your criteria.

5. Evaluate your X by matching X to each of the criteria.

ORGANIZING AN EVALUATION ARGUMENT

As you write a draft, you might find useful the following prototypical structures for evaluation arguments. Of course, you can always alter these plans if another structure better fits your material.

Plan 1 (Criteria and Match in Separate Sections)

- Introduce the issue by showing disagreements about how to evaluate a problematic X (Is X a good Y?).
- State your claim.
- Present your criteria for evaluating members of class Y.
  State and develop Criterion 1.
  State and develop Criterion 2.
  Continue with the rest of your criteria.
- Summarize and respond to possible objections to your criteria.
- Restate your claim asserting that X is (is not) a good member of class Y.
  Apply Criterion 1 to your case.
  Apply Criterion 2 to your case.
  Continue the match argument.
- Summarize and respond to possible objections to your match argument.
- Conclude your argument.

Plan 2 (Criteria and Match Interwoven)

- Introduce the issue by showing disagreements about how to evaluate a problematic X (Is X a good Y?).
- Present your claim.
  State Criterion 1 and argue that your X meets (does not meet) this criterion.
  State Criterion 2 and argue that your X meets (does not meet) this criterion.
  Continue with criteria-match sections for additional criteria.
- Summarize opposing views.
- Refute or concede to opposing views.
- Conclude your argument.

QUESTIONING AND CRITIQUING AN EVALUATION ARGUMENT

To strengthen your draft of an evaluation argument, you can role-play a skeptic by asking the following questions.

Will a skeptic accept my criteria?   Many evaluative arguments are weak because the writers have simply assumed that readers will accept their criteria. Whenever your audience's acceptance of your criteria is in doubt, you will need to make your warrants clear and provide backing in their support.

Are my criteria based on the "smallest applicable class" for X?   For example, the film *The Blair Witch Project* will certainly be a failure if you evaluate it in the general class "movies," in which it would have to compete with *Citizen Kane* and other great classics. But if you evaluated it as a "horror film" or a "low-budget film," it would have a greater chance for success and hence of yielding an arguable evaluation.

Will a skeptic accept my general weighting of criteria?   Another vulnerable spot in an evaluation argument is the relative weight of the criteria. How much anyone weights a given criterion is usually a function of his or her own interests relative to the X in question. You should always ask whether some particular group affected by the quality of X might not have good reasons for weighting the criteria differently.

Will a skeptic question my standard of reference?   In questioning the criteria for judging X, we can also focus on the standard of reference used—what's common versus what's ideal. If you have argued that X is bad because it doesn't live up to what's ideal, you can expect some readers to defend X on the basis of what's common. Similarly, if you argue that X is good because it is better than its competitors, you can expect some readers to point out how short it falls from what is ideal.

Will a skeptic criticize my use of empirical measures?   The tendency to mistake empirical measures for criteria is a common one that any critic of an argument should be aware of. As we have discussed earlier, what's most measurable isn't always significant when it comes to assessing the essential traits needed to fulfill whatever function X is supposed to fulfill. A 95-mph fastball is certainly an impressive empirical measure of a pitcher's ability. But if the pitcher doesn't get batters out, that measure is a misleading gauge of performance.

Will a skeptic accept my criteria but reject my match argument?   The other major way of testing an evaluation argument is to anticipate how readers might object to your stated reasons and grounds. Will readers challenge you by finding sampling errors in your data or otherwise find that you used evidence selectively? For example, if you think your opponents will emphasize Lillian Jones's abrasive management style much more heavily than you did, you may be able to undercut their arguments by finding counterexamples that show Ms. Jones acting diplomatically. Be prepared to counter objections to your grounds.

READING

The following essay, by student writer Pat Inglenook, evaluates the Spice Girl phenomenon of the late 1990s. At the time this essay was written, Ginger Spice had just left the band. Critics predicted a quick decline of Spice Girl popularity. Inglenook chooses to evaluate the Spice Girls not as musicians or entertainers but as marketers of an image.

The Spice Girls:
Good at Marketing but Not Good for Their Market
Pat Inglenook (Student)

When my eight-year-old sister asked for a Baby Spice talking doll (it plays Baby Spice's voice saying "In my bed I've got two teddies, a rabbit, two dollies" and "Fantastic. I love it"), and my eleven-year-old sister and her friends seemed to be dancing to Spice Girl CDs all the time, I started to wonder about this strange relationship between capitalism and culture in the late 1990s. What is it about the Spice Girls—Ginger Spice, Posh Spice, Baby Spice, Scary Spice, and Sporty Spice—that has attracted mobs of screaming, hysterical girls, aged seven to fourteen, and created for the Spice Girls a multi-million-dollar industry almost overnight? Clearly, my two sisters and their friends with their three-inch Spice Girl figurines ($3.99 each) and their seven-inch Spice Girl dolls ($7.99 each) and their Spice Girl Hair Play set, Nail Salon set, and Tattoo Graphix set ($9.97 each), to say nothing of the CDs ($16.85 each), have helped to support this industry. But why? As I have watched my sisters I have wondered, What is the fascination here? The Spice Girls do wear hip, hot-looking outfits, but the group's music is bubblegum for the brain. One critic says that the Spice Girl music is an "ideal hollow-commodity for a world increasingly obsessed with 'low': low-fat, low-sodium, low-calorie, low-IQ" (Crumley). Neither do they fare well in the category "actresses," where they won the anti-Oscar "Golden Raspberry Award" as "Worst Actress" for 1998. According to the judge, "They have the talent of one bad actress between them" ("Shiteworld"). 1

So if we place the Spice Girls in the categories "musician" or "actress," they fail miserably. But if we evaluate them in the category "marketers," they obviously excel. They are excellent marketers because, in targeting a specific audience of preteen girls, they have shrewdly created an image that appeals to that audience's interests and psychological desires. 2

Their first mark of excellence is that they understand girl psychology, which wants sexy fashion without sex. As any good marketer knows, the younger part of the Spice Girls' target audience values Barbie dolls, and so the Spice Girls created a Barbie image of décolletage and fashion without any Madonna-like interest in real sex. In their film "Spice World," the girls look music-video sexy, but they aren't seeking sex. When one of the directors tries to put some buff male dancers on the stage, the girls do an "Ick, Boys" routine and mock them. No real boyfriends intrude on this Barbie doll world. 3

Instead of sex, the Spice Girls value an endless slumber party where giggling girls share secrets. In *Spice World,* they bond together like fun-seeking little girls on vacation from the grown-up world of responsibility represented by their manager. In this intimate little girl world, they look out for each other like Care Bears. They are even willing to miss their concert date to stay with their friend who is having a baby. 4

Another example of their marketing shrewdness is the way that the Spice Girls appeal to individualism and the belief that any self has many sides. Just as it was a calculatingly clever marketing move for the Barbie people to create an astronaut Barbie, a teacher Barbie, 5 and a doctor Barbie, so was it brilliant to give each Spice Girl a different personality type and a different style of hot, sexy clothes. On any given day, your typical ten-year-old girl can live out her baby side, her posh side, her sporty side, her scary side, and her fun-loving Ginger side.

6   But their shrewdest marketing move is to create an illusion that a girl can be both a sex object and a liberated woman. Popular culture today pummels young girls with two contradictory messages. First, it tells girls to make themselves objects of sexual desire by being consumers of beauty and glamour products and purchasers of fashion magazines. Conversely, it tells girls to be liberated women, fully equal to men, with men's freedom and power and array of career choices. The Spice Girls, with their "girl power" logos on midriff T's worn over micro-skirts, send both messages simultaneously. Their girl-power side is acted out in *Spice World* by their defiance of the male authority figures. For instance, they "steal" a boat and go for a frolicking excursion on a speedboat. Later in the movie, their "heroic" bus ride (a parody of James Bond pursuit scenes) shows the girls having another adventure and taking control of their lives. Even their rise from poverty to fame in a music culture dominated by men demonstrates "girl power." Their object-of-sexual-desire side is portrayed constantly by their sexy clothes and dance routines. The effect is to urge young girls to become capitalist consumers of beauty products while believing they possess power as girls. Girls get the same illusion when they comb the hair of their astronaut Barbies.

7   Despite the overwhelming marketing success of the Spice Girls, I question whether monetary gain should be the main measure of this cultural product. Furthermore, although the Spice Girls sell themselves as models for young girls and appear to succeed, are they promoting models that can and should be imitated?

8   Some people would say that combining sexuality and girl power is good and beneficial. Critics of feminism often complain that hard-line feminists want women to give up beauty and sex appeal. These critics don't like that desexed view of women. They think a truly liberated woman should be able to use *all* her powers, and some of this power comes from her being a sex object. This view would say that beauty pageant contestants, topless dancers, and even prostitutes can be liberated women if they use their sexuality to get what they want and if they feel good about themselves. From this perspective, the Spice Girls use their sexuality in the name of liberation. This view perhaps led the United Nations to send Geri Halliwell (the former Ginger Spice) to be an ambassador of goodwill for the United Nations Population Fund to promote contraceptives in Third World countries ("Church Attacks").

9   But to me this argument doesn't work. I think the Spice Girls are confusing, even bad, models for helping young girls integrate sexuality and liberation. The sex is voyeuristic only. The Spice Girls flaunt their sexuality but don't show any signs of establishing healthy adult relationships. The projected scene of married life in *Spice World* shows fat or pregnant housewives bored out of their skulls—no love, no husbands, no families. Equally strange is the childbirth scene where the Spice Girls seem to know nothing about female bodies. It is closer to a stork delivery than the real thing: no messy water, blood, and umbilical cords. The cherubic, powdered baby pops out like toast from a toaster.

The Spice Girl image sends all kinds of mixed messages, urging preteens to become sex   10
objects while remaining little girls. I'm surprised that parents aren't up in arms (but they are
the ones, of course, who supply the money that drives the Spice enterprise). In a review of
Spice World from *Screen It: Entertainment Reviews for Parents,* the reviewers rated the
movie "mild" for sex/nudity (parents were cautioned primarily about naked male butts in
one scene), and under the criterion "topics to talk about" they found almost nothing in the
movie that needs discussion with one's children. On the lookout for things like visible nip-
ples, sex scenes, and violence, parents have failed to see the unhealthy, fragmented, and
warped view of womanhood the Spice Girls project to their young audience. Their strange
clashing mixture of sexuality and liberation promotes confusion, not health.

Near the end of *Spice World* the girls are stopped by a cop who aims to give them   11
a ticket for reckless driving. Undaunted, they turn to Baby Spice, who gives Daddy
Policeman her best I'm-a-sorry-little-girl smile, and his heart melts. Rather than face the
consequences of choice-making in an adult world, Baby Spice knows just the right daddy-
pleasing gesture to make all their troubles go away. I grant that the Spice Girls are great at
marketing themselves, but I don't think their product is good for their market. Maybe soon
all the Spice Girl dolls and CDs in my house will be given away like other outgrown, fad-
dish toys. I hope the next pop cultural sensation aimed at preteen girls has more wholesome substance than this mixture of illusory independence, sexiness, and lollipops.

Works Cited

"Church Attacks Ex-Spice Girl's Sex-Education Tour." *Seattle Times* 15 June 1999: A18.

Crumley, Bruce. "Spice Invaders." *Culture* Kiosque 12 June 1997. Paris. 23 Aug. 1999 <http://www.
      culturekiosque.com/nouveau/comment/rhespice.htm>.

Rev. of *Spice World.* dir. Bob Spiers. *Screen It! Entertainment Reviews for Parents* 12 Jan. 1998. 24
      Aug. 1999 <http://www.screenit.com/movies/1998/spice_world.html>.

"Shiteworld: The Movies." *New Musical Express Online.* 23 Aug. 1999 <http://nme.com/newsdesk/
      19990222143334news.html>.

WRITING ASSIGNMENT FOR CHAPTER 13

Write an argument in which you try to change someone's mind about the value
of X. The X you choose should be controversial or at least problematic. While you
are safe in arguing that a Mercedes is a good car or that smoking is bad for your
health, your claim is unlikely to surprise anyone. By "controversial" or "problematic," we mean that people are likely to disagree with your evaluation of X, that
they are surprised at your evaluation, or that you are somehow opposing the common or expected view of X. By choosing a controversial or problematic X, you will
be able to focus on a clear issue. Somewhere in your essay you should summarize
alternative views and either refute them or concede to them (see Chapter 8).

Note that this assignment asks you to do something different from a typical movie review, restaurant review, or product review in a consumer magazine. Many reviews are simply informational or analytical; the writer's purpose is to describe the object or event being reviewed and explain its strengths and weaknesses. In contrast, your purpose here is persuasive. You must try to change someone's mind about the worth or value of X.

14 Proposal Arguments

We Should (Should Not) Do X

EXAMPLE CASE

Many cultural commentators are alarmed by a new social disease brought on by addictive spending. Dubbed "affluenza" and "credititis," this disease is spreading through aggressive promotion of credit cards. Economic analysts are particularly concerned at the way credit card companies are deluging teenagers with credit card offers. Some argue that encouraging credit card debt among the young is highly irresponsible corporate behavior. To raise public awareness of the problem, a group of legislators proposed that the following warning label be placed prominently on all credit cards: "*Warning:* Failure to research interest rates and credit cards may result in personal financial loss or possible bankruptcy."*

THE NATURE OF PROPOSAL ARGUMENTS

Proposal arguments are among the most common arguments that you will encounter or be called on to write. Their essence is that they call for action. In reading a proposal, the audience is enjoined to make a decision and then to act on it—to *do* something. Proposal arguments are sometimes called *should* or *ought* arguments because these helping verbs express the obligation to act: "We *should* do X" or "We *ought* to do X."

---

*"Credit Cards: Wealth Hazard," *Seattle Times*, 4 Feb. 1999: B2.

For instructional purposes, we will distinguish between two kinds of proposal arguments, even though they are closely related and involve the same basic arguing strategies. The first kind we will call *practical proposals* which propose an action to solve some kind of local or immediate problem. A student's proposal to change the billing procedures for scholarship students would be an example of a practical proposal, as would an engineering firm's proposal for the design of a new bridge being planned by a city government. The second kind we will call *policy proposals*, in which the writer offers a broad plan of action to solve major social, economic, or political problems affecting the common good. An argument that the United States should adopt a national health insurance plan or that the terms for senators and representatives should be limited to twelve years would be examples of policy proposals.

THE GENERAL STRUCTURE AND STRATEGY OF PROPOSAL ARGUMENTS

Proposal arguments, whether practical proposals or policy proposals, generally have a three-part structure: (1) description of a problem, (2) proposed solution, and (3) justification for the proposed solution. Luckily, proposal arguments don't require different sorts of argumentative strategies from the ones you have already been using. In the justification section of your proposal argument, you develop *because* clauses of the kinds you have practiced all along throughout this text.

SPECIAL CONCERNS OF PROPOSAL ARGUMENTS

In their call for action, proposal arguments entail certain emphases and audience concerns that you don't generally face with other kinds of arguments. Let's look briefly at some of these special concerns.

The Need for Presence

It's one thing for a person to assent to a value judgment, but it's another thing to act on that judgment. The personal cost of acting may be high for many people in your audience. That means that you have to engage not only audience members' intellects but their emotions as well. Thus proposal arguments often require more attention to *pathos* than do other kinds of arguments (see pp. 109–15).

The effect of *pathos* is to give your argument presence as well as intellectual force. An argument is said to have *presence* when the problem being addressed ceases to be an abstraction. Pathetic appeals help the reader sense the urgency and realness of the problem addressed. In an argument with presence, the reader can share the writer's point of view—the writer's emotions, the force of the writer's personal engagement with the issue. Such arguments call the reader beyond assent toward action.

The Need to Overcome People's
Natural Conservatism

Another difficulty faced by a proposal maker is the innate conservatism of all human beings, whatever their political persuasion. One philosopher refers to this conservatism as the *law of inertia*, the tendency of all things in the universe, including human beings, to remain at rest if possible. The popular adage "If it ain't broke, don't fix it" is one expression of this tendency. Hence, proposers of change face an extraordinary burden of proof. Specifically, they have to prove that something needs fixing, that it can be fixed, and that the cost of fixing it will be outweighed by the benefits of fixing it.

The difficulty of proving that something needs fixing is compounded by the fact that frequently the status quo appears to be working. So sometimes when writing a proposal, you can't argue that what we have is bad, but only that what we could have would be better. Often, then, a proposal argument will be based not on present evils but on the evils of lost potential. And getting an audience to accept lost potential may be difficult indeed, given the inherently abstract nature of potentiality.

The Difficulty of Predicting
Future Consequences

Further, most proposal makers will be forced to predict consequences of a given act. As we've seen in our earlier discussions of causality, it is difficult enough to argue backward from event Y in order to establish that X caused Y. Think how much harder it is to establish that X will, in the future, cause certain things to occur. We all know enough of history to realize that few major decisions have led neatly to their anticipated results. This knowledge indeed accounts for much of our conservatism. All the things that can go wrong in a causal argument can go wrong in a proposal argument as well; the major difference is that in a proposal argument we typically have less evidence for our conjectures.

The Problem of Evaluating Consequences

A final difficulty faced by all proposal arguments concerns the difficulty of evaluating the consequences of the proposal. In government and industry, managers often turn to a tool known as *cost-benefit analysis* to calculate the potential consequences of a given proposal. As much as possible, a cost-benefit analysis tries to reduce all consequences to a single scale for purposes of comparison. Most often, the scale will be money. Although this scale may work well in some circumstances, it can lead to grotesquely inappropriate conclusions in other situations.

Just how does one balance the money saved by cutting Medicare benefits against the suffering of the people denied benefits? How does one translate the beauty of a wilderness area into a dollar amount? On this score, cost-benefit analyses often run into a problem discussed in the previous chapter: the seductiveness of empirical measures (see pp. 203–04). Because something can't be readily measured doesn't mean it can be safely ignored. And finally, what will be a cost for one group will often be a benefit for others. For example, if Social Security benefits are cut, those on Social Security will suffer, but current workers who pay for it with taxes will take home a larger paycheck.

These, then, are some of the general difficulties facing someone who sets out to argue in favor of a proposal. Although not insurmountable, they are at least daunting.

DEVELOPING A PROPOSAL ARGUMENT

Writers of proposal arguments must focus in turn on three main phases or stages of the argument: showing that a problem exists, explaining the proposed solution, and offering a justification.

Convincing Your Readers That a Problem Exists

There is one argumentative strategy generic to all proposal arguments: awakening in the reader a sense of a problem. Typically, the development of a problem occurs in one of two places in a proposal argument—either in the introduction prior to the presentation of the arguer's proposal claim or in the body of the paper as the first main reason justifying the proposal claim. In the second instance the writer's first *because* clause has the following structure: "We should do X *because* we are facing a serious problem that needs a solution."

At this stage of your argument, it's important to give your problem presence. You must get people to see how the problem affects people, perhaps through examples of suffering or other loss or through persuasive statistics and so forth. Your goal is to awaken your readers to the existence of a problem, a problem they may well not have recognized before.

Besides giving presence to the problem, a writer must also gain the readers' intellectual assent to the depth, range, and potential seriousness of the problem. Suppose, for illustration, that you wanted to propose a special tax to increase funding for higher education in your state. In trying to convince taxpayers in your state that a problem exists, what obstacles might you face? First of all, many taxpayers never went to college and feel that they get along just fine without it. They tend to worry more about the quality of roads, social services, elementary and secondary schools, police and fire protection, and so forth. They are not too convinced that they need to worry about professors' salaries or better-equipped research labs. Thus, it's not enough to talk about the importance of education in general or to cite figures showing how paltry your state's funding of higher education is.

To convince members of your audience of the need for your proposal, you'll have to describe the consequences of low funding levels in terms they can relate to. You'll have to show them that potential benefits to the state are lost because of inadequate funding. Perhaps you can show the cost in terms of inadequately skilled graduates, disgruntled teachers, high turnover, brain drain to other states, inadequate educational services to farmers and businesspeople, lost productivity, and so forth. Or perhaps you can show your audience examples of benefits realized from better college funding in other states. Such examples give life to the abstract notion of lost potential.

All of this is not to say that you can't or shouldn't argue that higher education is inherently good. But until your reader can see low funding levels as "problematic" rather than "simply the way things are," your proposal stands little chance of being enacted.

Showing the Specifics of Your Proposal

Having decided that there is a problem to be solved, you should lay out your thesis, which is a proposal for solving the problem. Your goal now is to stress the feasibility of your solution, including costs. The art of proposal making is the art of the possible. To be sure, not all proposals require elaborate descriptions of the implementation process. If you are proposing, for example, that a local PTA chapter should buy new tumbling mats for the junior high gym classes, the procedures for buying the mats will probably be irrelevant. But in many arguments the specifics of your proposal—the actual step-by-step methods of implementing it—may be instrumental in winning your audience's support.

You will also need to show how your proposal will solve the problem either partially or wholly. Sometimes you may first need to convince your reader that the problem is solvable, not something intractably rooted in "the way things are," such as earthquakes or jealousy. In other words, expect that some members of your audience will be skeptical about the ability of any proposal to solve the problem you are addressing. You may well need, therefore, to "listen" to this point of view in your refutation section and to argue that your problem is at least partially solvable.

To persuade your audience that your proposal can work, you can follow any one of several approaches. A typical approach is to lay out a causal argument showing how one consequence will lead to another until your solution is effected. Another approach is to turn to resemblance arguments, either analogy or precedent. You try to show how similar proposals have been successful elsewhere. Or, if similar things have failed in the past, you try to show how the present situation is different.

The Justification: Convincing Your Reader
That Your Proposal Should Be Enacted

This phase of a proposal argument will need extensive development in some arguments and minimal development in others, again depending on your particular problem and the rhetorical context of your proposal. If your audience already acknowledges the seriousness of the problem you are addressing and has simply been waiting for the right solution to come along, then your argument will be successful so long as you can convince your audience that your solution will work and that it won't cost too much. Such arguments depend on the clarity of your proposal and the feasibility of its being implemented.

But what if the costs are high? What if your readers don't think the problem is serious? What if they don't appreciate the benefits of solving the problem or the bad consequences of not solving it? In such cases you have to develop persuasive reasons for enacting your proposal. You may also have to determine who has the power to act on your proposal and apply arguments directly to that person's or agency's immediate interests. You need to know to whom or to what your power source is beholden or responsive and what values your power source holds that can be appealed to. You're looking, in short, for the best pressure points.

In the next two sections, we explain invention strategies you can use to generate persuasive reasons for proposal arguments and to anticipate your audience's doubts and reservations. We call these the "claim-type strategy" and the "stock-issues strategy."

USING THE CLAIM-TYPE STRATEGY TO DEVELOP A PROPOSAL ARGUMENT

In Chapter 9 we explained how a theory of claim types can help you generate ideas for an argument. Specifically, we explained how values claims often depend for their supporting reasons on the reality claims of category, cause, or resemblance. This principle leads to a powerful idea-generating strategy that can be schematized as follows:

Overview of Claim-Type Strategy

We should do X (proposal claim)

- because X is a Y (categorical claim)
- because X will lead to good consequences (causal claim)
- because X is like Y (resemblance claim)

With each of these *because* clauses, the arguer's goal is to link X to one or more good things the audience already values. For a specific example, suppose that you wanted insurance companies to pay for long-term psychological counseling for anorexia. The claim-type strategy could help you develop arguments such as these:

Insurance companies should pay for long-term psychological counseling for anorexia (proposal claim)

- because paying for such counseling is a demonstration of commitment to women's health (categorical claim)

- because paying for such counseling might save insurance companies from much more extensive medical costs at a later date (causal claim)
- because anorexia is like alcoholism or drug dependency, which is already covered by insurance (resemblance claim)

Proposal arguments using reality claims as reasons are very common. Here is another example, this time from a famous art exhibit controversy in the early 1990s when conservatives protested government funding for an exhibition of homoerotic photographs by artist Robert Mapplethorpe.

Taxpayer funding for the Mapplethorpe exhibit should be withdrawn (proposal claim)

- because the photographs are pornographic (a categorical claim linking the photographs to pornography, which the intended audience opposes)
- because the exhibit promotes community acceptance of homosexuality (a causal claim linking the exhibit to acceptance of homosexuality, which the intended audience opposes)
- because the photographs are more like political statements than art (a resemblance claim linking the exhibit to politics rather than art, a situation that the intended audience would consider unsuitable for arts funding)

Whatever you might think of this argument, it shows how the supporting reasons for a proposal claim can be drawn from claims of category, cause, and resemblance. Each of these arguments attempts to appeal to the value system of the audience. Each tries to show how the proposed action is within the class of things that the audience already values, will lead to consequences that the audience desires, or is similar to something that the audience already values. The invention procedure can be summarized in the following way.

Argument from Category

To discover reasons using this strategy, conduct the following kind of search:

We should (should not) do X because X is _____.

Try to fill in the blank with an appropriate adjective or noun (*good, just, ethical, criminal, ugly, violent, peaceful, wrong, inflationary, healing,* etc; *an act of kindness, terrorism, murder, true art, political suicide,* etc.). The point is to try to fill in the blank with a noun or adjective that appeals in some way to your audience's values. Your goal is to show that X belongs to the chosen class or category.

Argument from Consequence

To discover reasons using this category, conduct the following kind of search:

We should (should not) do X because X leads to these good (bad) consequences: _____, _____, _____, _____.

Then think of consequences that your audience will agree are good or bad as your argument requires.

Argument from Resemblance

To discover supporting reasons using this strategy, conduct the following kind of search:

We should (should not) do X because doing X is like _____.

Then think of analogies or precedents that are similar to doing X but that currently have greater appeal to your audience. Your task is then to transfer to X your audience's favorable or unfavorable feelings toward the analogy/precedent.

These three kinds of searches—supporting a proposal claim from the perspectives of category, consequence, and resemblance—are powerful means of invention. In selecting among these reasons, choose those most likely to appeal to your audience's assumptions, beliefs, and values.

▼ FOR CLASS DISCUSSION

1. Working individually or in small groups, use the strategies of category, consequence, and resemblance to create *because* clauses that support each of the following claims. Try to have at least one *because* clause from each of the claim types, but generate as many reasons as possible. Don't worry about whether any individual reason exactly fits the claim type. The purpose is to stimulate thinking, not fill in the slots.

EXAMPLE

CLAIM:	Pit bulls make bad pets.
REASON FROM CATEGORY:	because they are vicious

REASON FROM CONSEQUENCE:	because owning a pit bull leads to conflicts with neighbors
REASON FROM RESEMBLANCE:	because owning a pit bull is like having a shell-shocked roommate—mostly they're lovely companions but they can turn violent if startled

   a. Marijuana should be legalized.
   b. Division I college athletes should receive salaries.
   c. High schools should pass out free contraceptives.
   d. Violent video games should be made illegal.
   e. Parents should be heavily taxed for having more than two children.

2. Repeat the exercise, taking a different position on each issue.

USING THE STOCK-ISSUES STRATEGY TO DEVELOP A PROPOSAL ARGUMENT

Another effective way to generate ideas for a proposal argument is to ask yourself a series of questions based on the stock-issues strategy. Suppose, for example, you wanted to develop the following argument: "To solve the problem of students who won't take risks with their writing, the faculty at Weasel College should adopt a pass/fail method of grading in all writing courses." The stock-issues strategy invites the writer to consider stock ways (that is, common, usual, frequently repeated ways) that such arguments can be conducted.

Stock issue 1:   *Is there really a problem here that needs to be solved?* Is it really true that a large number of student writers won't take risks in their writing? Is this problem more serious than other writing problems such as undeveloped ideas, lack of organization, and poor sentence structure? This stock issue invites the writer to convince her audience that a true problem exists. Conversely, an opponent to the proposal might argue that a true problem does not exist.

Stock issue 2:   *Will the proposed solution really solve this problem?* Is it true that a pass/fail grading system will cause students to take more risks with their writing? Will more interesting, surprising, and creative essays result from pass/fail grading? Or will students simply put less effort into their writing? This stock issue prompts a supporter to demonstrate that the proposal will solve the problem, and it prompts an opponent to show that the proposal won't work.

Stock issue 3:   *Can the problem be solved more simply without disturbing the status quo?* An opponent of the proposal might agree that a problem exists and that the proposed solution might solve it. However, the opponent might say, "Are there not less radical ways to solve this problem? If we want more creative and risk-taking student essays, can't we just change our grading criteria so that we reward risky papers and penalize conventional ones?" This stock issue prompts supporters to show that *only* the proposed solution will solve the problem and that no minor tinkering with the status quo will be adequate. Conversely, opponents will argue that the problem can be solved without acting on the proposal.

Stock issue 4: Is the proposed solution really practical? Does it stand a chance of actually being enacted? Here an opponent to the proposal might agree that the proposal would work but that it involves pie-in-the-sky idealism. Nobody will vote to change the existing system so radically; therefore, it is a waste of our time to debate it. Following this prompt, supporters would have to argue that pass/fail grading is workable and that enough members of the faculty are disposed to it that the proposal is worth debating. Opponents might argue that the faculty at Weasel College is so traditional that pass/fail has utterly no chance of being accepted, despite its merits.

Stock issue 5: What will be the unforeseen positive and negative consequences of the proposal? Suppose we do adopt a pass/fail system. What positive or negative consequences might occur that are different from what we at first predicted? Using this prompt, an opponent might argue that pass/fail grading will reduce the effort put forth by students and that the long-range effect will be writing of even lower quality than we have now. Supporters would try to find positive consequences—perhaps a new love of writing for its own sake rather than for the sake of a grade.

▼ FOR CLASS DISCUSSION

The following collaborative task takes approximately two class days to complete. The exercise takes you through the process of creating a proposal argument.

1. In small groups, identify and list several major problems facing students in your college or university.

2. Decide among yourselves which are the most important of these problems and rank them in order of importance.

3. Take your group's number one problem and explore answers to the following questions. Group recorders should be prepared to present your group's answers to the class as a whole:
   a. Why is the problem a problem?
   b. For whom is the problem a problem?
   c. How will these people suffer if the problem is not solved? (Give specific examples.)
   d. Who has the power to solve the problem?

  e. Why hasn't the problem been solved up to this point?
  f. How can the problem be solved? (Create a proposal.)
  g. What are the probable benefits of acting on your proposal?
  h. What costs are associated with your proposal?
  i. Who will bear those costs?
  j. Why should this proposal be enacted?
  k. Why is it better than alternative proposals?

4. As a group, draft an outline for a proposal argument in which you:
  a. Describe the problem and its significance.
  b. Propose your solution to the problem.
  c. Justify your proposal by showing how the benefits of adopting that proposal outweigh the costs.

5. Recorders for each group should write their group's outline on the board and be prepared to explain it to the class.

ORGANIZING A PROPOSAL ARGUMENT

When you write your draft, you may find it helpful to have at hand some plans for typical ways of organizing a proposal argument. What follows are two common methods of organization. Option 1 is the plan most typical for practical proposals. Either Option 1 or Option 2 is an effective plan for a policy proposal.

Option 1

- Presentation of a problem that needs solving:
  Description of problem (Give the problem presence.)
  Background, including previous attempts to solve the problem
  Argument that the problem is solvable (optional)
- Presentation of writer's proposal:
  Succinct statement of the proposed solution serves as thesis statement.
  Explain specifics of the proposed solution.
- Summary and rebuttal of opposing views (In practical proposals, this section is often a summary and rejection of alternative ways of solving the problem.)
- Justification persuading the reader that the proposal should be enacted:
  Present and develop Reason 1.
  Present and develop Reason 2.
  Continue with additional reasons.
- Conclusion that exhorts the audience to act:
  Give presence to the final sentences.

Option 2

- Presentation of an issue, including background
- Presentation of the writer's proposal
- Justification:

  Reason 1: Show that the proposal addresses a serious problem.

  Reason 2: Show that the proposal will solve the problem.

  Reason 3: Give additional reasons for enacting the proposal.

- Summary and refutation of opposing views
- Conclusion that exhorts the audience to act

QUESTIONING AND CRITIQUING A PROPOSAL ARGUMENT

As we've suggested, proposal arguments need to overcome people's innate conservatism, the difficulty of anticipating all the consequences of a proposal, and so forth. What questions, then, can we ask about proposal arguments to help us anticipate these problems?

Will a skeptic deny that my problem is really a problem? The first question to ask of your proposal is "What's so wrong with the status quo that change is necessary?" The second question is "Who loses if the status quo is changed?" Be certain not to overlook the second question. Most proposal makers can demonstrate that some sort of problem exists, but often the problem exists only for certain groups of people. Solving the problem will thus prove a benefit to some people but a cost to others. Members of your audience who examine the problem from the perspective of the potential losers, rather than the winners, will often raise doubts about your proposal.

For example, one state recently held an initiative on a proposed "bottle bill" that would fight litter by permitting the sale of soda and beer only in returnable bottles. Sales outlets would be required to charge a substantial deposit on the bottles in order to encourage people to return them. Proponents of the proposal emphasized citizens as "winners" sharing in the new cleanliness of a landscape no longer littered with cans. To refute this argument, opponents showed consumers as "losers" burdened with the high cost of deposits and the hassle of collecting and returning bottles to grocery stores.

Will a skeptic doubt the effectiveness of my solution? Assuming that you've satisfied yourself that a significant problem exists for a significant number of people, a number of questions remain to be asked about the quality of the proposed solution to solve the problem. First, "Does the problem exist for the reasons cited, or might there be alternative explanations?" Here we return to the familiar ground of causal arguments. A proposal supposedly strikes at the cause of a problem. But perhaps striking at that "cause" won't solve the problem. Perhaps you've mistaken a symptom for a cause, or confused two commonly associated but essentially unlinked phenomena for a cause-effect relationship. For example, will paying teachers higher salaries improve the quality of teaching or merely attract greedier rather than brighter people? Maybe more good teachers would be attracted and retained if they were given some other benefit (fewer students? smaller classes? more sabbaticals? more autonomy? more prestige?).

Another way to test your solution is to list all the uncertainties involved. This might be referred to as "the Devil you know is better than the Devil you don't know" strategy. Remind yourself of all the unanticipated consequences of past changes. Who, for example, would have thought back in the days when aerosol shaving cans were being developed that they might lead to diminished ozone layers, which might lead to more ultraviolet rays getting through the atmosphere from the sun, which would lead to higher incidences of skin cancer? The history of technology is full of such cautionary tales that can be invoked to remind you of the uncertain course that progress can sometimes take.

Will a skeptic think my proposal costs too much? The most commonly asked question of any proposal is simply "Do the benefits of enacting the proposal outweigh the costs?" As we saw above, you can't foresee all the consequences of any proposal. It's easy, before the fact, to exaggerate both the costs and the benefits of a proposal. So, in asking how much your proposal will cost, we urge you to make an honest estimate. Will your audience discover costs you hadn't anticipated—extra financial costs or unexpected psychological or environmental or aesthetic costs? As much as you can, anticipate these objections.

Will a skeptic suggest counterproposals? Related to all that's been said so far is the counterproposal. Can you imagine an appealing alternative to both the status quo and the proposal that you're making? The more clearly your proposal shows that a significant problem exists, the more important it is that you be able to identify possible counterproposals. Any potential critic of a proposal to remedy an acknowledged problem will either have to make such a counterproposal or have to argue that the problem is simply in the nature of things. So, given the likelihood that you'll be faced with a counterproposal, it only makes sense to anticipate it and to work out a refutation of it before you have it thrown at you. And who knows, you may end up liking the counterproposal better and changing your mind about what to propose!

READING

The following reading, by student writer Stephen Bean, is a policy proposal written for the assignment on page 237. Bean's paper joins a heated social debate about what to do about the mentally ill homeless. In 1988, conservative columnist Charles Krauthammer published an influential article arguing that states should confine the mentally ill homeless—involuntarily if necessary—in state mental hospitals. Krauthammer argued that the huge rise of homeless people in the 1970s and 1980s was the result of the closing of state mental hospitals following court rulings that persons could not be involuntarily committed. In this researched policy argument, Bean aims to refute Krauthammer's argument and offer a counter-proposal. Bean's argument is formatted as a formal research paper using the documentation system of the Modern Language Association (MLA). A brief explanation of this system is given in Appendix 2, "A Concise Guide to Evaluating and Documenting Sources."

Stephen Bean

Professor Arness

English 110

1 June 199X

What Should Be Done about the Mentally Ill Homeless?

1   Winter paints Seattle's streets gray with misting rain that drops lightly but steadily into pools. Walking to work through one of Seattle's oldest districts, Pioneer Square, I see an incongruous mixture of people: both successful business types and a large population of homeless. Some walk to offices or lunches grasping cups of fresh ground coffee; others slowly push wobbling carts containing their earthly possessions wrapped carefully in black plastic. These scenes of homelessness have become common throughout America's urban centers--so common, perhaps, that despite our feelings of guilt and pity, we accept the presence of the homeless as permanent. The empty-stomach feeling of confronting a ragged panhandler has become an often accepted fact of living in the city. What can we do besides giving a few cents spare change?

2   Recently, a growing number of commentators have been focusing on the mentally ill homeless. In response to the violent murder of an elderly person by a homeless mentally ill man, New York City recently increased its efforts to locate and hospitalize dangerous homeless mentally ill individuals. New York's plan will include aggressive outreach--actively going out into the streets and shelters to locate mentally ill individuals and then involuntarily hospitalizing those deemed dangerous either to others or to themselves (Dugger, "Danger" B1). Although the New York Civil Liberties Union has objected to this action on the grounds that involuntary hospitalization may violate the rights of the mentally ill, many applaud the city's action as a first step in dealing with a problem that the nation has grossly ignored. One highly influential commentator, Charles Krauthammer, has recently called for wide-scale involuntary reinstitutionalization of the mentally ill homeless--

Bean 2

a seemingly persuasive proposal until one begins to do research on the mentally ill homeless. Adopting Krauthammer's proposal would be a dangerous and wrong-headed policy for America. Rather, research shows that community-based care in which psychiatrists and social workers provide coordinated services in the community itself is a more effective solution to the problems of the mentally ill homeless than wide-scale institutionalization.

In his article "How to Save the Homeless Mentally Ill," Charles Krauthammer   3
argues that the federal government should assist the states in rebuilding a national system of asylums. He proposes that the criteria for involuntary institutionalization be broadened: The state should be permitted to institutionalize mentally ill persons involuntarily not only if they are deemed dangerous to others or to themselves (the current criterion for institutionalization) but also if they are "degraded" or made helpless by their illness. He points to the large number of patients released from state institutions in the 1960s and 1970s who, finding no support in communities, ended up on the streets. Arguing that the mentally ill need the stability and supervision that only an institution can provide, Krauthammer proposes substantial increases in federal taxes to fund rebuilding of asylums. He argues that the mentally ill need unique solutions because of their unique problems; their homelessness, he claims, stems from mental illness not poverty. Finally, Krauthammer rebuts the argument that involuntary hospitalization violates civil liberties. He argues that "liberty" has no meaning to someone suffering from severe psychosis. To let people suffer the pains of mental illness and the pains of the street when they could be treated and recover is a cruel right indeed. He points to the project HELP program, in which less than a fifth of those involuntarily hospitalized protested their commitment; most are glad, he claims, for a warm bed, nutritious food, and a safe environment.

Krauthammer's argument, while persuasive on first reading, is based on four   4
seriously flawed assumptions. His first assumption is the widely accepted notion that deinstitutionalization of state mental hospitals in the 1960s and 1970s is a primary cause of the current homelessness problem in America. Krauthammer talks about the hundreds of thousands released from the hospitals who have become "an army of grate-dwellers" (24). However, recent research has shown that the relationship of deinstitutionalization to homelessness is vastly overstated.

Ethnologist Kim Hopper argues that while deinstitutionalization has partly contributed to increased numbers of mentally ill homeless its influence is far smaller than popularly believed. She argues that the data many used to support this claim were methodologically flawed and that researchers who found symptoms of mental illness in homeless people didn't try to ascertain whether these symptoms were the cause or effect of living on the street. Finally, she points out that a lag time of five years existed between the major release of state hospital patients and the rise of mentally ill individuals in shelters. This time lag suggests that other social and economic factors might have come into play to account for the rise of homelessness (156–57). Carl Cohen and Kenneth Thompson also point to this time lag as evidence to reject deinstitutionalization as the major cause of mentally ill homelessness (817). Jonathan Kozol argues that patients released from state hospitals in the late sixties and early seventies didn't go directly to the streets but went to single-room occupancy housing, such as cheap hotels or boarding houses. Many of these ex-patients became homeless, he argues, when almost half of single-room occupancy housing was replaced by more expensive housing between 1970 and 1980 (18). The effects of this housing shortage might account for the lag time that Hopper and Cohen and Thompson cite.

5   Krauthammer's focus on mental illness as a cause of much of the homelessness problem leads to another of the implicit assumptions in his argument: that the mentally ill comprise a large percentage of the homeless population. Krauthammer avoids mentioning specific numbers until the end of his article when he writes:

> The argument over how many of the homeless are mentally ill is endless. The estimates, which range from one-quarter to three-quarters, vary with method, definition, and ideology. But so what if even the lowest estimates are right? Even if treating the mentally ill does not end homelessness, how can that possibly justify not treating the tens, perhaps hundreds of thousands who would benefit from a partial solution? (25)

This paragraph is rhetorically shrewd. It downplays the numbers issue and takes the moral high road. But by citing estimates between one-quarter and three-quarters, Krauthammer effectively suggests that a neutral estimate might place the number around fifty percent--a high estimate reinforced by his leap from "tens" to "perhaps hundreds of thousands" in the last sentence.

Close examination of the research, however, reveals that the percentage of   6
mentally ill people on the streets may be even lower than Krauthammer's lowest figure of 25%. In an extensive study conducted by David Snow and colleagues, a team member lived among the homeless for 12 months to collect data on mental illness. Additionally, the researchers tracked the institutional histories of a random sample of homeless. The study found that only 10% of the street sample and 16% of the tracking sample showed mental illness. The researchers pointed to a number of reasons why some previous estimates and studies may have inflated the numbers of mentally ill homeless. They suggest that the visibility of the mentally ill homeless (their odd behaviors make them stand out) combined with the widespread belief that deinstitutionalization poured vast numbers of mentally ill onto the streets caused researchers to bias their data. Thus researchers would often interpret behavior such as socially inappropriate actions, depression, and sleeping disorders as indications of mental illness, when in fact these actions may simply be the natural response to living in the harsh environment of the street. Additionally, the Snow study points to the medicalization of homelessness. This phenomenon means that when doctors and psychiatrists treat the homeless they focus on their medical and psychological problems while ignoring their social and economic ones. Because studies of the mentally ill homeless have been dominated by doctors and psychologists, these studies tend to inflate the numbers of mentally ill on the streets (419–21).

Another persuasive study showing low percentages of mentally ill   7
homeless--although not as low as Snow's estimates--comes from Deborah Dennis and colleagues, who surveyed the past decade of research on mentally ill homeless. The combined findings of all these research studies suggest that the mentally ill comprise between 28% and 37% of the homeless population (Dennis et al. 1130). Thus we see that while the mentally ill make up a significant proportion of the homeless population they do not approach a majority as Krauthammer and others would have us believe.

Krauthammer's third assumption is that the causes of homelessness among   8
the mentally ill are largely psychological rather than socioeconomic. By this

thinking, the solutions to their problems involve the treatment of their illnesses rather than the alleviation of poverty. Krauthammer writes, "Moreover, whatever solutions are eventually offered the non-mentally ill homeless, they will have little relevance to those who are mentally ill" (25). Closer examination, however, shows that other factors play a greater role in causing homelessness among the mentally ill than mental illness. Jonathan Kozol argues that housing and the economy played the largest role in causing homelessness among the mentally ill. He points to two million jobs lost every year since 1980, an increase in poverty, a massive shortage in low-income housing, and a drop from 500,000 subsidized private housing units to 25,000 during the Reagan era (17–18). Cohen and Thompson also place primary emphasis on poverty and housing shortages:

> Data suggest that most homeless mentally ill persons lost their rooms in single-room-occupancy hotels or low-priced apartments not because of psychoticism but because they 1) were evicted because of renewal projects and fires, 2) were victimized by unscrupulous landlords or by other residents, or 3) could no longer afford the rent. (818)

Douglas Mossman and Michael Perlin cite numerous studies which show that mental illness itself is not the primary factor causing homelessness among the mentally ill; additionally, they point out that the severity of mental illness itself is closely linked to poverty. They argue that lack of private health care increases poor health and the frequency of severe mental illness. They conclude, "Homelessness is, if nothing else, a condition of poverty, and poor individuals in general are at increased risk for episodes of psychiatric illness" (952). Krauthammer's article conveniently ignores the role of poverty, suggesting that much of the homeless problem could be solved by moving the mentally ill back into institutions. But the evidence suggests that symptoms of mental illness are often the <u>results</u> of being homeless and that any efforts to treat the psychological problems of the mentally ill must also address the socioeconomic problems.

9   Krauthammer's belief that the causes of mentally ill homelessness are psychological rather than social and economic leads to a fourth assumption that the mentally ill homeless are a distinct subgroup who need different treatment from the other homeless groups. Krauthammer thus divides the homeless into three primary groups: (1) the mentally ill; (2) those who choose to live on the street;

and (3) "the victims of economic calamity, such as family breakup or job loss" (25). By believing that the mentally ill homeless are not also victims of "economic calamity," Krauthammer greatly oversimplifies their problems. As Cohen and Thompson show, it is difficult to separate the mentally ill homeless and the non-mentally ill homeless. "On closer examination, 'not mentally ill' homeless people have many mental health problems; similarly, the 'mentally ill' homeless have numerous nonpsychiatric problems that arise from the sociopolitical elements affecting all homeless people" (817). Because the two groups are so similar, it is counterproductive to insist on entirely different solutions for both groups.

Krauthammer's proposal thus fails on a number of points. It won't solve   10 nearly as much of the homelessness problem as he leads us to believe. It would commit valuable taxpayer dollars to building asylums rather than attacking the underlying causes of homelessness in general. And perhaps most importantly, its emphasis on involuntary confinement in asylums is not the best long-range method to treat the mentally ill homeless. Instead of moving the mentally ill homeless away from society into asylums, we would meet their needs far more effectively through monitored community-based care. Instead of building expensive institutions, we should focus on finding alternative low-cost housing for the mentally ill homeless and meet their needs through teams of psychiatrists and social workers who could oversee a number of patients' treatments, monitoring such things as taking medications and receiving appropriate counseling. Involuntary hospitalization may still be needed for the most severely deranged, but the majority of mentally ill homeless people can be better treated in their communities.

From a purely financial perspective, perhaps the most compelling reason to   11 prefer community-based care is that it offers a more efficient use of taxpayer dollars. In a letter to the New York Times on behalf of the Project for Psychiatric Outreach to the Homeless, Drs. Katherine Falk and Gail Albert give us the following statistics:

> It costs $105,000 to keep someone in a state hospital for a year. But it costs only $15,000 to $35,000 (depending on the intensity of services) to operate supported residences in the community with the necessary onsite psychiatrists, case workers, case managers, drug counselors, and other rehabilitation services. (A30)

It can be argued, in fact, that the cost of maintaining state hospitals for the mentally ill actually prevents large numbers of mentally ill from receiving treatment. When large numbers of mentally ill persons were released from state hospitals during the deinstitutionalization movement of the 1960s and 1970s, the original plan was to convert resources to community-based care. Even though the number of patients in state institutions has dramatically decreased over the past two decades, institutions have continued to maintain large shares of state funding. According to David Rothman of Columbia University, "Historically, the dollars have remained locked in the institutions and did not go into community mental health" (qtd. in Dugger, "Debate" B2). In fact, cutting New York's state hospital budget would provide enough money for over 20,000 units in supported community residences (Falk and Albert A30). Furthermore, Linda Chafetz points out that having the money to pay for such resources as clothes, bathing facilities, meals, and housing is the most urgent concern among caregivers in treating the mentally ill homeless. According to Chafetz, "The immediate and urgent nature of the resource dilemma can make other issues appear almost frivolous by comparison" (451). With such an obvious shortage of resources, pouring what money we have into the high-cost institutional system would be a grave disservice to the majority of the mentally ill homeless population and to the homeless population as a whole.

12   A second reason to adopt community-based care over wide-scale institutionalization is that the vast majority of the homeless mentally ill do not need the tight control of the hospital system. Cohen and Thompson cite a number of studies that show "that only 5%–7% of single adult homeless persons are in need of acute inpatient care" (820). Involuntarily hospitalizing a large number of homeless who don't demand institutionalized care is not only a waste of resources but also an unnecessary assault on individual freedom for many.

13   Finally, the community-based care system is preferable to institutionalization because it most often gives the best treatment to its patients. Although Krauthammer claims that less than a fifth of involuntarily hospitalized patients have legally challenged their confinement (25), numerous studies indicate there is widespread resistance to institutional care by the homeless mentally ill. Mossman and Perlin cite multiple sources indicating that many mentally ill have legitimate reasons to fear state hospitals. Moreover, they provide evidence that many would rather suffer the streets and their mental illness than suffer the conditions of state

hospitals and the side effects of medications. The horrible track record of conditions of state hospitals supports the logic of this thinking. On the other hand, Mossman and Perlin point out many mentally ill homeless persons will accept treatment from the type of alternative settings community-based care offers (953). Powerful evidence showing the success of community-based care comes from early evaluation reports of ACCESS (Access to Community Care and Effective Services), a community-based program of the Center for Mental Health. More than 11,000 mentally ill homeless have received services through this program, which reports "significant improvements in almost all outcome measures," such as "a 66 percent decrease in minor criminal activity" and "a 46 percent decrease in reported psychotic symptoms" ("Articles"). Given that institutionalization can leave mentally ill persons feeling humiliated and disempowered (Cohen and Thompson 819), community-based solutions such as ACCESS seem the best approach.

Given the advantages of community-based care, what is the appeal of   14
Krauthammer's proposal? Involuntary institutionalization appeals to our common impulse to lock our problems out of sight. As crime increases, we want to build more prisons; when we see ragged men and women mumbling in the street, we want to shut them up in institutions. But the simple solutions are not often the most effective ones. Institutionalization is tempting, but alternative methods have shown themselves to be more effective. Community-based care works better because it's based on a better understanding of the problem. Community-based care, by allowing the psychiatrist and social worker to work together, attacks both the mental and the social dimensions of the problem: The client receives not only psychological counseling and medication but also help on how to find affordable housing, how to manage money and shop effectively, and how to live in a community. Without roots in a community, a patient released from a mental asylum will quickly return to the streets. To pour scarce resources into the expensive project of rebuilding asylums--helping the few while ignoring the many--would be a terrible misuse of taxpayer dollars.

Krauthammer's argument appeals in another way also. By viewing the   15
homeless as mentally ill, we see them as inherently different from ourselves. We needn't see any connection to those mumbling bag ladies and those ragged men lying on the grates. When we regard them as mentally ill, we see ourselves as largely unresponsible for the conditions that led them to the streets. Those

professional men and women carrying their espresso Starbuck's coffees to their upscale offices in Seattle's Pioneer Square don't have to be reminded that this historic district used to contain a number of single-occupancy boarding houses. The professionals work where the homeless used to live. The rich and the poor are thus interconnected, reminding us that homelessness is primarily a social and economic problem, not a mental health problem. And even the most deranged of the mentally ill homeless are messengers of a nationwide scourge of poverty.

Works Cited*

"Articles to Focus on National Effort to Help People Who Are Homeless and Have Mental Illness." Press release. 3 Mar. 1997. National Mental Health Services Knowledge Exchange Network (KEN). 23 Apr. 1998. <http://www.mentalhealth.org./resource/praccess.htm>.

Chafetz, Linda. "Withdrawal from the Homeless Mentally Ill." Community Mental Health Journal 26 (1990): 449–61.

Cohen, Carl I., and Kenneth S. Thompson. "Homeless Mentally Ill or Mentally Ill Homeless?" American Journal of Psychiatry 149 (1992): 816–23.

Dennis, Deborah L., et al. "A Decade of Research and Services for Homeless Mentally Ill Persons: Where Do We Stand?" American Psychologist 46 (1991): 1129–38.

Dugger, Celia W. "A Danger to Themselves and Others." New York Times 24 Jan. 1993: B1+.

---. "A Debate Unstilled: New Plan for Homeless Mentally Ill Does Not Address Larger Questions." New York Times 22 Jan. 1993: B2.

Falk, Katherine, and Gail Albert. Letter. New York Times 11 Feb. 1993: A30.

Hopper, Kim. "More Than Passing Strangers: Homelessness and Mental Illness in New York City." American Ethnologist 15 (1988): 155–57.

Kozol, Jonathan. "Are the Homeless Crazy?" Harper's Sept. 1988: 17–19.

Krauthammer, Charles. "How to Save the Homeless Mentally Ill." New Republic 8 Feb. 1988: 22–25.

Mossman, Douglas, and Michael L. Perlin. "Psychiatry and the Homeless Mentally Ill: A Reply to Dr. Lamb." American Journal of Psychiatry 149 (1992): 951–56.

Snow, David A., et al. "The Myth of Pervasive Mental Illness among the Homeless." Social Problems 33 (1986): 407–23.

---

*When preparing your own essay using MLA style, begin the Works Cited list on a separate page.

WRITING ASSIGNMENTS FOR CHAPTER 14

OPTION 1: *A Practical Proposal Addressing a Local Problem*   Write a practical proposal offering a solution to a local problem. Your proposal should have three main sections: (1) description of the problem, (2) proposed solution, and (3) justification. You may include additional sections or subsections as needed. Longer proposals often include an *abstract* at the beginning of the proposal to provide a summary overview of the whole argument. (Sometimes called the *executive summary*, this abstract may be the only portion of the proposal read by high-level managers.) Sometimes proposals are accompanied by a *letter of transmittal*—a one-page business letter that introduces the proposal to its intended audience and provides some needed background about the writer.

Document design is important in practical proposals, which are aimed at busy people who have to make many decisions under time constraints. Because the writer of a practical proposal usually produces the finished document (practical proposals are seldom submitted to newspapers or magazines for publication), he or she must pay particular attention to the attractive design of the document. An effective design helps establish the writer's *ethos* as a quality-oriented professional and helps make the reading of the proposal as easy as possible. Document design includes effective use of headings and subheadings, attractive typeface and layout, flawless editing, and other features enhancing the visual appearance of the document.

OPTION 2: *A Policy Proposal as a Guest Editorial*   Write a two or three-page policy proposal suitable for publication as a feature editorial in a college or city newspaper or in some publication associated with a particular group or activity such as a church newsletter or employee bulletin. The voice and style of your argument should be aimed at general readers of your chosen publication. Your editorial should have the following features:

1. The identification of a problem (Persuade your audience that this is a genuine problem that needs solving; give it presence.)
2. A proposal for action that will help alleviate the problem
3. A justification of your solution (the reasons why your audience should accept your proposal and act on it)

OPTION 3: *A Researched Argument Proposing Public Policy*   Write an eight- to twelve-page proposal argument as a formal research paper, using research data for support. Your argument should include all the features of the shorter argument in Option 2 and also a summary and refutation of opposing views (in the form of alternative proposals and/or differing cost-benefit analyses of your proposal.) An example of a researched policy proposal is student writer Stephen Bean's "What Should Be Done about the Mentally Ill Homeless?" on pages 228–36.

15

Ethical Arguments

The line between ethical arguments ("Is X morally good?") and other kinds of values disputes is often pretty thin. Many apparently straightforward practical values issues can turn out to have an ethical dimension. For example, when deciding what kind of car to buy, most people would base their judgments on criteria such as cost, reliability, safety, comfort, and stylishness. But some people might feel morally obligated to buy the most fuel-efficient car or not to buy a car from a manufacturer whose investment or labor policies they found morally repugnant. Depending on how large a role ethical considerations played in the evaluation, we might choose to call this an *ethical argument* as opposed to a simpler kind of values argument. In any case, we here devote a separate chapter to ethical arguments because we believe they represent special difficulties to the student of argumentation. Let's take a look at some of those special difficulties.

SPECIAL DIFFICULTIES OF ETHICAL ARGUMENTS

One crucial difficulty with ethical arguments concerns the role of "purpose" in defining criteria for judgment. In Chapter 13, we assumed that every class of beings has a purpose, that the purpose should be defined as narrowly as possible, and that the criteria for judgment derive directly from that purpose. For example, the purpose of a computer repair person is to analyze the problem with my computer, to fix it, and to do so in a timely and cost-efficient manner. Once I formulate this purpose, it is easy for me to define criteria for a good computer repair person.

In ethics, however, the place of purpose is much fuzzier. Just what is the purpose of human beings? Before I can begin to determine what ethical duties I have to myself and to others, I'm going to have to address this question; and because the chance of reaching agreement on that question remains remote, many ethical arguments are probably unresolvable. In ethical discussions we don't ask what a "manager" or a "judge" or a "point guard" is supposed to do in situations relevant to the respective classes; we're asking what John Doe is supposed to be or what Jane Doe is supposed to do with her life. Who they are or what their social function is makes no difference to our ethical assessment of their actions or traits of character. A morally bad person may be a good judge and a morally good person may be a bad manager.

As the discussion so far has suggested, disagreements about ethical issues often stem from different systems of belief. We might call this problem the "problem of warrants"—that is, people disagree because they do not share common assumptions on which to ground their arguments.

If, for example, you say that good manners are necessary for keeping us from reverting to a state of raw nature, your implied warrant is that raw nature is bad. But if you say that good manners are a political tool by which a ruling class tries to suppress the natural vitality of the working class, then your warrant is that liberation of the working classes from the corrupt habits of the ruling class is good. It would be difficult, therefore, for people representing these opposing belief systems to carry on a reasonable discussion of etiquette—their assumptions about value, about the role of the natural self, and about political progress are different. This is why ethical arguments are often so acrimonious—they frequently lack shared warrants to serve as starting places for argument.

It is precisely because of the problem of warrants, however, that you should try to confront issues of ethics with rational deliberation. The arguments you produce may not persuade others to your view, but they should lay out more clearly the grounds and warrants of your own beliefs. Such arguments serve the purpose of clarification. By drafting essays on ethical issues, you begin to see more clearly what you believe and why you believe it. Although the arguments demanded by ethical issues require rigorous thought, they force us to articulate our most deeply held beliefs and our richest feelings.

AN OVERVIEW OF MAJOR
ETHICAL SYSTEMS

When we are faced with an ethical issue, such as the issue of whether terrorism can be justified, we must move from arguments of good or bad to arguments of right or wrong. The terms *right* and *wrong* are clearly different from the terms *good* and *bad* when the latter terms mean simply "effective" (meets purposes of class, as in "This is a good stereo system") or "ineffective" (fails to meet purposes of class, as in "This is a bad cookbook"). But *right* and *wrong* often also differ from what seems to be a moral use of the terms *good* and *bad*. We might say, for example, that warm sunshine is good because it brings pleasure and that cancer is bad because it brings pain and death, but that is not quite the same thing as saying that sunshine is "right" and cancer is "wrong." It is the problem of "right" and "wrong" that ethical arguments confront.

Thus it is not enough to say that terrorism is "bad"; obviously everyone, including most terrorists, would agree that terrorism is "bad" in that it causes suffering and anguish. If we want to condemn terrorism on ethical grounds, we have to say that it's also "wrong" as well as "bad." In saying that something's wrong, we're saying that all people ought to refrain from doing it. We're also saying that acts that are morally "wrong" are in some way blameworthy and deserve censure, a conclusion that doesn't necessarily follow a negative nonethical judgment, which might lead simply to our not buying something or not hiring someone. From a nonethical standpoint, you may even say that someone is a "good" terrorist in that he fully realizes the purposes of the class "terrorist": He causes great damage with a minimum of resources, brings a good deal of attention to his cause, and doesn't get caught. The ethical question here, however, is not whether this person is a good member of the class, but whether it is wrong for such a class to exist.

In asking the question "Ought the class 'terrorist' to exist?" or, to put it more colloquially, "Are there ever cases where terrorism is justified?" we need to seek some consistent approach or principle. In the phrase used by some philosophers, ethical judgments are typically "universalizable" statements—that is, when we oppose a terrorist act, our ethical argument (assuming it's a coherent one) should be capable of being generalized into an ethical principle that will hold for all similar cases. Ethical disputes usually involve clashes between such principles. For example, a pro-terrorist might say, "My ends justify my means," whereas an antiterrorist might say, "The sanctity of human life is not to be violated for any reason." The differences in principles such as these account for different schools of ethical thought.

There are many different schools of ethical thought—too many to present in this chapter. But to help you think your way through ethical issues, we'll look at some of the most prevalent methods of resolving ethical questions. The first of these methods, "naive egoism," is really less a method than a retreat from method. It doesn't represent a coherent ethical view, but it is a position that many people lapse into on given issues. It represents, in short, the most seductive alternative to rigorous ethical thought.

Naive Egoism

Back in Chapter 1, we touched on the morality of the Sophists and suggested that their underlying maxim was something like "Might makes right." In ethical terms, they were essentially egoists who used other people with impunity to realize their own ends. The appeal of this position, however repugnant it may sound when laid out like this, is that it rationalizes self-promotion and pleasure seeking: If we all follow the bidding of our egos, we'll be happy.

On examination, this philosophy proves to be incoherent. It should be noted, however, that philosophers don't reject naive egoism simply because they believe "selfishness is bad." Rather, philosophers tend to assess ethical systems according to such factors as their scope (How often will this system provide principles to guide our moral action?) and their precision (How clearly can we analyze a given situation using the tools of the system?) rather than their intuition about whether the system is right or wrong. Although naive egoism has great scope—You can always ask "What's in it for me?"—it is far from precise, as we'll try to show.

Take the case of young Ollie Unger, who has decided that he wants to quit living irrationally and to join some official school of ethical thought. The most appealing school at the moment—recommended to him by a philosophy major over at the Phi Upsilon Nu house—is the "I'm Number One!" school of scruples. He heads downtown to the school's opulent headquarters and meets with the school's guru, one Dr. Pheelgood.

"What's involved in becoming a member of your school?" Ollie inquires.

"Ahhh, my apple-cheeked chum, that's the beauty of it. It's so simple. You just give me all your worldly possessions and do whatever I tell you to do."

Ollie is puzzled. He had in mind something a bit more, well, gratifying. He was hoping for something closer to the philosophy of eat, drink, and make merry—all justified through rational thought.

"You seem disappointed," Pheelgood observes. "What's the matter?"

"Well, gee, it just doesn't sound like I'm going to be number one here. I thought that was the idea. To look out for *numero uno*."

"Of course not, silly boy. This is after all the "I'm Number One School of Scruples." And I, *moi*, am the I who's number one.

"But I thought the idea of your school was for everyone to have the maximum amount of enjoyment in life."

Peevishness clouds Pheelgood's face. "Look here, Unger, if I arrange things for you to have a good time, it's going to cost me. Next you'll be asking me to open soup kitchens. If I'm to look out for number one, then you've got to act entirely differently from me. I take, you give. *Capiche?*"

As should be obvious by now, it's very difficult to systematize egoism. You have two sets of demands in constant conflict—the demands of your own personal ego and those of everyone else's. It's impossible, hence, to universalize a statement that all members of the school could hold equally without contradicting all other members of the school.

Some egoists try to get around this problem by conceding that we must limit our self-gratification either by entering into contracts or institutional arrangements with others or by sacrificing short-term interests for long-term ones. We might, for example, give to the poor now in order to avoid a revolution of the masses later. But once they've let the camel's nose of concern for others into the tent, it's tough to hang onto egoistic philosophy. Having considered naive egoism, let's turn to a pair of more workable alternatives.

In shifting to the two most common forms of ethical thought, we shift point of view from "I" to "us." Both groups, those who make ethical judgments according to the consequences of any act and those who make ethical judgments according to the conformity of any act with a principle, are guided by their concern for the whole of humanity rather than simply the self.

Consequences as the Base of Ethics

Perhaps the best-known example of evaluating acts according to their ethical consequences is utilitarianism, a down-to-earth philosophy that grew out of nineteenth-century British philosophers' concern to demystify ethics and make it work in the practical world. Jeremy Bentham, the originator of utilitarianism, developed the goal of the greatest good for the greatest number, or "greatest happiness," by which he meant the most pleasure for the least pain. John Stuart Mill, another British philosopher, built on Bentham's utilitarianism using predicted consequences to determine the morality of a proposed action.

Mill's consequentialist approach allows you readily to assess a wide range of acts. You can apply the principle of utility—which says that an action is morally right if it produces a greater net value (benefits minus costs) than any available alternative action—to virtually any situation and it will help you reach a decision. Obviously, however, it's not always easy to make the calculations called for by the principle, since, like any prediction, an estimate of consequences is conjectural. In particular, it's often very hard to assess the long-term consequences of any action. Too often, utilitarianism seduces us into a short-term analysis of a moral problem simply because long-term consequences are very difficult to predict.

Principles as the Base of Ethics

Any ethical system based on principles will ultimately rest on one or two moral tenets that we are duty-bound to uphold, no matter what the consequences. Sometimes the moral tenets come from religious faith—for example, the Ten Commandments. At other times, however, the principles are derived from philosophical reasoning, as in the case of German philosopher Immanuel Kant. Kant held that no one should ever use another person as a means to his or her own ends and that everyone should always act as if his or her acts were the basis of universal law. In other words, Kant held that we were duty bound to respect other people's sanctity and to act in the same way that we would want all other people to act. The great advantage of such a system is its clarity and precision. We are never overwhelmed by a multiplicity of contradictory and difficult-to-quantify consequences; we simply make sure we are not violating a principle of our ethical system and proceed accordingly.

The Two Systems Compared

In the eyes of many people, a major advantage of a system such as utilitarianism is that it impels us to seek out the best solution, whereas systems based on principle merely enjoin us not to violate a principle by our action. In turn, applying an ethical principle will not always help us resolve necessarily relativistic moral dilemmas. For instance, what if none of our available choices violates our moral principles? How do we choose among a host of permissible acts? Or what about situations where none of the alternatives is permitted by our principles? How might we choose the least bad alternative? To further our comparison of the two systems, let's ask what a Mill or a Kant might say about the previously mentioned issue of terrorism.

The Kantian position is clear: To kill another person to realize your own ends is palpably evil and forbidden. A follower of Mill will face a less clear choice. A utilitarian could not automatically rule out terrorism or any other means so long as it led ultimately to the greatest good for the greatest number. If a nation is being slowly starved by those around it, if its people are dying, its institutions are crumbling, and its future is disappearing, who is to say that the aggrieved nation is not justified in taking a few hundred lives to improve the lot of hundreds of thousands? The utilitarian's first concern is to determine if terrorism will most effectively bring about that end. So long as the desired end represents the best possible net value and the means are effective at bringing about the end, the utilitarian can, in theory anyway, justify almost any action.

Given the shared cultural background and values of most of us, not to mention our own vulnerability to terrorism, the Kantian argument is probably very appealing here. Indeed, Kantian ethical arguments have overwhelming appeal for us when the principle being invoked is already widely held within our culture, and when violation of that principle will have clear and immediate negative consequences for us. But in a culture that doesn't share that principle and for whom the consequences of violation are positive rather than negative, the argument will undoubtedly appear weaker, a piece of fuzzy-headed idealism.

FOR CLASS DISCUSSION

Working as individuals or in small groups:

1. Try to formulate a utilitarian argument to persuade terrorist leaders in the Middle East, the Balkans, Ireland, or elsewhere to stop terrorist action.

2. Try to formulate an ethical principle or rule that would permit terrorism.

Some Compromise Positions between Consequences and Principles

In the end, most of us would not be entirely happy with an ethic that forced us to ignore either principles or consequences. We all have certain principles that we simply can't violate no matter what the consequences. Thus, for example, some of us would not have dropped the bomb on Hiroshima even if doing so did mean saving many lives ultimately. And certainly, too, most of us will compromise our principles in certain situations if we think the consequences justify compromise. For instance, how many of us would not deceive, harm, or even torture a kidnapper to save the life of a stolen child? Indeed, over the years, compromise positions have developed on both sides to accommodate precisely these concerns.

Some "consequentialists" have acknowledged the usefulness of general rules for creating more human happiness over the long run. To go back to our terrorism example, a consequentialist might oppose terrorist action on the grounds that "Thou shalt not kill another person in the name of greater material happiness for the group." This acknowledgment of an inviolable principle will still be based on a concern for consequences—for instance, a fear that terrorist acts may lead to World War III—but having such a principle allows the consequentialist to get away from a case-by-case analysis of acts and to keep more clearly before himself the long-range consequences of acts.

Among latter-day ethics of principle, meanwhile, the distinction between absolute obligation and what philosophers call *prima facie* obligation has been developed to take account of the force of circumstances. An *absolute* obligation would be an obligation to follow a principle at all times, no matter what. A *prima facie* obligation, in contrast, is an obligation to do something "other things being equal"—that is, in a normal situation. Hence, to use a classic moral example, you would not, other things being equal, cannibalize an acquaintance. But if there are three of you in a lifeboat, one is dying, and the other two will surely die if they don't get food, your *prima facie* obligation not to eat another might be waived. (However, the Royal Commission, which heard the original case, took a more Kantian position and condemned the action of the seamen who cannibalized their mate.)

These, then, in greatly condensed form, are the major alternative ways of thinking about ethical arguments. Let's now briefly summarize the ways you can use your knowledge of ethical thought to develop your arguments and critique those of others.

DEVELOPING AN ETHICAL ARGUMENT

To help you see how familiarity with these systems of ethical thought can help you develop an ethical argument, let's take an example case. How, for example, might we go about developing an argument in favor of abolishing the death penalty? Our first task is to examine the issue from the two points of view just discussed. How might a utilitarian or a Kantian argue that the death penalty should be abolished?

The argument on principle, as is usually the case, would appear to be the simpler of the two. Taking another life is difficult to justify under most ethical principles. For Kant, the sanctity of human life is a central tenet of ethics, and under

Judeo-Christian ethics we are told that "Vengeance is Mine, saith the Lord" and "Thou shalt not kill." But, unfortunately for our hopes of simplicity, Kant argued in favor of capital punishment:

> There is no sameness of kind between death and remaining alive even under the most miserable conditions, and consequently there is no equality between the crime and the retribution unless the criminal is judicially condemned and put to death.*

Kant is here invoking an important principle of justice: Punishments should be proportionate to the crime. He appears to be saying that this principle must take precedence over his notion of the supreme worth of the individual.

Some philosophers think Kant was being inconsistent in taking this position. Certainly, in establishing your own position, you could support a case against capital punishment based on Kant's principles even if Kant himself did not reach the same conclusion. But you'd have to establish for your reader why you are at odds with Kant. Kant's apparent inconsistency here illustrates how powerfully our intuitive judgments can affect our ethical judgment.

Likewise, with the Judeo-Christian position, passages can be found in the Bible that would support capital punishment—notably, the Old Testament injunction to take "an eye for an eye and a tooth for a tooth." That principle is simply a more poetic version of "Let the punishment fit the crime": Retribution should be of the same kind as the crime. And the commandment "Thou shalt not kill" is often interpreted as "Thou shalt not commit murder," an interpretation that not only permits just wars or killing in self-defense but also is consistent with other places in the Bible that suggest that people have not only the right but the obligation to punish wrongdoers and not leave their fate to God.

So there appears to be no clearcut argument in support of abolishing capital punishment on the basis of principle. What about an argument based on consequences? How might abolishing capital punishment result in a net good that is at least as great as allowing it?

A number of possibilities suggest themselves. First, in abolishing capital punishment, we rid ourselves of the possibility that someone may be wrongly executed. To buttress this argument, we might want to search for evidence of how many people have been wrongly convicted of or executed for a capital crime. In making arguments based on consequence we must, whenever possible, offer empirical evidence that the consequences we assert exist—and exist to the degree we've suggested. There are also other possible consequences that a utilitarian might mention in defending the abolition of capital punishment. These include leaving open the possibility that the person being punished will be reformed, keeping those charged with executing the murderer free from guilt,

---

*From Immanual Kant, *The Metaphysical Elements of Justice.*

and putting an end to the costly legal and political process of appealing the conviction.

But in addition to calculating benefits, you will need also to calculate the costs of abolishing the death penalty and to show that the net result favors abolition. Failure to mention such costs is a serious weakness in many arguments of consequence. Moreover, in the issue at hand, the consequences that favor capital punishment—deterrence of further capital crimes, cost of imprisoning murderers, and so forth—are well known to most members of your audience.

In our discussion of capital punishment, then, we employed two alternative ways of thinking about ethical issues. In pursuing an argument from principle, we looked for an appropriate rule that permitted or at least did not prohibit our position. In pursuing an argument from consequence, we moved from what's permissible to what brings about the most desirable consequences. Most ethical issues, argued thoroughly, should be approached from both perspectives, so long as irreconcilable differences don't present themselves.

Should you choose to adopt one of these perspectives to the exclusion of the other, you will find yourself facing many of the problems mentioned here. This is not to say that you can't ever go to the wall for a principle or focus solely on consequences to the exclusion of principles; it's simply that you will be hard pressed to convince those of your audience who happen to be of the other persuasion and demand different sorts of proof. For the purpose of developing arguments, we encourage you to consider both the relevant principles and the possible consequences when you evaluate ethical actions.

TESTING ETHICAL ARGUMENTS

Perhaps the first question you should ask in setting out to analyze your draft of an ethical argument is "To what extent is the argument based on consequences or on ethical principles?" If it's based exclusively on one of these two forms of ethical thought, then it's vulnerable to the sorts of criticism discussed here. A strictly principled argument that takes no account of the consequences of its position is vulnerable to a simple cost analysis. What are the costs in the case of adhering to this principle? There will undoubtedly be some, or else there would be no real argument. If the argument is based strictly on consequentialist grounds, we should ask if the position violates any rules or principles, particularly such commandments as the Golden Rule—"Do unto others as you would have others do unto you"—which most members of our audience adhere to. By failing to mention these alternative ways of thinking about ethical issues, we undercut not only our argument but our credibility as well.

Let's now consider a more developed examination of the two positions, starting with some of the more subtle weaknesses in a position based on principle. In practice people will sometimes take rigidly "principled" positions because they live in fear of "slippery slopes"—that is, they fear setting precedents that might lead to ever more dire consequences. Consider, for example, the slippery slope leading from birth control to euthanasia if you have an absolutist commitment to the sanctity of human life. Once we allow birth control in the form of condoms or pills, the principled absolutist would say, then we will be forced to accept birth control "abortions" in the first hours after conception (IUDs, "morning after" pills), then abortions in the first trimester, then in the second or even the third trimester. And once we have violated the sanctity of human life by allowing abortions, it is only a short step to euthanasia and finally to killing off all undesirables.

One way to refute a slippery-slope argument of this sort is to try to dig a foothold into the side of the hill to show that you don't necessarily have to slide all the way to the bottom. You would thus have to argue that allowing birth control does not mean allowing abortions (by arguing for differences between a fetus after conception and sperm and egg before conception), or that allowing abortions does not mean allowing euthanasia (by arguing for differences between a fetus and a person already living in the world).

Consequentialist arguments have different kinds of difficulties. As discussed before, the crucial difficulty facing anyone making a consequentialist argument is to calculate the consequences in a clear and reliable way. Have you considered all significant consequences? If you project your scenario of consequences further into the future (remember, consequentialist arguments are frequently stronger over the short term than over the long term, where many unforeseen consequences can occur), can you identify possibilities that work against the argument?

As also noted, consequentialist arguments carry a heavy burden of empirical proof. What evidence can you offer that the predicted consequences will in fact come to pass? Do you offer any evidence that alternative consequences won't occur? And just how do you prove that the consequences of any given action are a net good or evil?

In addition to the problems unique to each of the two positions, ethical arguments are vulnerable to the more general sorts of criticism, including consistency, recency, and relevance of evidence. Obviously, however, consequentialist arguments will be more vulnerable to weaknesses in evidence, whereas arguments based on principle are more open to questions about consistency of application.

READING

In the following essay, "The Case for Torture," philosopher Michael Levin argues that torture not only can be justified but is positively mandated under certain circumstances.

The Case for Torture
Michael Levin

1   It is generally assumed that torture is impermissible, a throwback to a more brutal age. Enlightened societies reject it outright, and regimes suspected of using it risk the wrath of the United States.

2   I believe this attitude is unwise. There are situations in which torture is not merely permissible but morally mandatory. Moreover, these situations are moving from the realm of imagination to fact.

3   **Death:** Suppose a terrorist has hidden an atomic bomb on Manhattan Island which will detonate at noon on July 4 unless . . . (here follow the usual demands for money and release of his friends from jail). Suppose, further, that he is caught at 10 A.M. of the fateful day, but—preferring death to failure—won't disclose where the bomb is. What do we do? If we follow due process—wait for his lawyer, arraign him—millions of people will die. If the only way to save those lives is to subject the terrorist to the most excruciating possible pain, what grounds can there be for not doing so? I suggest there are none. In any case, I ask you to face the question with an open mind.

4   Torturing the terrorist is unconstitutional? Probably. But millions of lives surely outweigh constitutionality. Torture is barbaric? Mass murder is far more barbaric. Indeed, letting millions of innocents die in deference to one who flaunts his guilt is moral cowardice, an unwillingness to dirty one's hands. If *you* caught the terrorist, could you sleep nights knowing that millions died because you couldn't bring yourself to apply the electrodes?

5   Once you concede that torture is justified in extreme cases, you have admitted that the decision to use torture is a matter of balancing innocent lives against the means needed to save them. You must now face more realistic cases involving more modest numbers. Someone plants a bomb on a jumbo jet. He alone can disarm it, and his demands cannot be met (or if they can, we refuse to set a precedent by yielding to his threats). Surely we can, we must, do anything to the extortionist to save the passengers. How can we tell 300, or 100, or 10 people who never asked to be put in danger, "I'm sorry, you'll have to die in agony, we just couldn't bring ourselves to . . . ."

6   Here are the results of an informal poll about a third, hypothetical, case. Suppose a terrorist group kidnapped a newborn baby from a hospital. I asked four mothers if they would approve of torturing kidnappers if that were necessary to get their own newborns back. All said yes, the most "liberal" adding that she would like to administer it herself.

7   I am not advocating torture as punishment. Punishment is addressed to deeds irrevocably past. Rather, I am advocating torture as an acceptable measure for preventing future evils. So understood, it is far less objectionable than many extant punishments. Opponents of the death penalty, for example, are forever insisting that executing a murderer will not bring back his victim (as if the purpose of capital punishment were supposed to be resurrection, not deterrence or retribution). But torture, in the cases described, is intended not to bring anyone back but to keep innocents from being dispatched. The most powerful argument against using torture as a punishment or to secure confessions is that such prac-

tices disregard the rights of the individual. Well, if the individual is all that important—and he is—it is correspondingly important to protect the rights of individuals threatened by terrorists. If life is so valuable that it must never be taken, the lives of the innocents must be saved even at the price of hurting the one who endangers them.

Better precedents for torture are assassination and pre-emptive attack. No Allied leader would have flinched at assassinating Hitler, had that been possible. (The Allies did assassinate Heydrich.) Americans would be angered to learn that Roosevelt could have had Hitler killed in 1943—thereby shortening the war and saving millions of lives—but refused on moral grounds. Similarly, if nation A learns that nation B is about to launch an unprovoked attack, A has a right to save itself by destroying B's military capability first. In the same way, if the police can by torture save those who would otherwise die at the hands of kidnappers or terrorists, they must.   8

Idealism: There is an important difference between terrorists and their victims that should mute talk of the terrorists' "rights." The terrorist's victims are at risk unintentionally, not having asked to be endangered. But the terrorist knowingly initiated his actions. Unlike his victims, he volunteered for the risks of his deed. By threatening to kill for profit or idealism, he renounces civilized standards, and he can have no complaint if civilization tries to thwart him by whatever means necessary.   9

Just as torture is justified only to save lives (not extort confessions or recantations), it is justifiably administered only to those *known* to hold innocent lives in their hands. Ah, but how can the authorities ever be sure they have the right malefactor? Isn't there a danger of error and abuse? Won't We turn into Them?   10

Questions like these are disingenuous in a world in which terrorists proclaim themselves and perform for television. The name of their game is public recognition. After all, you can't very well intimidate a government into releasing your freedom fighters unless you announce that it is your group that has seized its embassy. "Clear guilt" is difficult to define, but when 40 million people see a group of masked gunmen seize an airplane on the evening news, there is not much question about who the perpetrators are. There will be hard cases where the situation is murkier. Nonetheless, a line demarcating the legitimate use of torture can be drawn. Torture only the obviously guilty, and only for the sake of saving innocents, and the line between Us and Them will remain clear.   11

There is little danger that the Western democracies will lose their way if they choose to inflict pain as one way of preserving order. Paralysis in the face of evil is the greater danger. Some day soon a terrorist will threaten tens of thousands of lives, and torture will be the only way to save them. We had better start thinking about this.   12

a p p e n d i x   1

Informal Fallacies

In this appendix we examine *informal fallacies*, which can fool us into thinking that an inconclusive argument is conclusive. Informal fallacies are quirky; they identify classes of less conclusive arguments that recur with some frequency, but they do not contain formal flaws that make their conclusions automatically illegitimate. An informal fallacy makes an argument more or less fallacious, and determining the degree of fallaciousness is a matter of judgment.

In arranging the fallacies, we have, for convenience, put them into three categories derived from classical rhetoric: *pathos, ethos,* and *logos.* Fallacies of *pathos* rest on a flawed relationship between what is argued and the audience for the argument. Fallacies of *ethos* rest on a flawed relationship between the argument and the character of those involved in the argument. Fallacies of *logos* rest on flaws in the relationship among statements of an argument.

FALLACIES OF *PATHOS*

Argument to the People
(Appealing to Stirring Symbols)

An argument to the people appeals to the fundamental beliefs, biases, and prejudices of the audience in order to sway opinion through a feeling of group solidarity. For example, when a politician says, "My fellow Americans, I stand here, draped in this flag from head to foot, to indicate my fundamental dedication to the values and principles of these sovereign United States," he's linking himself to the prime symbol of the group's nationalistic values, the flag.

Provincialism (Appealing to the Belief That
the Known Is Always Better than the Unknown)

Here is an example from the 1960s: "You can't sell small cars in the United States. Americans love their big cars. Those cramped little Japanese tin boxes will never win the hearts of American consumers." Although we may inevitably feel more comfortable with familiar things, ideas, and beliefs, we are not necessarily better off for sticking with them.

Appeal to Emotional Premises
(Appealing to Comforting Reasons
That Have No Basis in Logic)

This mode of short-circuiting reason may take one of three forms. In all three cases, we say that something is right, good, or necessary based on the comforting but irrational reason that it is common, traditional, or popular.

1. *Appeal to common practice.* (It's all right to do X because everyone else does it.) "Of course I borrowed money from the company slush fund. Everyone on this floor has done the same in the last eighteen months."

2. *Appeal to traditional wisdom.* (It's all right because we've always done it this way.) "We've got to require everyone to read *Hamlet* because we've always required everyone to read it."

3. *Appeal to popularity—the bandwagon appeal.* (It's all right because lots of people like it.) "You should buy a Ford Escort because it's the best-selling car in the world."

Red Herring (Shifting the Audience's Attention
from a Crucial Issue to an Irrelevant One)

The *red herring* fallacy deliberately raises an unrelated or irrelevant point to throw an audience off the track. Politicians often employ this fallacy when they field questions from the public press. "You raise a good question about my support of continuing air strikes in country X. Let me tell you about my admiration for the bravery of our pilots."

FALLACIES OF *ETHOS*

Appeals to False Authority and Bandwagon Appeals
(Appealing to the Authority of a Popular Person
or to the "Crowd" Rather Than to an Expert)

False authority fallacies offer as support for an argument the fact that a famous person or "many people" support it. Unless the supporters are themselves authorities in the field, their support is irrelevant. "Buy Freeble oil because Joe Quarterback always uses it in his fleet of cars." "How can abortion be wrong if millions of people support a woman's right to choose?"

Keep in mind, however, that occasionally the distinction between a false authority fallacy and an appeal to legitimate authority can blur. Suppose that Tiger Woods were to praise a particular company's golf club. Because he is an expert on golf, perhaps he speaks from authority about a truly superior golf club. But perhaps he is being paid to endorse a club that is no better than its competitors'. We could better determine the argument's conclusiveness if Woods presented an *ad rem* ("to the thing") argument showing us scientifically why the golf club in question is superior.

Appeal to the Person or *Ad Hominem* (Attacking the Character of the Arguer Rather Than the Argument Itself)

Literally, *ad hominem* means "to the person." When people can't find fault with an argument, they sometimes attack the arguer, substituting irrelevant assertions about that person's character for an analysis of the argument itself. It is better for an argument to be *ad rem* rather than *ad hominem*. Thus an *ad rem* critique of a politician would focus on her voting record, the consistency and cogency of her public statements, her responsiveness to constituents, and so forth. An *ad hominem* argument would shift attention to irrelevant features of her personality or personal life, perhaps a recent divorce or a long-ago reckless driving conviction.

But not all *ad hominem* arguments are *ad hominem* fallacies. It's not always fallacious to address your argument to the arguer. There are indeed times when the credibility of the person making an opposing argument is at issue. Lawyers, for example, in questioning expert witnesses who give damaging testimony, will often make an issue of their motives and credibility—and rightfully so.

Straw Man (Greatly Oversimplifying an Opponent's Argument to Make It Easier to Refute or Ridicule)

In committing a *straw man* fallacy, you basically make up the argument you *wish* your opponents had made and attribute it to them because it's so much easier to refute than the argument they actually made. Some political debates consist almost entirely of straw man exchanges, such as "You may think that taxing people out of their homes and onto park benches is the best way to balance the budget, but I don't," or "While my opponent would like to empty our prisons of serial killers and coddle kidnappers, I hold to the sacred principles of swift and sure justice."

FALLACIES OF *LOGOS*

Begging the Question (Supporting a Claim with a Reason That Is Really a Restatement of the Claim in Different Words)

We *beg the question* when we use as a reason the same assertion we make in our claim. "Abortion is murder because it involves the intentional killing of an unborn human being." Since murder is defined as the "intentional killing of a human being," the argument says, in effect, "Abortion is murder because it's murder."

False Dilemma/Either-Or
(Oversimplifying a Complex Issue So
That Only Two Choices Appear Possible)

A good extended analysis of this fallacy is found in sociologist Kai Erikson's analysis of President Harry Truman's decision to drop the A-bomb on Hiroshima. His analysis suggests that the Truman administration prematurely reduced numerous options to just two: either drop the bomb on a major city or suffer unacceptable losses in a land invasion of Japan. Erikson, however, shows there were other alternatives. Typically, we encounter *false dilemma* arguments when people try to justify a questionable action by creating a false sense of necessity, forcing us to choose between two options, one of which is clearly unacceptable.

But of course not all dilemmas are false. People who reject all binary oppositions are themselves guilty of a false dilemma. There are times when we might determine through a rational process of elimination that only two possible choices exist. Deciding whether a dilemma is truly a dilemma or only an evasion of complexity often requires a difficult judgment. Although we should initially suspect any attempt to convert a complex problem into an either/or choice, we may legitimately arrive at such a choice through thoughtful deliberation.

Confusing Correlation for Cause or *Post Hoc, Ergo*
Propter Hoc (After This, Therefore Because
of This—Assuming That Event X Causes Event Y
Because Event X Preceded Event Y)

Here are two examples in which this fallacy may be at work:

Cramming for a test really helps. Last week I crammed for a psychology test and I got an A on it.

I am allergic to the sound of a lawnmower because every time I mow the lawn I start to sneeze.

We treat this fallacy at length in Chapter 11 in our discussion of correlation versus causation (pp. 174–76). The *post hoc, ergo propter hoc* fallacy occurs when a sequential relationship is mistaken for a causal relationship. The conjunction may be coincidental, or it may be attributable to some as-yet-unrecognized third factor. For example, your A on the psych test may be caused by something other than your cramming. Maybe the exam was easier, or perhaps you were luckier or more mentally alert. And perhaps a lawnmower makes you sneeze because it stirs up pollen rather than because it makes a loud noise.

Slippery Slope (Once We Move Slightly toward an Unpleasant End, We Will Eventually Have to Go All the Way)

The *slippery-slope* fallacy appeals to the fear that once we take a first step in a direction we don't like, we will have to keep going.

> We don't dare send weapons to Country X. If we do so, next we will send in military advisers, then a special forces battalion, and then large numbers of troops. Finally, we will be in all-out war.

> Look, Blotnik, no one feels worse about your need for open-heart surgery than I do. But I still can't let you turn this paper in late. If I were to let you do it, then I'd have to let everyone turn in papers late.

The slippery-slope fear is that an apparently harmless first step in a dangerous direction dooms us to slide right out of sight.

The problem, of course, is that not every slippery-slope argument exhibits the slippery-slope fallacy. We all know that some slopes *are* slippery and that we sometimes have to draw the line, saying "to here, but no farther." And it is true also that making exceptions to rules is dangerous; the exceptions soon get established as regular procedures. The slippery slope becomes a fallacy, however, when we forget that some slopes don't have to be slippery unless we let them be slippery. Often we do better to imagine a staircase with stopping places all along the way. The assumption that we have no control over our descent once we take the first step makes us unnecessarily rigid.

Hasty Generalization (Making a Broad Generalization on the Basis of Too Little Evidence)

A *hasty generalization* occurs when we leap to a conclusion on insufficient evidence: "The food stamp program supports mostly freeloaders. Let me tell you about my worthless neighbor." But what constitutes "sufficient" evidence is a knotty problem. No generalization arrived at through empirical evidence would meet a logician's strict standard of certainty.

The Food and Drug Administration (FDA), for example, proceeds cautiously before certifying a drug as "safe." However, whenever doubts arise about the safety of an FDA-approved drug, critics accuse the FDA of having made a hasty generalization. At the same time, patients eager to get a new drug, or manufacturers eager to sell it, may lobby the FDA to quit dragging its feet and get the drug to market. Hence, the point at which a hasty generalization about drug safety passes over into the realm of a prudent generalization is nearly always uncertain and contested.

Mistaking the Part for the Whole or *Pars Pro Toto* (Assuming That What Is True for a Part Will Be True for the Whole)

We use the *pars pro toto* fallacy when we attack the whole of something by focusing on a part we don't like. Thus, critics who want to abolish the National Endowment for the Arts might focus on several controversial grants and use them as justification for wiping out all NEA programs.

False Analogy (Claiming That Because X Resembles Y in One Regard, X Will Resemble Y in All Regards)

Arguments by analogy are tricky because there are almost always significant differences between any two things being compared. If the two things differ greatly, the analogy can mislead rather than clarify. "You can't force a kid to become a musician any more than you can force a tulip to become a rose." For further discussion of reasoning by analogy, see Chapter 12.

Non Sequitur (Making a Claim That Doesn't Follow Logically from the Premises, or Supporting a Claim with Irrelevant Premises)

The *non sequitur* (literally, "it does not follow") fallacy is a miscellaneous category that includes any claim that doesn't follow logically from its premises or that is supported with irrelevant premises. Typically, *non sequitur* fallacies take the following forms:

An illogical leap: "Clambake University has one of the best faculties in the United States because a Nobel Prize winner used to teach there." (How does the fact that a Nobel Prize winner used to teach at Clambake University make its present faculty one of the best in the United States?)

Irrelevant premises: "I should not receive a C in this course because I have received B's or A's in all my other courses (here is my transcript for evidence) and because I worked exceptionally hard in this course (here is my log of hours worked)." (Even though the arguer has solid evidence to support each premise, the premises themselves are irrelevant to the claim. Course grades should be based on actual performance, not on previous grades or on effort.)

a p p e n d i x 2

A Concise Guide to Evaluating and Documenting Sources

When you research material for your arguments, you must be able to evaluate possible sources for reliability and document your sources effectively so that readers can retrace your steps. The problem of evaluating sources is particularly acute when you retrieve materials from the World Wide Web. This appendix provides brief instruction on evaluating sources, followed by instruction on how to avoid plagiarism, how to cite your sources in the body of your paper, and how to prepare a complete bibliographic list at the end of your paper. The section on documentation gives an overview of both the MLA (Modern Language Association) and the APA (American Psychological Association) systems. For more complete information, consult a composition handbook or the most recent editions of the *MLA Handbook for Writers of Research Papers* or the *Publication Manual of the American Psychological Association.*

EVALUATING WEB SITES AND OTHER SOURCES

When you interview someone personally or when you read a book, magazine, or scholarly journal from your library, you have direct clues about the timeliness, accuracy, reliability, and bias of the source. For example, when you look at an article in a magazine, the features of the magazine itself—its format, its table of contents, its editorial information, its advertisements, its use of photographs, the length and range and style of its articles—can help you infer valuable information about the article's author, intended audience, and political bias. In contrast, when you print materials from the Internet, these contextual clues are lost: An article from a scholarly journal can look the same as mindless rant from Joe's Web page. (In fact, if Joe is skilled at hypertext formatting, his piece can look more flashy, interesting, and professional than dense pages of text from a scholarly article.) It is essential, therefore, that you learn how to evaluate Internet sources by

257

understanding the logic of Internet searching and by learning the criteria that experienced researchers use to evaluate Web sites.

The Logic of Internet Searching

To understand the logic of Internet searching, you should realize that the Internet is divided into a restricted section open only to those with special access rights (for example, library online catalogs and general databases that subscribers have to pay for) and a free-access section. Web search engines such as Yahoo and Infoseek search only the free-access portion of the Internet; they do not have access to licensed databases or the holdings of libraries.

Let's explain this important point more fully. A Web search engine won't retrieve for you the contents of your institution's library—the books on its shelves, the magazine or journal articles in its periodical collections, or the information in its numerous reference works. To retrieve information on your library's book holdings, you would use its online catalog (which replaces card catalogs). Similarly, to learn the titles of magazine or journal articles on your subject, you would use one of the licensed databases that your library subscribes to, such as Infotrac, EBSCOhost, or Lexis-Nexis (which replace print indexes such as *Reader's Guide*). However, to retrieve information posted to the Web by users of the world's networked computers—government agencies, corporations, advocacy groups, information services, individuals with their own Web sites, you would use a Web search engine such as Yahoo or AltaVista.

The following example will quickly show you the difference between the two kinds of searches. When we entered the keyword "policewomen" into our library's licensed database (EBSCOhost), we received sixty-seven "hits" showing the titles of sixty-seven articles on the subject of policewomen that had appeared in recent magazines, newspapers, or scholarly journals (see Figure AP2.1). In contrast, when we entered the same keyword into the Web search engine Infoseek, we received 3,941 hits—all the Web sites available to Infoseek that had the word "policewomen" appear somewhere in the site. When we plugged the same word into AltaVista, another search engine, we received 2,704 hits, and only two of the first ten hits from AltaVista matched the first ten from Infoseek. Figure AP2.2 shows the first seven hits from yet another Web search engine, GoTo.com.

◆ FOR CLASS DISCUSSION

Working in small groups or as a whole class, compare the items on "policewomen" retrieved from the licensed database EBSCOhost (Figure AP2.1) and the Web search engine GoTo.com (Figure AP2.2).

1. Explain in your own words why the results from GoTo.com are different from those from EBSCOhost. Give some specifics to show how the amount and kind of information differ.

Mark	Full Text	Select Result For More Detail
☐	📄	<u>Who Are the New Beat Poets? Hint: They're Blue.</u>; By: Grace, Julie., Time, 09/13/99, Vol. 154 Issue 11, p20, 1/5p, 1c **Note:** We subscribe to this magazine.
☐		<u>Officer Charged in Sexual Abuse of Ex-Companion.</u>; By: Cooper, Michael., New York Times, 08/31/99, Vol. 148 Issue 51631, pB4, 0p **Note:** We subscribe to this magazine.
☐		<u>Ban on Skirts For Guards Is Challenged.</u>; By: Herszenhorn, David M.., New York Times, 08/26/99, Vol. 148 Issue 51626, pB6, 0p **Note:** We subscribe to this magazine.
☐	📄	<u>Women face 'blue wall' of resistance.</u> (cover story); By: Marks, Alexandra., Christian Science Monitor, 08/18/99, Vol. 91 Issue 184, p1, 0p, 1c **Note:** We subscribe to this magazine.
☐	📄	<u>Affirmative Action, Political Representation, Unions, and Female Police Employment.</u>; By: Sass, Tim R., and Troyer, Jennifer L.., Journal of Labor Research, Fall99, Vol. 20 Issue 4, p571, 17p, 4 charts **Note:** We do not subscribe to this magazine.
☐	📄	<u>Do women make better peacekeepers?</u>; By: DeGroot, Gerard J.., Christian Science Monitor, 07/14/99, Vol. 91 Issue 159, p9, 0p, 1 cartoon **Note:** We subscribe to this magazine.
☐	📄	<u>She goes 'mano a mano' with drug lords.</u> (cover story); By: Marks, Alexandra., Christian Science Monitor, 06/01/99, Vol. 91 Issue 129, p1, 0p, 1c **Note:** We subscribe to this magazine.
☐		<u>Iran to Train *Policewomen.*</u>, New York Times, 05/27/99, Vol. 148 Issue 51535, pA5, 0p **Note:** We subscribe to this magazine.
☐	📄	<u>News Digest.</u>, Workforce, May99, Vol. 78 Issue 5, p18, 1/3p **Note:** We do not subscribe to this magazine.
☐		<u>A municipal mother: Portland's Lola Greene Baldwin, America's first policewoman.</u>; By: Myers, Gloria E., Peace Research Abstracts Journal, 2/1/99, Vol. 36, Issue 1, p0, 0p **Note:** We subscribe to this magazine.

FIGURE AP2.1   Sample results list for a search using EBSCOhost

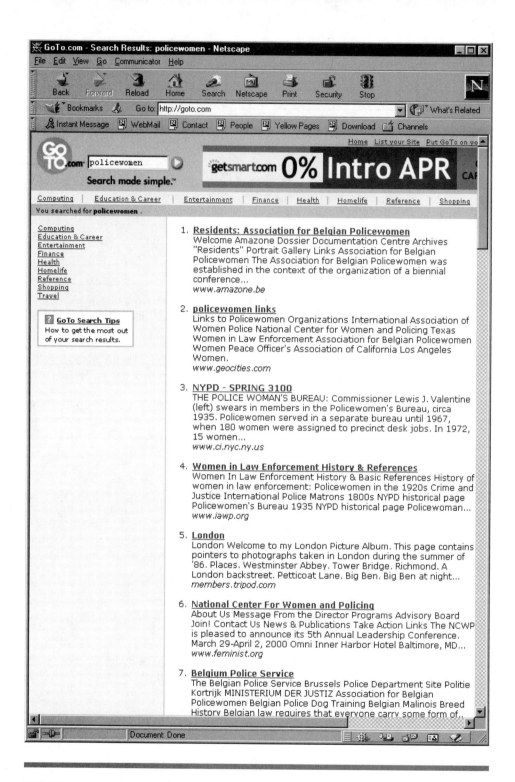

FIGURE AP2.2   Web search using GoTo.com

2. At the end of this appendix is student writer Lynnea Clark's researched argument asking whether a physically weak woman can be a good police officer. Which of the Web sites from GoTo.com or the articles from EBSCOhost might be useful for Lynnea's research?

Evaluating Web Sites

Despite the preponderance of garbage on the World Wide Web, its resources for writers of argument are breathtaking. At your fingertips you have access to government documents and statistics, legislative white papers, court cases, persuasive appeals of advocacy groups, MOO's and chat rooms, newspaper articles— the list seems endless. Moreover, the hypertext structure of Web sites lets Web designers create links to other sites so that users can read an argument from an advocacy group in one Web site and then have instant links to the argument's sources at other Web sites.

Although the Web is an exciting, inexhaustible source of information, it also contains lots of junk, so you need to evaluate Web material carefully. Anyone with hypertext skills can put up a Web page that furthers his or her own agenda. Flashy graphics and other design elements can sometimes overwhelm the information that is being presented on Web pages or lend an air of authority to an otherwise suspect argument or position.

When you look at a Web site, begin by asking the following two questions:

- *What kind of Web site is it?* Web sites can have distinctly different purposes. Business/marketing Web sites are aimed at attracting and serving customers as well as creating a favorable public image. Informational/ government Web sites are aimed at providing basic data ranging from traffic information to bills being debated in Congress. News Web sites supplement coverage in other media. Advocacy Web sites (often indicated by *.org* at the end of their URL address) attempt to influence public opinion on disputed issues. Special interest Web sites are aimed at connecting users with common interests ranging from recent film reviews to kayaking. Personal home pages are created by individuals for their own purposes.

- *What is my purpose in using this Web site?* Am I trying to get an initial understanding of the various points of view on an issue, looking for reliable data, or seeking expert testimony to support my thesis? Joe's Web page— let's say Joe wants California to secede from the United States—may be a terrible source for reliable data about the federal government but an excellent source for helping you understand the views of fringe groups.

One of the most challenging parts of using the Web is determining whether a site offers gold or glitter. Sometimes the case may not be clearcut. How do you sort out reliable, worthwhile sites from unreliable ones? We offer the following criteria developed by scholars and librarians as points to consider when you are using Web sites.

Criterion 1: Authority

- Is the author or sponsor of the Web site clearly identified?
- Does the site identify the occupation, position, education, experience, and credentials of the site's authors?
- Does the introductory material reveal the author's or sponsor's motivation for publishing this information on the Web?
- Does the site provide contact information for the author or sponsor such as an e-mail or organization address?

Criterion 2: Objectivity or Clear Disclosure of Advocacy

- Is the site's purpose (to inform, explain, or persuade) clear?
- Is the site explicit about declaring its author's or sponsor's point of view?
- Does the site indicate whether its author is affiliated with a specific organization, institution, or association?
- Does the site indicate whether it is directed toward a specific audience?

Criterion 3: Coverage

- Are the topics covered by the site clear?
- Does the site exhibit suitable depth and comprehensiveness for its purpose?
- Is sufficient evidence provided to support the ideas and opinions presented?

Criterion 4: Accuracy

- Are the sources of information stated? Can you tell whether this information is original or taken from someplace else?
- Does the information appear to be accurate? Can you verify this information by comparing this source with other sources in the field?

Criterion 5: Currency

- Are dates included in the Web site?
- Do the dates apply to the material itself or to its placement on the Web? Is the site regularly revised and updated?
- Is the information current or at least still relevant for the site's purpose?

To illustrate how these criteria can help you deal with the good points and deficiencies of Web material, we give an example of how to use the criteria to assess the value of Web information. We wanted to investigate U.S. involvement in the exploitation of workers in sweatshops. We specifically wanted to investigate this question: "To what extent are caps and shirts with university logos produced under sweatshop conditions?"

To start our investigation of the link between university-licensed clothing and sweatshops, we entered the keyword "sweatshop" into Yahoo, our selected search engine. We discovered a vast anti-sweatshop movement with a number of promising sites for our first-step initiation into the issues. We decided to investigate the site of "NMASS," which we discovered was the abbreviation for "National Mobilization against Sweatshops" (http://www.nmass.org). Figure AP2.3 shows you the initial Web page of this site. Using the criteria for evaluating Web sites, we were able to identify the strengths and weaknesses of this site in the light of our question and purpose.

This site does well when measured against our first two criteria: "authority" and "clear disclosure of advocacy." On the home page, the organization name "National Mobilization against Sweatshops" boldly announces this organization's perspective. Information in the bulleted list openly declares its purpose: "Become a sweatshop buster!" The links then provide more detailed information on the goals of the organization. In the "Mission Statement" link, the site forthrightly declares:

> The National Mobilization against Sweatshops (NMASS) is a grassroots educational effort by and for working people and youth of all backgrounds and communities. NMASS was first started by members and supporters of the Chinese Staff and Workers' Association, an independent workers' center in New York's Chinatown.

Links mentioned on the home page indicate that this site is directed toward both members and prospective members; it seeks to rally the members of the organization and to win new supporters. The site does provide contact information by giving an address for comments and suggestions: nmass@yahoo.com.

This site also does well in "coverage," our third criterion. We found that this site provides good coverage of material for its purpose, even though it does not specifically address our research question. Particularly, the link called "8 Myths about Sweatshops" introduced us to important sweatshop issues such as the existence of sweatshops in the United States, the exploitation of immigrant workers, the level of government involvement in addressing the problem, and the ineffectiveness of unions. Several of these links identify industries involved with sweatshops, but the site does not give specific information about university-licensed clothing and sweatshops.

Our fourth criterion, "accuracy," enabled us to identify some problems with the accuracy of the site's information for our purposes. The links called "Global

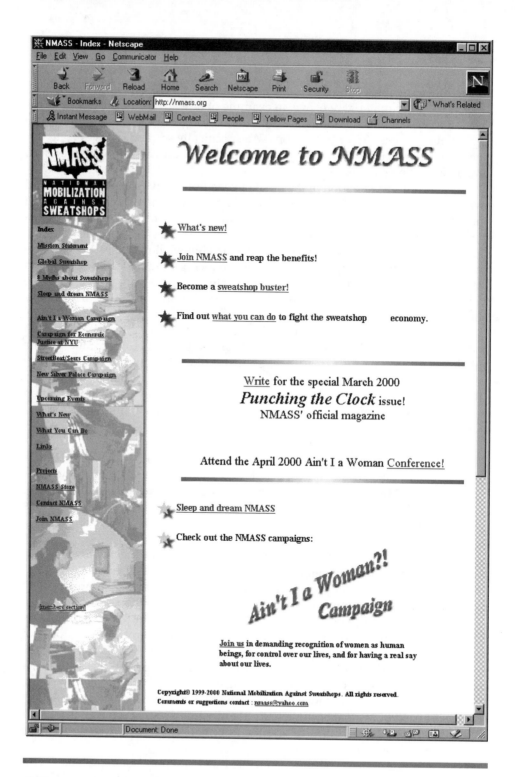

FIGURE AP2.3 Home page for NMASS

Sweatshop" and "8 Myths about Sweatshops" offer a number of facts and figures about the origin and history of sweatshops and about current working conditions, yet no specific sources are cited. These statements are startling and compelling, but are they accurate? And what opposing information should be considered?

Finally, the site seemed satisfactory though a little vague with regard to "currency," our fifth criterion. Although the links revealed sources with recent, up-to-date copyright dates, the site itself has no indication of how often it is updated.

In short, we found this site helpful in a "first stop" way to acquaint us with the stakes in the anti-sweatshop movement, but we concluded that this site's information is too broad for our purposes. Furthermore, this site could not stand as a major, unverified source. Using the evaluation criteria helped us recognize our need for more in-depth research and follow-up investigations. We realized, particularly, that we would need to investigate sweatshops from the perspective of industry (such as the American Apparel Manufacturers Association at www.americanapparel.org) and government regulatory agencies (such as the Bureau of International Labor Affairs at www.dol.gov/dol/ilab).

Whether a source comes from the Web or from materials retrieved directly from the library, once you have decided to use a source in your argument, you need to use that source responsibly by avoiding plagiarism, citing it properly in the body of your paper, and including it in the bibliographic list at the end. We turn now to these issues.

HOW TO AVOID PLAGIARISM

Before discussing how to cite and document your sources, we need to take a brief excursion into the realm of ethics to explain plagiarism. *Plagiarism* occurs whenever you take someone else's work and pass it off as your own. Plagiarism can happen in two ways: by borrowing another person's *ideas* without giving credit through a proper citation and by borrowing another writer's *language* without giving credit through quotation marks or block indentation.

The second kind of plagiarism is far more common than the first, perhaps because inexperienced writers don't appreciate how much they need to change the wording of a source to make the writing their own. It is not enough to change the order of phrases in a sentence or to replace a few words with synonyms. In the following example, compare an acceptable rewording of a passage with unacceptable plagiarism.

ORIGINAL PASSAGE (FROM AN ARTICLE ON VIOLENCE
IN THE OLD WEST BY ROGER D. MCGRATH)

There is considerable evidence that women in Bodie were rarely the victims of crime. Between 1878 and 1882 only one woman, a prostitute, was robbed, and there were no reported cases of rape. (There is no evidence that rapes occurred but were not reported.)

ACCEPTABLE REWORDING

According to Roger D. McGrath, women in Bodie rarely suffered at the hands of criminals. Between 1878 and 1882, the only female robbery victim in Bodie was a prostitute. Also rape seemed nonexistent, with no reported cases and no evidence that unreported cases occurred (20).

PLAGIARISM

According to Roger D. McGrath, there is considerable evidence that women in Bodie were seldom the victims of crime. Between 1878 and 1882 only one woman, a prostitute, was robbed, and there were no reported rapes. There is no evidence that unreported cases of rape occurred (20).

Although the writer of the plagiarized passage correctly used the MLA citation system (see next section) to indicate that his data comes from page 20 in the McGrath article, he nevertheless plagiarized his source because he copied its language directly without showing the borrowing with quotation marks.

HOW TO CITE SOURCES

When academic writers cite a source, they use the conventions appropriate to their discipline. In the sciences, citation systems often emphasize the date of a research study and refer to researchers only by last names and first initials. In the humanities, citation systems often emphasize the full names of scholars and place less emphasis on dates. Two of the most extensively used systems are those of the Modern Language Association (MLA) in the humanities and the American Psychological Association (APA) in the social sciences. In both systems, complete bibliographic information on all cited sources is placed at the end of the paper—in a Works Cited list (MLA) or a References list (APA). For in-text citations, both systems place reference information in parentheses directly in the text, not in footnotes or endnotes. However, the two systems differ somewhat in the way parenthetical reference information is selected and structured.

MLA System of In-Text Citation

In the MLA system, you place the author's last name and the page number of the cited source in parentheses. (If the author's name is mentioned in a preceding attributive tag such as "according to Michael Levin" or "says Levin," only the page number should be placed in parentheses.)

> Torture, claims one philosopher, should be applied only to those "known to hold innocent lives in their hands" and only if the person being

> tortured is clearly guilty and clearly can prevent a terrorist act from
> occurring (Levin 13).

or

> Torture, claims Michael Levin, should be applied only to those "<u>known</u> to
> hold innocent lives in their hands" and only if the person being tortured
> is clearly guilty and clearly can prevent a terrorist act from occurring (13).

If your readers wish to follow up on this source, they will look for the Levin article in the Works Cited list at the end of your essay. If you use more than one work by Levin as a source in the essay, include in the in-text citation a shortened version of the title of the work following Levin's name:

> (Levin, "Torture" 13)

Once Levin has been cited the first time and it is clear that you are still quoting from Levin, you need put only the page number in parentheses.

APA System of In-Text Citation

In the APA system, you place the author's last name and the publication date of the cited source in parentheses. If you are quoting a particular passage or citing a particular table, include the page number where the information is found. Use a comma to separate each element in the parenthetical citation, and use the abbreviation *p.* or *pp.* before the page number. (If the author's name is mentioned in a preceding attributive tag, only the date needs to be placed in parentheses.)

> Torture, claims one philosopher, should be applied only to those
> "<u>known</u> to hold innocent lives in their hands" and only if the person
> being tortured is clearly guilty and clearly can prevent a terrorist act
> from occurring (Levin, 1982, p. 13).

or

> Torture, claims Michael Levin, should be applied only to those
> "<u>known</u> to hold innocent lives in their hands" and only if the person
> being tortured is clearly guilty and clearly can prevent a terrorist act
> from occurring (1982, p. 13).

If your readers wish to follow up on this source, they will look for the 1982 Levin article in the References section at the end of your essay. If you cite two works by Michael Levin published in 1982, list the works in alphabetical order by title in your References list, and add a lowercase *a* to the date of the first one and a lowercase *b* to the date of the second one. Your in-text parenthetical citation will be either

> (Levin, 1982a)

or

> (Levin, 1982b)

In APA style, if an article or book has more than one author, the word *and* is used to join the authors' names in the text, but an ampersand (&) is used to join them in the parenthetical reference:

> Smith and Peterson (1983) found that . . .
>
> More recent data (Smith & Peterson, 1983) have shown . . .

Citing a Quotation or Other Data from a Secondary Source

Occasionally, you may wish to use a quotation or other kinds of data from a secondary source. Suppose you are writing an argument that the United States should reconsider its trade policies with China. You read an article entitled "China's Gilded Age" by Xiao-huang Yin appearing in the April 1994 issue of the *Atlantic*. This article contains the following passage appearing on page 42:

> Dual ownership has in essence turned this state enterprise into a private business. Asked if such a practice is an example of China's "socialist market economy," a professor of economics at Nanjing University, where I taught in the early 1980's, replied, "Nobody knows what the concept means. It is only rhetoric, and it can mean anything but socialism."

In citing material from a secondary source, it is always best, when possible, to locate the original source and cite your data directly from it. But in the case above, no other source is likely to be available. Here is how you would cite the internal quotation in the MLA and APA systems.

MLA: According to an economics professor at Nanjing University, the term "socialist market economy" has become confused under capitalistic influence. "Nobody knows what the concept means. It is only rhetoric, and it can mean anything but socialism" (qtd. in Yin 42).

APA: According to an economics professor at Nanjing University, the term "socialist market economy" has become confused under capitalistic influence: "Nobody knows what the concept means. It is only rhetoric, and it can mean anything but socialism" (cited in Yin, 1994, p. 42).

Using either system, you would place a full citation to the Yin article in your end-of-text bibliographic list.

HOW TO PROVIDE BIBLIOGRAPHIC INFORMATION AT THE END OF YOUR PAPER

In this section we briefly describe the format for end-of-text bibliographic entries under Works Cited (MLA) or References (APA).

MLA Works Cited Page

Figure AP2.4 shows a sample Works Cited page that would go at the end of a paper using the MLA system. On this page, we illustrate the formats for the most commonly used kinds of sources: a book with a single author; a book in a second or later edition; a book with two or more authors; an article in an anthology; an article in a scholarly journal; an article in a weekly or biweekly popular magazine; an article in a monthly, bimonthly, or quarterly magazine; an Internet Web site; and a newspaper article. To see how a Works Cited list is appended to a complete researched argument written in MLA style, see Stephen Bean's paper on pages 228–36.

APA References Page

Figure AP2.5 shows a sample References page that would go at the end of a paper using the APA system. It contains the same information as the MLA page, transformed into APA style and format. Note that the APA system places the date in parentheses immediately after the author's name; that it uses only initials rather than first and middle names; that it capitalizes only the first word and proper nouns in article and book titles; that it does not enclose article titles in quotation marks; and that it puts *p.* or *pp.* in front of page numbers.

EXAMPLE OF A RESEARCHED ARGUMENT IN APA STYLE

Pages 272–78 provide an example of a fully documented argument using the APA style. For an example of an argument in the MLA style, see Stephen Bean's "What Should Be Done about the Mentally Ill Homeless?" (pp. 228–36).

Ross 27

Works Cited

Adler, Freda. <u>Sisters in Crime</u>. New York: McGraw, 1975.

Andersen, Margaret L. <u>Thinking about Women: Sociological</u>
<u>Perspectives on Sex and Gender</u>. 3rd ed. New York:
Macmillan, 1993.

Bart, Pauline, and Patricia O'Brien. <u>Stopping Rape: Successful</u>
<u>Survival Strategies</u>. New York: Pergamon, 1985.

Durkin, Kevin. "Social Cognition and Social Context in the
Construction of Sex Differences." <u>Sex Differences in</u>
<u>Human Performances</u>. Ed. Mary Anne Baker. New York:
Wiley, 1987. 45–60.

Fairburn, Christopher G., et al. "Predictors of Twelve-Month
Outcome in Bulimia Nervosa and the Influence of
Attitudes to Shape and Weight." <u>Journal of Consulting</u>
<u>and Clinical Psychology</u> 61 (1993): 696–98.

Kantrowitz, Barbara. "Sexism in the Schoolhouse." <u>Newsweek</u>
24 Feb. 1992: 62.

Langewiesche, William. "The World in Its Extreme." <u>Atlantic</u>
Nov. 1991: 105–40.

National Law Center. "Selected Rights of Homeless Persons."
<u>National Law Center on Homelessness and Poverty</u>. 19
Apr. 1998. <http://www.nlchp.org/rights2.htm>.

Taylor, Chuck. "After Cobain's Death: Here Come the Media
Ready to Buy Stories." <u>Seattle Times</u> 10 Apr. 1994: A1+.

In upper right corner, writer's last name and page number.

Book by one author. Use standard abbreviations for common publishers.

Book in a second or later edition.

Book by two or three authors. For more than three, name only the first and use *et al.*, as in Jones, Peter, et al.

Article in anthology. Author begins the entry; editor cited after the book title. Inclusive page numbers come after the period following the year.

Article in scholarly journal paginated consecutively throughout year. This article has more than three authors.

Weekly or biweekly popular magazine. Abbreviate all months except May, June, and July.

Monthly, bimonthly, or quarterly magazine.

Online document with corporate author. Title in quotation marks; Web site underlined; date of access; Web address in angle brackets

Newspaper article with identified author. If no author, begin with title.

FIGURE AP2.4   Works Cited list: MLA style for the most commonly used kinds of sources

Women, Health, and Crime   27

References

Adler, F. (1975). Sisters in crime. New York: McGraw-Hill.

Andersen, M. L. (1993). Thinking about women: Sociological

perspectives on sex and gender (3rd ed.). New York:

Macmillan.

Bart, P., & O'Brien, P. (1985). Stopping rape: Successful survival

strategies. New York: Pergamon Press.

Durkin, K. (1987). Social cognition and social context in the

construction of sex differences. In M. A. Baker (Ed.), Sex

differences in human performances (pp. 45–60). New

York: John Wiley & Sons.

Fairburn, C. G., Pevaler, R. C., Jones, R., & Hope, R. A. (1993).

Predictors of 12-month outcome in bulimia nervosa and

the influence of attitudes to shape and weight. Journal of

Consulting and Clinical Psychology, 61, 696–698.

Kantrowitz, B. (1992, February 24). Sexism in the schoolhouse.

Newsweek, p. 62.

Langewiesche, W. (1991, November). The world in its extreme.

Atlantic, pp. 105–140.

Selected rights of homeless persons. National Law Center on

Homelessness and Poverty. Retrieved April 19, 1998 from

the World Wide Web: http://www.nlchp.org./rights2.htm

Taylor, C. (1993, April 10). After Cobain's death: Here come the

media ready to buy stories. Seattle Times, pp. A1+.

Marginal annotations:

In upper right corner, running head and page number separated by five spaces.

Book by one author. Don't abbreviate publisher but omit unnecessary words.

Book in a second or later edition.

Book by fewer than six authors. Uses ampersand instead of and before last author's name. Authors' names listed last name first.

Article in anthology. No quotation marks around article title. Name of editor before book title.

Article in scholarly journal paginated consecutively throughout year. APA style lists all authors in the References rather than using et al.

Weekly or biweekly popular magazine. Spell out all months.

Monthly, bimonthly, or quarterly magazine.

Online document with corporate author. Roman title; date if known in parentheses; no period after Web address. (No date is available for this source.)

Newspaper article with identified author. If no author, begin with title followed by date.

FIGURE AP2.5   References list: APA style for the most commonly used kinds of sources

Women Police Officers:

Should Size and Strength Be Criteria for Patrol Duty?

Lynnea Clark

English 301

November 15 , 199X

This research paper follows the APA style for format and documentation.

Women Police Officers:

Should Size and Strength Be Criteria for Patrol Duty?

A marked patrol car turns the corner at 71st and Franklin Avenue and　　1
cautiously proceeds into the parking lot of an old shopping center. About a dozen
gang members, dressed in their gang colors, stand alert, looking down the alley
that runs behind the store. As the car moves toward the gathering, they suddenly
scatter in all directions. Within seconds, several shots are fired from the alley.
Switching on the overhead emergency lights, the officer bolts from the car when he
sees two figures running past him. "Freeze! Police!" the officer yells. The men dart
off in opposite directions. Chasing one, the policeman catches up to him, and,
observing no gun, tackles him. After a violent struggle, the officer manages to
handcuff the man, just as the backup unit comes screeching up.

This policeman is my friend. The next day I am with him as he sits at a cafe　　2
with three of his fellow officers, discussing the incident. One of the officers
comments, "Well, at least you were stronger than he was. Can you imagine if
Connie Jones was on patrol duty last night?" "What a joke," scoffs another officer.
"How tall is she anyway?" "About 4'10" and 90 pounds," says the third officer.
"She could fit in my backpack." Connie Jones (not her real name) has just
completed police academy training and has been assigned to patrol duty in _____ .
Because she is so small, she has to have a booster seat in her patrol car and has
been given a special gun, since she can barely manage to pull the trigger of a
standard police-issue .38 revolver. Although she passed the physical requirements
at the academy, which involved speed and endurance running, situps, and monkey
bar tests, most of the officers in her department doubt her ability to perform
competently as a patrol officer. But nevertheless she is on patrol because men and
women receive equal assignments in most of today's police forces. But is this a
good policy? Can a person who is significantly small and weak make an effective
patrol officer?

Because the "small and weak" people in question are almost always women,　　3
the issue becomes a woman's issue. Considerable research has been done on
women in the police force, and much of it suggests that women, who are
on the average smaller and weaker than men, can perform competently in law
enforcement, regardless of their size or strength. More specifically, most research
concludes that female police workers in general perform just as well as their fellow

officers in patrolling situations. A major study by Bloch and Anderson (1984), commissioned by the Urban Institute, revealed that in the handling of violent situations, women performed well. In fact, women and men received equally satisfactory evaluation ratings on their overall performances.

4   In another more recent study (Grennan, 1987) examining the relationship between outcomes of police-citizen confrontations and the gender of the involved officers, female officers were determined to be just as productive as male officers in the handling of violent situations. In his article on female criminal justice employment, Potts (1981) reviews numerous studies on evaluation ratings of policewomen and acknowledges that "the predominant weight of evidence is that women are equally capable of performing police work as are men" (p. 11). Additionally, female officers score higher on necessary traits for leadership (p. 10), and it has been often found that women are better at dealing with rape and abuse victims. Again, a study performed by Grennan (1987), concentrating on male and female police officers' confrontations with citizens, revealed that the inborn or socialized nurturing ability possessed by female police workers makes them "just as productive as male officers in the handling of a violent confrontation" (p. 84).

5   This view has been strengthened further by the achievement of Katherine P. Heller, who was honored by receiving the nation's top award in law enforcement for 1990 (Proctor, 1990). Heller, a United States park policewoman, risked her life by stepping in the open to shoot dead an assailant while he leveled his gun to shoot at her fellow police officer. Five feet three inches and 107 pounds, Heller is not only the first woman to be awarded with Police Officer of the Year, but she is also the smallest recipient ever. Maybe Heller's decisiveness will help lay to rest doubts about many women's abilities as police workers.

6   However, despite the evidence provided by the above-cited research, I am not convinced. Although these studies show that women make effective police officers, I believe the studies must be viewed with skepticism. My concern is public safety. In light of that concern, the evidence suggests that police departments should set stringent size and strength requirements for patrol officers, even if these criteria exclude many women.

7   First of all, the research studies documenting the success of women as patrol officers are marred by two major flaws: The amount of evidence gathered is scanty and the way that the data have been gathered doesn't allow us to study factors of

size and strength. Because of minimal female participation in patrol work prior to the past decade, limited amounts of research and reports exist on the issue. And of the research performed, many studies have not been based on representative samples. Garrison, Grant, and McCormick (1988) found that

> [l]iterature on women in patrol or nontraditional police roles tends to be idiosyncratic. . . . Many of the observations written about a relatively small number of women performing successfully in a wider range of police tasks support the assumption that they are exceptions rather than the norm. (p. 32)

Similarly, Bloch and Anderson (1984) note that in the course of their study

> it was not possible to observe enough incidents to be sure that men and women are equally capable in all such situations. It is clear from the incidents which were described that women performed well in the few violent situations which did arise. (p. 61)

Another problem with the available research is that little differentiation has   8 been made within the large group of women being considered; all women officers seem to be grouped and evaluated based on only two criteria: that they are on the police force and that they are female. But like men, women come in all shapes and sizes. To say that women as a class make effective or ineffective police workers is to make too general a claim. The example of women officers such as Katherine Heller proves that some women make excellent patrol cops. But, presumably, some women probably would not make good patrol cops just as some men would not. The available data do not allow us to determine whether size and strength are factors. Because no size differentiation has been made within the groups of women officers under observation in the research studies, it is impossible to conclude whether or not smaller, weaker women performed patrol duties as well as larger, stronger women did. In fact, for Bloch and Anderson's study (which indicates that, from a performance viewpoint, it is appropriate to hire women for patrol assignments on the same basis as men) both men and women had to meet a minimum height requirement of 5'7". Therefore, the performance of smaller, weaker women in handling violent situations remained unevaluated. Thus the data show that many women are great cops; the data do <u>not</u> show that many small women with minimal strength make great cops.

The case of Katherine Heller might seem to demonstrate that smaller women   9 can perform patrol duties successfully. Heller acknowledged in an interview in

Parade magazine that ninety percent of her adversaries will be bigger than she (Proctor, 1990, p. 5). But she is no fluttering fluffball; rather, she has earned the reputation for being an extremely aggressive cop and has compensated for her size by her bearing. But how many women (or men) of Heller's size or smaller could maintain such "officer presence"? How can we be certain that Heller is in fact representative of small women rather than being an exception?

10   This question leads to my second reason for supporting stringent size and strength requirements: Many police officers, both male and female, have real doubts about the abilities of small and physically weak patrol workers, most of whom are women. For example, police officer Elizabeth Demetriou, a six-year veteran of the New York Police Department, said in an interview, "Women on the job still depend on men to help them during confrontations, more so than men do. Male police officers want their partners to be 'tough' or big so that automatically excludes women" (Kennedy, 1996). In a study done by Vega and Silverman (1982), almost 75% of male police officers felt that women were not strong enough to handle the demands of patrol duties, and 42% felt women lacked the needed assertiveness to enforce the law vigorously (p. 32). Unfortunately, however, because of frequent media reports of discrimination and sexism among police personnel and because of pressure from the Equal Employment Opportunity Commission (EEOC) on police agencies and other employers (Vega & Silverman, 1982; Lord, 1986), these reservations and attitudes have not been seriously taken into account.

11   The valid concerns and opinions of police workers who feel that some women officers are not strong enough to deal effectively with violent situations have been asphyxiated by the smoldering accusations of civil rights activists and feminists, who see only layers of chauvinism, conservatism, cynicism, and authoritarianism permeating our law enforcement agencies. These activists view the problem as being only a "women" issue rather than a "size" issue. But the fact remains that both male and female officers think that many patrol workers are incapable of handling violent situations because of small stature and lack of physical strength. Another policewoman belonging to the same department as Connie Jones explained, "She [Jones] doesn't have the authoritarian stance needed to compensate for her size. She's not imposing and is too soft spoken. Once she responded to a call and was literally picked up and thrown out the door" (anonymous personal communication, October 6, 1990).

Finally, patrol duties, unlike other areas of police work, constitute one of the   12
few jobs in our society that may legitimately require above-average strength.
Because the job involves great personal risk and danger, the concern for public
safety overrides the concern for equal rights in this instance. Patrolling is a high-
visibility position in police departments as opposed to jobs such as radio
dispatching, academy training, or clerical duties. Patrol workers directly face the
challenges presented by the public, and violence is always a threat for officers on
patrol (Vega & Silverman, 1982; Grennan, 1987). Due to the nature of patrol work,
officers many times must cope with violent situations by using physical force, such
as that needed for subduing individuals who resist arrest. However, pressure from
liberal groups has prevented special consideration being given to these factors of
patrol duty. As long as student officers pass the standard academy Physical Ability
Test (in addition to the other academy requirements), then they are eligible for
patrol assignments; in fact, everyone out of the academy <u>must</u> go on patrol. But
the minimum physical requirements are not challenging. According to Lord (1986),
police agencies "struggle to find a nondiscriminatory, empirically valid entry
level physical agility test which does not discriminate against women by
overemphasizing upper body strength" (p. 91). In short, the liberal agenda leading
to women on patrol has forced the lowering of strength requirements.

Without establishing minimum size and strength requirements for patrol   13
workers, police departments are not discharging their duties with maximum
competency or effectiveness. Police training programs stress that police officers
should be able to maintain an authoritarian presence in the face of challenges and
possess the ability to diffuse a situation just by making an appearance. But some
individuals who are able to pass basic training programs still lack the size needed
to maintain an imposing physical stance. And as many citizens obviously do not
respect the uniform, police workers must possess the strength to efficiently handle
violent encounters. Even if size and strength requirements have a disproportionate
impact on women, these physical standards are lawful, so long as they relate to the
demands of the job and "constitute valid predictors of an employee's performance
on the job" (Steel & Lovrich, 1987, p. 53). Patrol duties demand highly capable and
effective workers, and in order to professionalize law-enforcement practices and to
maintain the degree of order necessary for a free society, police agencies must
maintain a high level of competency in their street-patrol forces.

References

Bloch, P., & Anderson, D. (1984). Police women on patrol: Final report. Washington, DC: Police Foundation.

Garrison, C., Grant, N., & McCormick, K. (1988). Utilization of police women. The Police Chief, 55 (9), 32–73.

Grennan, S. (1987). Findings on the role of officer gender in violent encounters with citizens. Journal of Police Science and Administration, 15 (1), 78–84.

Kennedy, E. A. (1996, Spring). Defensive tactics and the female officer. Women-Police. Retrieved May 4, 1996 from the World Wide Web: http://www. mwarrior.com/DT-fem2.htm

Lord, L. (1986). A comparison of male and female peace officers' stereotypic perceptions of women and women peace officers. Journal of Police Science and Administration, 14 (2), 83–91.

Potts, L. (1981). Equal employment opportunity and female criminal justice employment. Police Studies, 4 (3), 9–19.

Proctor, P. (1990, September 30). I didn't have time to taste the fear. Parade, pp. 4–5.

Steel, B., & Lovrich, N., Jr. (1987). Equality and efficiency tradeoffs in affirmative action--real or imagined? The case of women in policing. Social Science Journal, 24 (1), 53–67.

Vega, M., & Silverman, I. (1982). Female police officers as viewed by their male counterparts. Police Studies, 5 (1), 31–39.

index

Checklist for Peer Reviewers

Understanding the Writer's Intentions

- What is the issue being addressed in this essay?
- What is the writer's major thesis/claim?
- Where does the writer present this thesis/claim? (See pp. 69–71, 125–32.)
- Who disagrees with this claim and why?
- Who is the primary audience for this argument? How resistant is this audience to the writer's claim? Does the writer regard this audience as supportive, undecided, or resistant? (See pp. 117–19.)
- Does the writer show awareness of the obstacles preventing the audience from accepting the writer's claim?
- If proposing an action, does the writer address a specific, appropriate group of decision makers? Is the writer aware of the constraints operating on these decision makers?

Reconstructing the Writer's Argument

- Can you summarize the writer's argument in your own words? Can you summarize it in one sentence as a claim with *because* clauses? (See pp. 68–69.) If you have trouble summarizing the argument, where is the source of difficulty?
- Can you make an outline, flow chart, or tree diagram of the writer's argument? If not, where do you have trouble perceiving the argument's structure?

Identifying the Argument's Claim Type

- Is the writer's main claim one of the claim types discussed in Part Three (category or definition, cause, resemblance, evaluation, proposal)?
- If so, does the writer use argumentative strategies appropriate to that claim type (for instance, using examples to support a categorical claim; using criteria-match arguing for definitional or evaluative claims; describing causal links for cause/consequence claims; arguing from category, consequence, or resemblance to support a proposal claim)?
- How well does the argument anticipate and respond to possible objections associated with each claim type?